JUST LIKE A SOLDIER

A TRUE STORY OF FAMILY, FARMING, AND FINDING HOPE IN ORDINARY FOLK

ROBERT STARK

ISBN: 979-8-9861780-6-6 (Paperback)
ISBN: 979-8-9861780-7-3 (Hardcover)
ISBN: 979-8-9861780-5-9 (Ebook)

Front cover image by Najdan Mancic
Book design by Najdan Mancic

First printing edition 2024

For Savanna—
my girl

ALSO BY ROBERT STARK

*Warflower: A True Story of Family,
Service, and Life in Alaska*

7 PRINCIPLES OF A U.S. ARMY SOLDIER

Loyalty
Duty
Respect
Selfless Service
Honor
Integrity
Personal Courage

"We are not youth any longer. We don't want to take the world by storm. We are fleeing. We fly from ourselves. From our life. We were eighteen and had begun to love life and the world; and we had to shoot it to pieces."

—ERICH MARIA REMARQUE
All Quiet on the Western Front

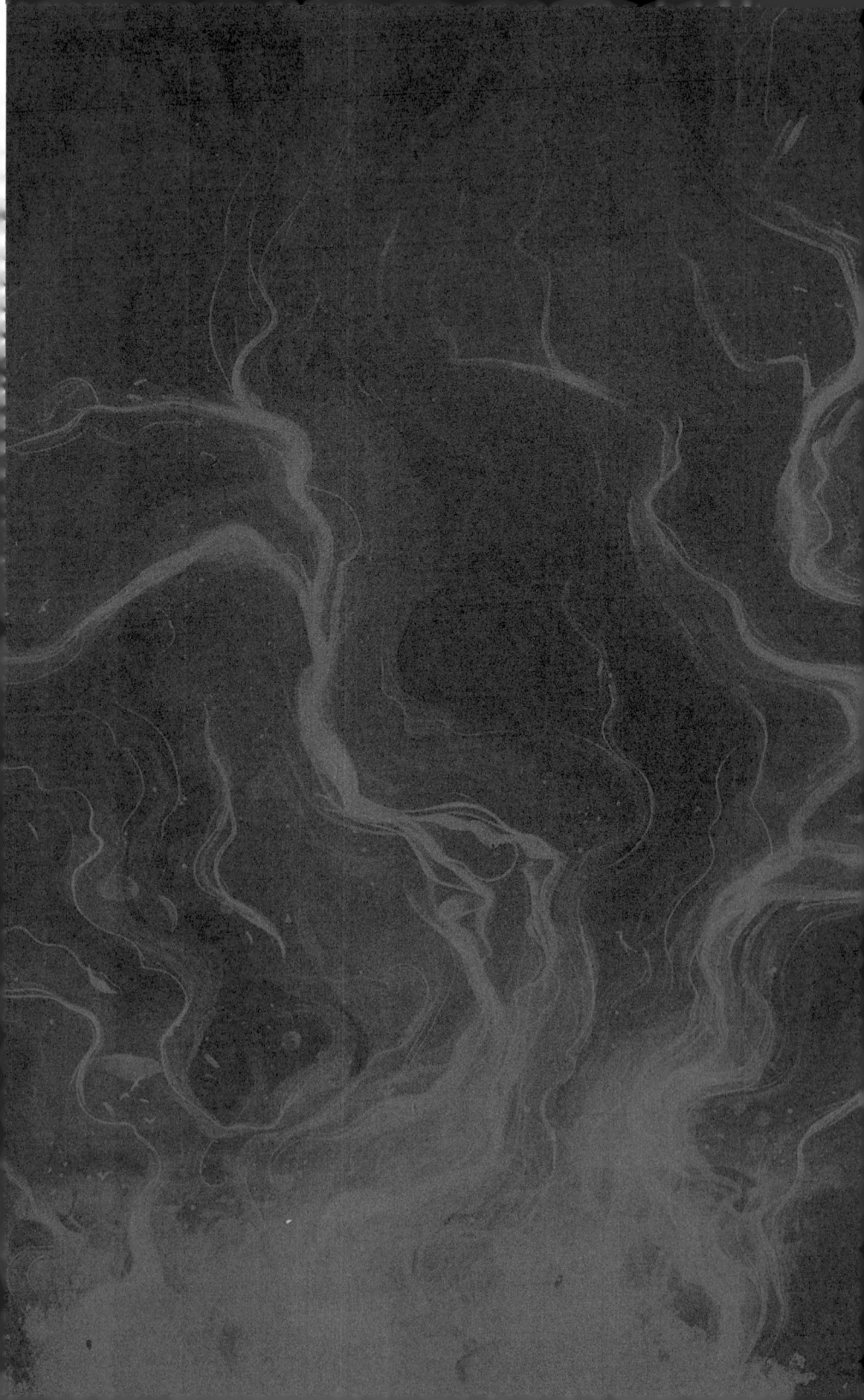

PART I

KINDNESS
OF STRANGERS

1

Seward, Alaska

SEPTEMBER, 2015

I left my home on the farm in Happy Valley to visit my mother's haunted apartment in the coastal town of Seward. When I entered the apartment, a large black man walked past me with a backpack and a grin.

Great, I thought. *She's still dating him. I'll bet he's still living on her couch without paying rent and beating her up like he used to.*

I removed my shoes and entered the living room where my mother sat on a two-cushion hide-a-bed couch with a camouflage duck hunting pattern.

"Hi, Mom. How you doing?" I leaned down to hug her.

"I'm okay, son." She smiled and strained to turn her head as I sat beside her. "Better now that you're here."

"I had to come and see my beautiful mother. I miss you."

"I miss you too, son. I am glad you're here."

I watched her to see if she looked any better than when she visited the farm a few weeks prior, but she didn't. Her neck and face were swollen and she was still in pain. She winced with every move.

"Are you still not working, Ma?"

"Not yet," she said. "And it's driving me flippin' crazy. I wish my back would heal, but it doesn't want to cooperate."

"Did you see a doctor yet?"

No response.

"Mom?"

No response.

"Did you see a doctor yet?"

Her back pain had been there for months yet she still stocked shelves, used a deep-fryer, and ran the register at the local grocery store—until the pain was so bad that she took paid leave to stay home. For a person who had not used paid leave or taken a sick day in thirteen years, to miss work was a big deal.

"You need to see the doctor to make sure it's nothing major."

"I know, I know. I will next week."

"This has been going on for months now, Ma. How do you cope with the pain?"

"I grin and bear it." She laughed. "And I move very slowly."

A tear ran down her cheek and she wiped it away. "It was better after seeing the chiropractor, but a week later it was worse than before."

"Damn it," I said. "He is the best in the state." I stood to look out of the open south facing window at white capped waves on Resurrection Bay. "Maybe you can see him again? Or his brother, the acupuncturist?"

"I tried, but I need an x-ray before they will see me."

"Doesn't your insurance cover that?"

"Yeah."

"So..."

"I will, I will." Another tear ran down her cheek. "Next week."

"What's the matter, ma?" I sat and swung my arm over her shoulders. "I have only seen you cry twice in thirty years. So why the tears?"

She stared at the TV as a robot with a pistol shot at people.

"I'm tired of being in pain," she said. "And I feel worthless not being able to work."

"I'm sorry, Ma." I rubbed her back. "I know you don't like missing work, but sometimes you have to. That's why they made paid leave and sick leave. Let's call the doctor and see if we can get you in."

No response.

"The last time you visited the farm, you snored so loud I could hardly sleep. That is unusual for you."

She wiped her eyes. "I know, and it's only gotten worse.

Some nights I go to sleep and I can hardly breathe, and I don't think I'll wake up in the morning."

"Damn."

"So much for quitting smoking fifteen years ago. I'm worse off now than I was back when I smoked."

I stood to look west at two spruce covered mountains towering over downtown. A tiny speck-of-a-human was over a thousand feet high on the Mount Marathon race trail. I scanned for bears and goats and then lowered my gaze to look across the street, past a building being used as a gym, where I could see the roof of an art and gift shop named Ranting Raven.

I remembered a stormy winter day fifteen years prior after Mother and I had first moved to Seward. We were living at the Murphy's Motel near the harbor in a room that never got warm. Mother spent her days looking for work, filing divorce papers, and visiting her new boyfriend in prison. He was big and black and in prison for life without parole for murdering a white man in a hate crime. He was in the same maximum security prison as my eighteen year old brother, James, who had robbed a liquor store at gunpoint when he was sixteen and was sentenced to seven years. He was the youngest inmate at Spring Creek Correctional Center, the harbor of nightmares. The infamous serial killer, Butcher Baker, was his barber. I was alone most of the time because I did not know anybody in Seward, and I could not stand hearing my mother whisper into the phone with her boyfriend. They were always on the phone. I was pissed off about moving from my friends and our suburban life in Eagle River to a tiny fishing town where everything smelled like fish guts and they didn't have high school baseball. I wished I was a senior, but I was only a sophomore.

I walked around town despite the weather and found shelter in covered pavilions and big wooden chairs under the eave of The Fish House in the harbor. I sat and smoked and read books. I hardly went to school, I did not want the students to know me or the teachers to pity me. One day while I was skipping school, I was out walking in a blizzard so thick that I could barely see my hands. I found shelter in a coffee shop I had walked past dozens of times but had been too afraid to enter. I climbed a creaky, wooden flight of stairs, flicked a cigarette into the wind, and opened the door. It flew out of my hands and almost ripped off the hinges. I struggled to close it, and when I finally did, I felt like Macaulay Culkin entering the library in *The Pagemaster*.

"Come in, come in," said a pretty lady at the counter around my mother's age. "Get out of that awful blizzard and get warm. Nobody should be outside on a day like this."

Heat mixed with the smell of baked goods and coffee. I approached the counter and noticed a crock pot with soup, a glass case full of ham and cheese savories, and oversized cookies. I dug deep in my jeans pockets with red, shaky hands and I could barely feel the coins. I held three quarters in my left hand while struggling to remove my wallet from my back pocket. I had two dollar bills and seventy-five cents.

"I would like a cup of black coffee, please."

The lady with kind eyes and a gentle smile said, "Is that all you'll be having on a blustery day like this?"

I will never forget what she said, because it was the first time in my thirteen years that somebody used the word "blustery" in real life.

"Yes ma'am," I said. "I'm not hungry."

She held out her hand and looked at me straight-in-the-face, in a way that most adults did not.

"I don't see many new faces around here during wintertime. My name is Jenn, Jenn Headtke. Who do I have the pleasure of meeting today?"

I shook her soft, warm hand with a cracked, icy hand. I wanted to hold on for hours.

"My name is Robert." I lowered my head. "Robert Stark. People call me, Bob."

"It is a pleasure to meet you, Robert." She smiled. "I mean, Bob." She looked at me even though I had turned my gaze away.

"You as well, ma'am."

"Call me, Jenn. I am certainly not old enough to be a "ma'am". Did your family move to Seward or are you here for a day trip?"

"My mother and I just moved here."

"Welcome to our Alaskan hamlet. I may be biased, but it is the most beautiful town in the state."

I will never forget what she said, because it was the first time in my thirteen years that somebody used the word "hamlet" in real life.

"I will make you a deal," she said. "How about I treat you

to a bowl of soup, a savory, and a cookie to accompany your coffee? As a welcome gift to my new friend."

"That's nice and all," I said, flushed with embarrassment while searching her face for pity. "But I'm not hungry." It was a lie, of course. It was almost two in the afternoon and I had smoked my breakfast and lunch.

"I insist." She dipped a ladle into a steaming pot of broccoli cheddar soup and poured its contents into a bowl. She cut two slices of bread and coated them with a slab of butter before gently placing the bread, the bowl, and the spoon on a plate on the counter next to the register. "We are closing in a few hours, so we need to eat the soup—or else I will be feeding it to my dog."

"In that case, I am happy to help."

"Which cookie would you prefer?"

She stood behind the counter with her warm hands embraced in front of her apron and a smile on her face.

Ginger molasses is my favorite of all time, I thought, *but I've only had it twice. You can't go wrong with chocolate chip, though.*

"Ginger molasses, please. It's my favorite."

She grabbed a cookie and a savory and set them on a small plate.

"I don't think you'll mind having an extra cookie." She carefully reached in the case with tongs and pulled out a chocolate chip cookie to set on the ginger molasses cookie.

"It's like the ginger molasses cookie and the chocolate chip cookie are hugging to stay warm on this blustery day," I said, without thinking.

She stopped, looked at me, and giggled.

"You know, you're right."

I kicked myself for having spoken so freely. She grabbed the small plate with the cookies and pastry in one hand, and the big plate with the soup, bread and butter in the other hand, and then led us into the dining room.

"This is the warmest seat in the house." She set the plates on a wooden table in the back corner without a sound. "On a day like this, you want the warmest seat. Stay until closing time, if you'd like. It's nice to have company on a day like this."

"Thank you so much, ma'am."

She raised an eyebrow.

"I mean, Jenn." I smiled. "You are too young to be a 'ma'am.'"

She smiled and grabbed a mug from the counter to fill with coffee from a dispenser.

"And your coffee."

I held the warm mug in my trembling hands and tried not to cry.

"Thank you," I said, lowering my head. "Thank you so much."

"Welcome to our little hamlet by the sea, my new friend, Bob. I hope to see you around here more often."

She left and I could hear the swinging door as she entered the kitchen.

My eyes welled with tears and I pinched the top of my leg to stop crying. I removed my ripped snowboard jacket and hung it on the back of the chair like a classy person. It was my second time being in a coffee shop, the first time was less than a year prior when my ex-girlfriend's parents had threatened a restraining order after finding out that we lost our virginity to each other after three years of dating.

Don't think about it, I thought. *Don't think about your brother, your mom's new boyfriend, your ex-girlfriend, your former friends, your former dreams of being a pro baseball player, your former step-father, or your real dad who wants nothing to do with you. Don't think about any of it. It'll just make you sad. Just focus on the coffee and the food.*

"What did you come to Seward for, son?" Mother asked, interrupting my daydream. "Who's feeding my chickens?"

"To visit you, Ma." I leaned down to hug her. "What do you think? A neighbor is taking care of the birds, it's not big deal. What movie are you watching, anyway? And do you mind if I bring the dogs up?"

She shook her head and tightened her lips. "I don't know, son—it's something on. Bring my dogs in, I miss them. Don't ask next time."

Our legs touched on the couch as she rubbed her thumbs together on her belly. I had not seen the movie, but it had the crazy rappers from South Africa and a robot gangster. How my mother picked out movies was beyond me, but she barely watched them anyway.

A high-pitched whistling sound came from somewhere in the apartment.

"What was that?"

She shrugged and stared at the screen.

"Did you hear that whistling sound?"

She shrugged and set her jaw forward in a slight frown.

I examined the baseboard heaters in the kitchen, the refrigerator and freezer, and the large, south facing windows for wind passing through cracks in the trim. I searched with eyes and ears for the culprit yet I found nothing. I was distracted by dozens of magnets on the refrigerator door. A picture of us in Sedona, Arizona taken two weeks after my discharge from the army. A magnet of Paul Bunyan with an axe over his shoulder read, "Trees of Mystery—Redwood Highway." A magnet of Bigfoot read, "Bigfoot Country, Oregon." They were mementos from our road trip ten years prior, a road trip that I hoped to duplicate. A whistling sound came from the living room. Mother's eyes were down with a guilty look on her face.

"Mother, is that whistling sound coming from you?"

She shrugged and stared at the carpet.

"If you are making that sound, please tell me. I am no doctor, but I am EMT certified. A whistle from the lungs can indicate that your body is not getting enough oxygen. If your body is not getting enough oxygen, your brain is not getting enough oxygen. You don't want to be a vegetable, do ya, Mom?"

"It's only been a couple of days," she said. "I was going to tell you, but I don't want you to worry."

"I'm not worried. Let's call Doctor Ursel at Glacier Family Medicine and see if he can squeeze you in."

"We can wait until next week. Maybe it will get better."

"We are talking about your brain here, Ma. Do you

want to live the rest of your life like a withered spud in a wheelchair?" She shook her head. "I didn't think so."

I dialed the number as she pinched her leg with one hand and wiped away tears with another.

2

I helped Mother stand from the couch, put her shoes on, and leave the apartment. She leaned on me and the handrail as we went down an outdoor flight of stairs to ground level and then walked to the car where I opened the passenger side door for her.

"You're treating me like an old lady. And I sure feel like one."

"I'm not trying to, Ma. I just want to help."

"You are a big help, son. Always have been, and I appreciate it."

I left the parking space directly in front of her apartment building and turned right to go past the new library down to the skatepark. I turned left on Ballaine Boulevard and drove slowly past the empty campgrounds where seagulls and ravens searched for scraps left behind by tourists. Two weeks prior the campgrounds were full with hundreds of people in RVs and tents. Where had they gone? Everywhere but here. Prison lights across the bay reminded me of our family's past. My mother's ex-husband was still in there, and he would be until death.

"You ever talk to Victor?"

"Nope."

We drove past the public restrooms and the softball fields until reaching a stop sign with Murphy's Motel on the left and Bayside Apartments on the right. We turned right and drove past the equal housing opportunity apartments where we lived after moving out of the motel. We lived in the bottom right apartment, 1015 B. I sat on the deck railing under the overhang smoking for hours while staring at the mountains and the sea. We went through the harbor, past sailboats and fishing boats moored after working all summer, past where I used to kick hacky sack with older kids and drink vodka in the public restroom until I was knocked out by a 45 year old black man I had never seen before and never saw again. We passed Ray's Waterfront and Chinook's, two restaurants where I had worked, and a railroad car at the end of the street with a bike shop. At a stop sign, I glanced right and remembered working on the docks as a longshoreman earning union wages to unload tourist's luggage from cruise ships to be loaded onto the train. Those are good folks working on the docks. We turned left and merged onto the

Seward Highway, the only road leading out of town, past two grocery stores and a gas station.

"I'll bet they're happy it slowed down at the store," Mother said. "It is so busy in the summertime."

"I'll bet they miss having you around."

"I miss them."

"You'll be back at work in no time."

"Maybe."

"Maybe?"

"Maybe."

We drove north surrounded by mountains, past the cemetery where a handful of friends were buried too young, past the chamber of commerce, the army recreation camp, and the tennis courts where I once did a half-cab kickflip over a lowered tennis net first try. Past the airport, where dozens of planes were fueled up ready to fly. Past mountains of sand and gravel just before crossing the three bridges that span Resurrection River, and past the turnoff to the prison on Nash Road. We turned right near a big log building into the Glacier Family Medical parking lot and I helped mother out of the car and up to the entrance where we were greeted by my nephew's aunt. Seeing her reminded me that I had not seen him in over a year, and that I am probably the worst uncle in the world.

If I could only reach out to him without pissing off my brother or causing a riff in his mother's new relationship. Breakups ruin families, and my poor nephew will never get to know his uncle, or his father, and we will never get to know him.

She led us to an exam room where we waited less than a

minute for the doctor. Mother and him spoke like old friends, and I questioned their relationship. As he palpated her throat and behind her ears, she wiped tears off her cheeks.

"Why the tears, Sheri?"

"I know it's bad."

"There is obvious swelling of the lymph nodes that may indicate a larger issue." He placed his hairy hand on hers. "But we don't know anything yet—only God does. So let's take an X-ray to find out more."

After she used his arm to stand and walk out of the room, I texted my brother—even though we had not spoken in over a year.

"Mom and I are at the clinic. I am worried. She is getting an X-ray now. I will keep you posted. Have you heard her breathing?"

To my surprise, he replied within seconds, "Mom okay?"

"Don't know. I will call after. I love you."

"Love you."

When they returned fifteen minutes later, Mother grimaced with each step. She stood shifting her weight from leg to leg, waiting for the results. The same lady I had car camped with all over the west coast—the brunette babe customers always flirted with—was fifty pounds overweight and barely able to move. She looked miserable and afraid. Her dyed strawberry blonde hair was faded and her silver roots were an inch long. She wore gray Mickey Mouse sweatpants and a dark blue Chicago Cubs sweatshirt. She had dark rings under her eyes with pale cracked skin. She bit her cheek and rubbed her thumbs together. We did not speak or make eye contact. *What could be said in a time like this?* I wondered. It was not the time for humor, theories, or small talk. After ten minutes, the doctor returned with a clenched jaw and downcast eyes.

"Here is what we know." He slapped the X-ray up on the wall and flipped on a light. "Please sit down."

Mother leaned on the edge of the exam table.

"You have a growth in your lungs that measures roughly the size of a softball." He pointed with a pencil at a tumor in her lungs. "And you have more in your spine." We saw dozens of small circles in her spine. "Which is probably why your back hurts so bad and your lungs are working extra hard. We do not know if they are cancerous, but tomorrow morning you will do a test that will tell us more. I can say this—" He put his hand on her shoulder. "The tumors in your spine appear to have destroyed parts of your spinal column, which may have caused your vertebrae to collapse onto one another and cause grinding. This would explain the pain." He rubbed her shoulder and then held her hand while shifting his gaze between us. "Whatever your family needs, whether today, tomorrow, or in the future, do not hesitate to call. Here is my number." He handed me a card. "I will be over any time, day or night."

"Thank you."

"And Sheri," he held her shoulders and faced her. "You are the brightest light this town has ever seen." She lowered her head. "I visit the store every day just because your presence makes my life better." Tears streamed down her face yet she made no sound. "Call the store—request more leave—paid leave, if you have it. You need time off. No matter what happens in the next few weeks, keep your light shining. God did not make bright lights like yours to hide away."

He hugged her as she wept. It was the first time I had seen her cry since she told me that she was moving to Seward to pursue a new relationship and to get divorced. When the doctor turned, I was surprised to see tears streaming down his face. Perhaps he was surprised to see my dry face.

"Remember what I said." He touched my shoulder. "Call if you need anything, anything at all, and please take care of this special woman."

"I will. Thank you."

"You are the luckiest guy in Alaska to call Sheri your mother."

"Don't I know it."

He opened the door to leave and turned around.

"I will see you both tomorrow after the results are sent over. I will review them, and then call you in."

"Sounds good."

"Thank you, Brent," said Mother. "Thank you so much."

"It is the least that I can do after all that you have done for our community."

He walked out.

We rode to Mother's place in silence. I helped her up the stairs and into the apartment building where the dogs greeted us with wagging tails and shaking bodies. I put on *Field of Dreams* as she went to the restroom in her bedroom and then sat on the couch.

"Do you want something to eat, Ma?"

"No thank you, son."

"Any coffee?"

"I'm fine, thanks."

"Okay. I'm going to the coffee house to write. If that's okay with you?"

"Please son, we both need time to process this."

"Amen. I'll take the dogs out when I get back. It won't be long."

"Take your time. Just make sure they have food and water and they will be just fine."

They were sprawled out on the living room floor, taking up the entire space.

The wonderful thing about having Saint Bernards is that they will lie around all day if you let them, I thought.

I kissed her forehead and lips before patting the dogs and leaving. I walked a couple of blocks to the coffee house where I ordered a black coffee and climbed the creaky, narrow stairs to be alone in the loft.

How the fuck am I going to deal with this? I wondered. *My cornerstone, my best friend, my only parent, is about to die?*

I heard friends talk and laugh downstairs, I stayed upstairs to stare out of the big picture windows at Fox Island and Resurrection Bay. A pen was in my hand and an open notebook on my lap, but nothing came out. I stared outside for an hour.

How will I ever write about this? My mother is going to fucking die, and she is only fifty-six.

3

There is a battle going on for your mother's soul," said the cashier while ringing up my carton of ice cream. "A battle between good and evil. Evil so evil that no horror film does it justice."

"Oh really?" I couldn't believe that she was talking like this while customers waited in line behind me. "And how do you know this?" I wanted her to be viewed as crazy.

"Because I was visited by the good and evil forces, and they warned me to stay away from your mother. So I cannot visit—please tell her why—and tell her that I am praying for her."

"Will do. Thanks for the prayers." *You crazy ass.*

We went to the hospital the next morning for testing. She moved slower than the day prior, and was in more pain.

She explained that somebody she once knew had received the same test and then died two weeks later.

"Was it because of the illness or the dye?" I asked.

She shrugged. She did not want to take the test. Hell, she did not want to be in the hospital with a softball in her lungs and dozens of tumors, but it was what it was. She took a hospital gown from the receptionist and walked to the restroom to change.

"You need a hand changing, Ma?"

She raised an eyebrow and gave me a look that said, "Don't be crazy?"

I thought about Heaven and Hell, purgatory, hungry spirits, Buddhist realms, bardos, reincarnation, karma, fate, and God.

Where will her spirit go after she dies, I wondered. *She always said that she would come back as an eagle to soar over the mountains and water and to watch her family grow. Can we so easily choose our next lives?*

She left the bathroom in a light blue hospital gown with her clothes draped over an arm.

"At least they gave you a nice color."

"I would have preferred pink."

She smiled and wiped a tear from her cheek.

"Thanks for being here, son. You've always been here for me."

"I wasn't there for you when I was in Iraq, or during the many years that I spent drunk and stoned."

"I still owe you thousands of dollars for helping me move from Alaska to Arizona while you were in Iraq."

"Get over it. For all that you have done for me, you don't owe me a dime."

"Thanks, son. We all go through a drinking phase. I am just glad that you stopped before it killed you or somebody else."

"Me too."

"Have you talked to your brother?"

"I texted him yesterday and will call when we get the results."

She bit her cheek and rubbed her thumbs together.

"I am worried about his drinking. He is going hard again."

"Aren't you always? It seems like you have other things to worry about."

"No shit. Maria called last week asking for advice. He drinks all day, even when he's watching the baby."

"And she continues to leave the baby with him to go to work?"

She shrugged. "He passes out around noon and then wakes up to drink again at night. His neighbor stopped by the other day and found him passed out on the floor while Liam crawled around the house alone. He could have died! He tried to wake James up, but he couldn't. So he brought Liam home and took care of him until Maria got off work."

"That's a good neighbor. What did you tell her to do?"

"Call the police. What else can you do? We have tried everything with that boy, and nothing works. He is just too hard headed to admit that he has a problem and too blind to see that it is affecting everybody around him."

"He needs to quit drinking, and to find friends who don't

drink. Somebody to talk to about the shit in his head could do him a lot of good, too."

"He should get what he wants," she said. "To go back to prison to live on government handouts and to be left alone for the rest of his life. He learned a bad habit in there that is hard to break, that you don't have to work hard to make it in this world. All you have to do is manipulate people, and that is what he continues to do with these poor women."

"He has been working on the docks as a longshoreman earning a great pay."

"He only works as much as he needs to so he can claim unemployment. He never learned how to work, son. Not like you did."

"I don't know about that, Mom. He worked at the brewery in Juneau for years after prison. He has held jobs longer than I have, no doubt. Prison just made him worse, it didn't rehabilitate him at all."

"Does prison rehabilitate anybody?"

"That is the million dollar question, Mother."

"Sheri Stern," said a plump nurse with a clipboard. Mother stood. "Please follow me."

My sick mother shuffled forward to take a test to determine her fate.

I remembered when she was lean and happy, tan and young, living at a gated trailer court in Coolidge, Arizona in her forties. She would sit on a lawn chair in a tank top and shorts covered in tanning oil. A tiny flower box bloomed beside her in a patch of gravel that was her yard. All the old men and women stopped to chat with the Taylor Swift of the trailer park.

If the doc would have said a golf ball instead of a softball, I would be more hopeful. But a softball—Hell, she is done for.

I texted my brother. "Back at hospital for testing. Not looking good, brother. I will text more later."

I had distanced myself from him ever since our joint land purchase fell through in Happy Valley, and then he accused me of trying to steal his ex-girlfriend and told me to stay away from his family. Soon after they split, he started dating a newly widowed Russian immigrant who got pregnant shortly after. They were soon married. I did not attend the wedding even though I was invited. He had two sons with two women in a small prison town where he regularly ran into former correctional officers who abused him in ways he only spoke of when blacked out drunk. He hated living in Seward because of the constant reminders of the dark past, so he either tried to hide from the thoughts by drinking and using or chose to wallow in the pain. His only thoughts of the future had to do with where he would get his next fix. It was a tough season for my big brother, James, who seemed to be in a twenty year stretch of a hard season. I could not be around him because there was nothing that I could do for him, and I did not want to be around him when he became violent—and he always became violent when he drank too much.

My phone rang, it was him.

"Bobby," he said, inhaling and exhaling a cigarette. "How's it going?"

"Not good. Mom has a softball size tumor in her lungs and a bunch more in her spine. We are at the hospital now. They are testing them for cancer."

Silence.

"Fuck—" He spoke with shortness of breath. "Fuck, fuck, fuck." He wailed, as I sat with a straight face. "When will we know if it's cancer?"

"Later today."

Silence.

I pictured my big, strong brother wiping tears from his cheeks with tattooed arms and hands like I had watched him do so many times before. He took deep breaths with long exhalations to try and regain control.

"Brother, you there?" I asked.

"Yeah. Should I come there right now? Is she going to fucking die?"

I wanted to say, 'Walk the two blocks up here so we can smoke outside and cry together.' But instead, I said, "I'll call when we know more."

"Okay, little brother—call later and let's meet up."

"Roger."

"I love you, Robert. And I miss you."

"I love you too, brother. Hang in there."

I took a deep breath and hung up while subconsciously pinching my leg with my left hand and rubbing my fingers together with my right. I stared at the wall trying not to think about Iraq. Fighting every damn urge and impulse to spiral into darkness, a darkness that held me for eight years after my discharge from the army.

If I start thinking about Iraq, every shitty thing from childhood will find a way in and I will end up depressed and drunk.

Mother hobbled into the waiting room in worse shape than before. She was so pale that it looked like she had lost half of her blood. Her lips were blue and cracked and the lines in her forehead were deep and grey. She stared at the ground and faked a half-smile.

"How'd it go?"

"I wouldn't wish that on my worst enemy."

Is she referring to the pain of the test or the mental agony of not knowing the results? I wondered.

"Good thing you don't have any enemies. I talked with James. I will call him after we meet with Doctor Ursel." I stood and put my arm around her shoulders. "We'll get through this."

"In one way or another, we will get through this. Dead or alive."

"You need help changing back into your clothes, Ma?"

She raised her eyebrow and gave me a look that said, 'You must be crazy.'

I laughed, and she did not.

4

We drank coffee on the couch while listening to Matchbox Twenty and Alicia Keys. The doctor called around 11 and we drove straight to the clinic where he greeted us at the front door. *This can't be good,* I thought. He led us to the same exam room and we sat in the same seats as the day prior. His body language was distant and he was more silent than before. Out of nowhere, I almost started to cry.

Push back the fucking tears, Robert. Now is not the time, I told myself.

"How is the pain, Sheri?"

"It hurts like hell, Brent, but I will manage."

"You will have a stronger medication soon." He leaned on

the counter near the sink and then sat on a stool to roll beside Mother. "I had a chance to look over the tests."

"And?"

He took a contemplative breath.

"You know in the movies when the doctor says, "I have some good news and some bad news—- which do you want to hear first?" Well—life is not always like the movies."

"Just give me the news, Brent."

He stood and set his hand on my mother's shoulder.

"There is no good news."

And with those seven words, all of the fire in the universe was extinguished as my breath and spirit seemed to leave my body.

"You have stage four lung cancer that has metastasized throughout your body." He paused. "It is in your bones, too, Sheri, and it is the reason for the pain in your spine." He paused again, letting the news sink in. I tried to imagine not having a mother for the rest of my life, I could not. "You could try chemotherapy—but I do not believe that it will do anything more than make you sick and make your hair fall out. Alternative treatments exist, some are proving quite successful, but your cancer is so far advanced that I am doubtful any would work. Not to mention, most insurance plans don't cover them."

Mother let out a full bodied, hysterical laugh that seemed to turn the doctor and I into statues.

"If you're going to do something, do it right," she said. "That's what my daddy always said."

"Well you, missus, certainly did it right." The doctor smiled and held her hand.

I stared at the floor, a master of detachment.

"How long do I have, Brent?"

"That is a tough question that I do not like to answer. But out of respect for you, Ms. Sheri, I would say that you have anywhere from two weeks to two months."

A heavy silence fell over our lives, like that which comes after the last bullets of a firefight have been fired and you realize that you are alive and uninjured and it is not a dream but a terrifying reality that will haunt you all of your life.

I pictured my mother and brother walking on the beach in Nome when I was only 4 or 5. She had spent all day panning for gold on the beach with a metal detector until she was just about to give up and she found a $100 bill under a log. She was happier than I had ever seen her. She was Team Mom for my baseball teams, at every game with snacks for all of the players. She caught my wild pitches in our makeshift pitching mound in the backyard, bruises covered her shins and knees. When I was fresh out of the army at twenty-two, I fell asleep at a vortex site in Sedona, Arizona after we hiked to every one. I was processing so much shit from my two tours in Iraq that I could not speak, and then I awoke and saw her shining face as she smiled while seated on a large rock surrounded by tiny hoodoos and trees.

She has always been there for me, even when my father was nowhere to be found. And then "POOF!"—she will be gone.

The doctor held her hand as I pinched my leg and came back to reality.

"We will make sure that you do not feel the pain. And when it becomes too difficult to stand to use the restroom, I will come to your home to insert a catheter." She nodded. "And for you." He turned to face me. "Are you willing and able to care for your mother at this time, or do you need additional support?"

I looked at her to see if she would talk or give a sign.

"I can handle it. If I need help, I will call you."

"Don't hesitate. Day or night, any hour, I will be there in less than ten minutes. Sheri, these may be the last weeks of your life—but you know that that it is not the end."

"Just another step on the journey." She smiled as tears rolled down her cheeks. "A wonderful journey it is."

"I am sorry that you are in such pain, and like I said— we will relieve the pain today. Robert, you are in charge of administering very powerful pain medication on a strict schedule. Otherwise, as the cancer progresses, your mother will be in excruciating pain. Can you handle that responsibility?"

I remembered my final weeks of high school before leaving for basic training. I had stolen and snorted a bottle of her pain pills to curb the cravings for marijuana and alcohol. But I was not a teenager anymore, and I had not drank alcohol or used any drugs in over a year.

"I can handle it."

"Good. I believe that you can." He wrapped his arm around my mother's shoulders. "Do you mind if we pray?"

"Please do," said Mother.

"Dear Heavenly Father,

We come to you today to ask for your protection and guidance as this bright lamp of a woman, Ms. Sheri, your blessed servant, transitions out of this body—one that has done so much work to bring goodness to the Earth—into a new body. Dear Lord, be with her as she begins the journey home. Keep her brave, and make her transition from this life to the next, painless. Send your heavenly angels to journey alongside her. In your son's name, amen."

"Amen."

S

Leaving the Doctor's Office | Staring at the Prison Towers | Let's Go to the Beach | A Run-In With an American Hardworking Man | Barefooted on the Beach

W e left the clinic in silence and drove toward town.
"Turn on Nash Road, would ya, son?"

I turned on the two-lane road surrounded by spruce trees and sparse habitations. Snow-capped mountains towered on the left, the waters of Resurrection Bay flowed on the right. I was muddled in the middle. Streams of light passed through clouds illuminating dust near my face. We passed a trailer park, climbed hills, and made wide turns before descending into an open area with an old metal tower on pilings in the bay near a large concrete pad with abandoned infrastructure. We approached the road that leads to the prison.

"Stop here, son. On the other side of the road, please."

"Yes, ma'am."

I pulled over and we stared down the long road at the

only maximum security prison in Alaska. Guard towers with gunmen towered over razor wire fences.

James was only sixteen when he pointed a gun at a liquor store clerk for three-hundred dollars and two bottles of Tequila, I thought. He was sent here to be raised by serial killers, serial rapists, and serial convicts. People commit worse crimes every day and get away with them. Our justice system is bullshit.

Mother was still staring at the prison.

"What are you thinking, ma?"

She sighed, "Oh, nothing, son. Nothing at all. Let's go to the beach, I love driving by the boats back there."

"Yes, ma'am."

We past the turnoff to Spring Creek, where fishermen gather every year to catch silver salmon, until arriving at the dry dock area where big boats on blocks were being worked on by men in XtraTuf boots and Carhartts. We drove at 5 MPH through the boat yard. Shipping containers stacked three high formed walls with trusses and a roof to provide a dry place to work. Most of the boats were outside of the shipping container structure, some had been there for years just waiting for the right person to fix them. A black haired man in a Red Sox cap wearing a face mask and safety goggles looked in our direction. He waved with a palm sander. Mother waved back. He shut down the sander, lowered the mask, raised the goggles, and walked over.

"Stop here, son."

Mother rolled down the window as the man lit a cigarette and approached.

"Hi Rich, it is a nice surprise to see you out here. You see me at work almost every day, and this is the first time I get to see you at work."

"What a pleasant surprise, Ms. Sheri." He had an east coast accent. "I haven't seen you at the store in over a week. Where you been? You doing alright?"

"I've been playing hooky." Mother laughed.

He held the cigarette away from the window and leaned in to talk.

"I doubt that. You ain't the type of gal to skip out on work, I know that. I've been worried about ya—we all have."

Two guys waved with their sanders, Mother waved back.

"You don't have to worry about me, honey. I'm in good hands. Rich, this is my youngest son, Robert."

He stuck his leathery, greasy hand past mother's face and shook mine.

"Pleased to meet ya, Robert. You're a lucky kid to have a mom like this one."

"Don't I know it." He couldn't have been older than me by more than a few years, yet he looked like an old man. "Good to meet you, Rich."

"Your mother is the most caring lady I've ever come across, and I've crossed paths with many-a-women."

"I am a lucky son."

"No, but seriously—where ya been, Sheri? I've been going to the store every day hoping to see you, but you haven't been around. That's not normal for you. You are usually there every day, rain or shine."

"I have been taking a little time off is all."

He looked at her with a look of self-restraint and wonder. Her face flushed and she pinched her leg and looked away.

"Okay, Ms. Sheri." He patted her shoulder. "This old boat ain't going to sand itself. It brings me great joy to see you out here. I hope to see you back at the store soon."

"It's nice to run into you, too, Rich. Now get back to work and quit slacking."

He laughed and kissed her cheek.

"You know me well. The slacker—if only that were true. I wouldn't be so beat up at such a young age."

He backed away, flicked a cigarette, lit another, and walked toward the boat.

"Hey Rich," Mother called. He turned around. A spruce covered mountain towered in the background and a handful of fishing boats were on blocks in the foreground. He had deep lines on his face full of dried paint, safety goggles on his forehead that pulled back his greasy black hair, a respirator mask over his neck, a full beard that almost hid the cigarette dangling from his lips, thick blackened fingers with knobby knuckles, and paint stained overalls with holes in the knees. Fabric strands blew in the wind. He looked like a real-life Norman Rockwell painting of a hardworking American man. "Don't work yourself to death. You are a good man, a kind and gentle man. Do not forget that."

He bit his lower lip, lowered his head, and nodded.

"Thank you, Ms. Sheri." He signed the cross and kissed a crucifix that he pulled out from under his shirt. "I doubt that my kids and wife think that. Hell, maybe it's time to give them a call. I will be seeing you soon, Ms. Sheri, I hope."

He walked to the boat, raised the mask, lowered the goggles, and sanded.

We followed the dirt road around a break wall to park near the beach.

"Moving to Seward was one of the best decisions I ever made." Mother opened the door and swung her legs out. "Spread my ashes in Resurrection Bay, son. I love it here."

"Will do, Ma."

I helped remove her shoes and socks before doing the same, and then we held hands and walked barefoot on the beach for the last time.

b

False Beliefs | Non-Judgment | Visitors from Far and Wide | Simply Kind | A Family Reunion | From Ashamed to Honored | Do What You Love, Every Day | Anchorage Oncology Center | Peaceful Pictures in Back | Treatment Suggestions | Aunt Kathy Saves the Day | Death Flight | Crying Together | The First Time I Met an Angel

I grew up believing that the only people who changed people's lives were doctors, teachers, coaches, athletes, musicians, authors, scientists, millionaires, and holy people. My mother proved me wrong. She was a grocery store clerk for nearly two decades who shared a glowing smile with dozens each day. She asked about people's lives and listened when they answered, later asking follow-up questions to make sure people were okay. By smiling and talking with customers, she spread kindness, joy, and non-judgment every day. Because of her kindness, dozens of people arrived to the tiny apartment to visit with her. They brought food, stories, tissues, and more. They took turns being alone with her in the bedroom—praying, coloring, snuggling, braiding her hair, reading aloud, and talking. Mother complimented their appearances and accomplishments, encouraging them to pursue their own dreams and goals rather than anybody else's.

Her coworkers at the grocery store filled a photo album with self-portraits for Mother to look at from bed. Her four siblings reunited for the first time in over twenty years. Uncle Joe and Aunt Gwen came from Idaho, Uncle Don from Minnesota, and Aunt Kathy from California. Their youngest brother, Uncle Ronnie, had tragically died in his twenties yet he was still there in spirit, Mother said. Cousins arrived from Anchorage and Willow. Old friends drove out from Glacierview and Peters Creek. A former pimp covered in gold jewelry touched the cheek of a two-week-old baby leaving with a young mother. Even my old drinking buddy from high school, Bruce Rockefeller, called from who-knows-where to sing a final version of Blind Melon's "No Rain." I could hear Mother cry-laughing from the bedroom. Money was collected from the townspeople that amounted to over five-thousand dollars to pay for food, plane tickets, cremation expenses, and whatever else our family needed.

"I enjoy coloring more than anything else," Mother said, while coloring beside a co-worker, "besides roller skating, of course. Unfortunately, I didn't do either after I was a teenager. Remember this, son, do what you love every day. Don't put it on the back burner just because it doesn't make money. Do what makes you happy."

My mother was married to my birth father and had their

first child by the time she was twenty-one. She had her second child when she was twenty-four. She left my father at a trailer park in California after he became too abusive due to drugs and alcohol and refused to quit, when she moved her sons to Nome, Alaska to live with her brother, my Uncle Don, until she met her second husband. For eight years she was a lonely wife in a loveless marriage to a man who would rather be golfing with Masons than spending time with his wife and step-sons. She left him in Eagle River and moved to Seward as a single mom with one son in prison and another on the way, months away from marrying a man in prison without parole. She did not know anybody in Seward, yet she moved there anyway despite her family's disapproval. And I, her youngest son, was so embarrassed by her decisions that I hated her.

I was so ashamed of her back then, I thought, while watching people come and go from her bedroom while crying. *But look at her now, twenty years later, surrounded by people who love and respect her. A revered member of the community that extends behind the prison walls to hundreds of inmates and their rejected families. My mother made a difference in the lives of so many without being a doctor, a teacher, a coach, an athlete, a musician, an author, a scientist, a millionaire, or a holy person. It didn't matter what she was, what mattered was who she was.*

After years of carrying a thousand pound rucksack full of shame and embarrassment, I saw her for who she was rather than who I thought she was. And for the first time in my life, after hearing it hundreds of times from friends and strangers alike, I was proud to be her son.

A week after the diagnosis, my aunt arrived from Lodi, California with her adopted son, Anthony, to take care of Mother. Aunt Kathy is a professional caregiver with a lifetime of experience taking care of people who cannot take care of themselves. She adopted a brain damaged native Alaskan girl over thirty years ago who is still unable to feed and bathe herself, and then recently adopted a Cambodian-American boy with brain damage, a bad limp, and a cockeyed wrist caused by a mother who could not stand the crying of her baby any longer. On top of it all, she works in a live-in facility where she takes care of elderly patients. She administered medication, bathed her little sister and braided her hair, and sat with her for hours each day.

I was in charge of Mother's advanced directive, the belongings, the life insurance, the treatment plan, and the remains. Treatment plans were brought to my attention daily by people who passed through the door. While I was grateful for their compassion, I believed Doctor Ursel—the cancer was too far progressed. After a late-night discussion with Aunt Kathy while her son watched *Lion King* in the background, we decided to get the opinion of an oncologist in Anchorage.

We laid the back seats down in Mother's car and used pillows to prop her up for the two and a half hour drive to Anchorage. The fit, young doctor could not guarantee that chemotherapy would help, but it was a possibility.

"Your insurance won't cover all of the costs, but we can tap into your life insurance to cover the difference. After two or three sessions we will have to figure out another payment method."

Mother stood from the wheelchair to look the young doctor in the eyes.

"So what you're telling me is that you guys will take one hundred and sixty four thousand dollars from my sons in exchange for making me go flipping bald?" She laughed. "You've got to be kidding."

Aunt Kathy and I laughed as the doctor's face flushed. I had the impression that he was not used to people talking back.

"Listen Cheryl—" He looked at the clipboard. "I mean, Sheri—I mean, Ms—"

"Let's get the hell out of here, son."

Aunt Kathy opened the door and I pushed the wheelchair to the car where we loaded Mother in back for the return trip to Seward.

I was furious on the drive. Angry at cancer profit centers, insurance companies, fraudulent doctors, unfair pay scales, classism, nepotism, and God. I couldn't stop picturing my mother's friend, Rich, standing by the boat with a cigarette in his mouth, busting his ass for pennies compared to what the rich-kid doctor made. I was fucking pissed that my fifty-six year-old mother was dying and I couldn't stop it.

I've read the Bible, I know about the healings. I've been to Christian Science churches where people make testimonies about miracles of healing through prayer. So why the hell isn't God healing my mother? What has she done to deserve this?

While I was angry in the driver's seat, Mother was at peace in the back. We stopped half a dozen times to open the hatch so she could take pictures

"What's the matter, son? You're not enjoying the fall colors?"

"I am dedicating my life to taking down these fraudulent cancer-cure-mother-fuckers. They are robbing people while killing them at the same time."

"If you dedicate your life to that, you will be mad every day." She paused to take a picture of a bald eagle in a spruce tree. "And I hate to say it, but you can't beat them. Focus on what brings joy to your life. Make changes that are in your control. Live a good life, son. Please, do it for me."

I pinched my leg and kept driving.

Some of her co-workers pushed the idea of an alternative cancer treatment center in Arizona that was covered by their insurance plan. I listened and then contemplated the option as Mother snored in bed. She was bedridden, unable to use the restroom, and on oxygen full time unless asleep.

Doctor Ursel arrived as mother was waking up. After taking her vitals, he sat by the bed and held her hand while stroking her hair. Aunt Kathy entered the room crying.

"Can I ask you a question, Doc?" I asked.

"Of course."

"People come in and out of here to visit my ma with good intentions." I looked outside and saw Uncle Joe and

Uncle Don smoking on the sidewalk below. "Because of their love for her, they urge us to try different treatments for her cancer. We brought her to the Anchorage Oncology center and we decided that we weren't going that route. Well, the newest idea brought to our attention is an alternative cancer treatment center in Arizona that is covered by her insurance. So my question is this—Should we go to Arizona for treatment, and what is the likelihood that it will work?"

He took a deep breath, closed his eyes, and lowered his head.

"I don't like to say this, but I will—since you asked. Sheri, I doubt that the airlines will allow you to board a plane in your condition. It would be too much of a liability. And if you were able to, you would probably be dead by the time you landed." Anthony laughed at the TV from the living room. "You can pursue any route that you want to take, it is your decision. But that is my opinion, since you asked for it."

Everybody in the room cried, including the doctor, as Anthony continued to laugh at the TV in the living room.

"'I'm watching you, Wazowski,'" he said, quoting *Monsters Inc.* "'Always watching.'"

Doctor Ursel wiped his eyes and hugged my mother. He hugged Aunt Kathy, and then he hugged me before leaving the apartment for the last time.

7

"Satan and his Legion are trying to take your mother's soul," said the crazy cashier at the grocery store. "Last night, I was visited at home by a host of them, and they told me to stay away from her or risk possession."

"Damn, you don't want that. In that case, it's best if you don't come by."

"There is a battle between good and evil taking place—"

"Can't I just pay for the fucking ice cream." Her eyes went wide with disbelief. "You said the same fucking thing last time."

"Oh—" She batted her fake eyelashes that were weighted down with thick blue eye shadow. "Excuse me. How is Sheri?"

I pictured her barely breathing with eyes barely open. Bedridden with a catheter, high on fentanyl, the rhythm of the oxygen machine as a metronome of death.

"She's okay."

"Tell her that I say, 'Hello,' and that I will be praying for her." I nodded.

Fuck off you crazy psycho, I thought.

The cashier had been talking to everybody about the battle between good and evil for my mother's soul, and while I did not believe that she was visited and warned by Satan and God's angels, one cannot be too cautious when dealing with the forces of good and evil. So I went to Sacred Heart Catholic Church to speak with the priest about mother's last rites, and despite her not being an active member of the Catholic Church, he agreed to perform the rituals.

I met Father Tero outside and we walked upstairs and inside without a word. He nodded and raised his hand to Aunt Kathy before being led through the living room toward the bedroom where Anthony was lying on the hide-a-bed in his pajamas laughing at *Toy Story*. The priest stopped to look at the boy and at the TV.

"Hi, I'm Anthony." Anthony smiled and waved his good hand.

"Hello, Anthony. It is nice to meet you."

"Nice to meet you."

Father Tero opened the bedroom door just enough to enter closing it behind him. Twenty minutes later, he left with a wave of the hand. What happened during that time, we will never know. I went in and sat by Mother's bed until she tapped on the blanket beside her.

"Closer, son." She barely had the strength to whisper.

I kissed her clammy forehead and touched her greasy hair. She tried to lift her arms to hug me but she was too weak. Her eyes were closed as I leaned forward and hugged her for a long time until resting my head on her upper chest. I focused on trying to remember her smell, but it was nothing like the smell of roses, coffee, and candles that I had always known.

"Thank you, son. For everything. You made my life so rich."

"I love you, Ma." Tears fell down my face. "I will miss you so much."

"I am so proud of you, son. You are a good man. I will always be with you."

"Thank you for taking such good care of me."

"Anytime." The oxygen machine was no longer making the annoying sound. We turned it off earlier that day upon her request. "My little brother, Ronnie, is here with me now. He is taking me to be with my Daddy again. We will all be together again soon."

I held her cold hand as she fell asleep, and then I kissed her cold forehead and lips.

"I love you, Mother. I will make you proud and honor you."

My brother opened the bedroom door and I could smell the deadly combination of alcohol, pot, and cigarettes. He could barely stand. We pressed our heads together and wept, before he asked to be alone with Mother.

Aunt Kathy looked at me from the hide-a-bed with a paper towel in her hands and tears on her eyes.

"I'll be back in a few," I said.

She nodded.

I walked with the dogs to the beach to smoke and stare.

How will I go on without her? I wondered. *Who will I call and talk with? Who will check on me and make sure that I'm okay? Who will hold me accountable for the dumb shit that I do? We never visited Europe like we wanted to, or took the second road trip. It's a damn shame. We were always too busy to make plans to do things outside of the daily grind. What if I have a family one day—my kids and wife will never know her. That is so fucking sad. What will come of my brother and I? Where will her soul go? If Heaven is for real, I can guarantee that my mother will be there.*

Loud voices came from outside of Tony's Bar, and I pondered having a drink for a brief moment before remembering that it only numbed me for a few hours until I eventually had to face reality with a hangover. My telepathic Saint Bernard, Nala, whined as a reminder of where my mind went when I drank. I patted her head and rubbed her belly.

"Thanks, girl."

She wagged her tail.

Her son, Charger, snuggled beside her on the gravel while staring behind us like a good, guard dog. I patted his thick back.

"Good boy."

He wagged his tail.

I guess this is going to be my only family for a while, I thought. *Me and my dogs.*

I tried to pray but I had no words. I tried to cry but the well was dry. I thought about calling somebody but I could not put my feelings into words. So I stared at the prison lights reflecting off of Resurrection Bay.

When I returned to the apartment, James was asleep on the living room floor with a hoodie as a pillow. Aunt Kathy and Anthony laid on the hide-a-bed watching *Michael*.

"There's food in there for you, honey."

"Thanks Aunt Kathy, I'm not hungry though."

"I understand."

"Thanks for coming to help." I patted her foot. "It means a lot."

"Anytime, honey."

I laid on the floor by my brother and fell asleep as the Archangel Michael descended the stairs in nothing but boxers while smoking a cigarette with his wings out.

Mother died sometime between midnight and six a.m. on October 1st, 2015. She waited until we were asleep to keep us wondering about white lights and spirits rising. James and I sat by her body as her lips turned gray taking turns with our ears over her mouth to hear the emptiness. We kissed her forehead and touched her hair. When a hearse arrived two hours later, we zipped the body in a black bag, rolled it onto a stretcher, and carried it outside to load in the hearse. James pulled out a pack of smokes and handed me one.

He lit the smoke and said, "Mom was a hell-of-a-lot-heavier than she looked." And we laughed-out-loud for a few seconds before falling into silence. "I guess I will see you later, little brother." He hugged me and rubbed his head against mine really hard. "I'm headed home to the fam." He searched his pockets with both hands and pulled out a handful of nickels, dimes, and cigarette butts.

"Take care of yourself, brother," I said. "I love you."

"I love you, too, Robert."

He walked to the corner of the building and stopped to look both ways. Right was the way home, left was the way downtown.

He went left.

PART II

FROM THE FOREST TO A CAMPFIRE

TWO YEARS PRIOR

"Wars are not paid for in wartime,
the bill comes later."

BENJAMIN FRANKLIN

1

THE WORLD'S LARGEST OUTDOOR INSANE ASYLUM RV PARK

Pinos Altos, New Mexico

NOVEMBER 8, 2013

Winter Hawk | North Slope Work | Meeting the
Neighbors | Tinkerbell Scratches | Sweet Smells |
Homicidal Thoughts | Bratwursts on Sticks | Tinkerbell
| "After Good Taco, Good Tobacco" | Dragons and Rats
| Five Gray Heads | Drug Runner's Alley | Dry Mouth,
Shaky Hands | Boyd Cleans His Pistol | Laundry
Day | Bottle of Booze | "I Never Stink" | Shake Out
the Apples | "Too Tall" | Five Gallon Buckets | Dry
Drunk | Varmints and Birds | "Suck the Juice" | Sliced
Apples Drying in the Sun | Beat Them to the Apples!
| Motorcycle Ride | Ben Tilly | Mangas Coloradas |
Inside the Hawk's Nest | The Importance of Listening

1

"They call this place, 'The World's Largest Outdoor Insane Asylum RV Park,'" exclaimed the self-proclaimed leader and chef of the trailer park. Sam Hawkins was his name, Winter Hawk his nickname. He was a couple of inches shorter than me, two hundred and fifty pounds solid, and fully capable of wrestling a full-grown black bear.

"When I first started working on the north slope," he said, referring to the oil rig jobs in northern Alaska, "I was a weakling of a man. A hundred and forty pounds soaking wet." He poked the fire with a stick and then rolled sausage links sizzling in a cast iron pan on a metal grate over the fire. "But after twenty-three years of eating the slop they serve without working out, I became a serious husky fucker." He gyrated his hips against an empty lawn chair, rubbed his big bare belly, and made weird movements with his eyes and lips. He silently laughed so hard that I thought his face would explode.

Two other old timers sat hunched over in lawn chairs beside a small campfire under a loaded apple tree. It was one of over fifty apple trees in the Continental Divide RV Park in Pinos Altos, New Mexico with heavy branches weighted down with red, yellow, green, and striped apples. The sweet smell of apples was part of the everyday setting at the park, mixed with cooking sausage, eggs, and wood smoke—it may have been the best-smelling two weeks of my life.

"Anything bent over is good with me," said a man with a hoarse voice and a wide-open, bloodshot blue eye. He was hunched down so low in the lawn chair that it looked like he was going to fall out and take a nap on the ground. He had a chest-length silver beard, collar-length silver hair, and one closed eye that looked an inch lower than the other due to a cocked head.

Sam and the other man looked at each other and shook their heads in disapproval. I looked over and noticed a man cleaning a pistol on the steps of a school bus.

"Is that right, Jimmy?" said Sam, poking the fire with a stick. "What do you say to that, Richard?"

Sam nudged Richard, who appeared to be somewhere between eighty and a hundred years old. Richard wore two pairs of glasses, the outer pair were dark sunglasses that matched his ponytail and cane, while the inner pair were thick bifocals. His face was covered in pockmarks and his hands shook terribly.

"I want nothing to do with him," said Richard, shaking his head with disgust. "He is nothing but a sick drunk. He starts the day sicker than Pol Pot and ends it sicker than Herod's niece."

"Don't go bending over in front of Ol' One-Eye Jimmy," said Sam, red in the face with laughter, "or you might get stuck."

Richard's hands and head shook as Sam laughed. I could not see Richard's eyes, but he sat facing Jim with the look of a man ready to kill.

"Oh yeah," said Jim, speaking in a loud voice that felt out

of place among songbirds and a crackling campfire. "I like 'em thin and flat-butted. The smaller the better!"

Sam poked the coals with his stick as sausage grease sizzled and popped. He poured a bowl of whipped eggs and milk over the sausage links as an apple fell to the ground and rolled to Jim's feet. Jim groaned and leaned forward to pick it up. He examined the apple for a few seconds before taking a bite and chewing loudly.

"Who is that guy?" I asked, referring to the guy cleaning a pistol and staring around the park in paranoia.

"His name is Boyd," said Sam. "He wants nothing to do with any of us. He sits over there every day and cleans his pistol."

"It's true," Jim continued, spitting out pieces of apple skin. "I am a pedophile, there's no shame in it." He removed a blue trucker hat to scratch his flaky head with swollen fingers. He wore faded blue overalls that were covered in holes and stains with snakeskin cowboy boots that were so scuffed, his big toe showed in his left boot and his pinky toe showed in the right. He wore the same clothes every day while I was there. "I admit it," he said. "I like little boys. Hey everybody, I am a pedophile! I like little boys!"

"Jimmy, stop!" said Sam.

"Shut the hell up," said Richard, who picked up his cane and whacked Jim across the shins. "You freakin' sicko."

"Ouch!" said Jim, as he rubbed his leg and bit into the apple.

"Keep your sick mouth shut," said Richard, waving

his cane in Jim's face, "next time I'll hit you where the sun don't shine."

"Maybe the sun don't shine on your privates, Mr. Dick, but it sure as shit shines on mine."

"Quiet down, Jimmy," said Sam, "or you won't get breakfast. If you wake the spirit of Mangas Coloradas, you'll be in big trouble."

Jim stared at the ground chewing his apple and pouting.

Maybe I've come to the wrong place, I thought. *I can be around almost anybody for a short time, but I have my limits. Hell, I am the one who snitched on my brother when I was twelve and sent him to prison for 8 years. I am the one who hated my mother for remarrying a man doing life in prison, and then went to the visiting room to play poker with him. I am the one who joined the Army at 17 to escape the shame of home life, only to spend the next year as an infantryman in Iraq wreaking terror on thousands. So what if I got out of the Army in 2006 and spent the next 7 years exploring Yoga, Buddhism, sobriety, healthy living, and life while traveling the world and earning a few college credits. I am just another war veteran trying to live a decent life after doing some shitty things to people. Who am I to judge?*

A tiny chihuahua that I imagined as the retired Taco Bell mascot scratched the window of a twenty-four-foot Jayco travel trailer parked beside Sam's bus. The trailer and the dog were both owned by a guy named Moose whom I did not see a single time. The dog's tiny paw and bark could barely be heard from a few feet away. Someone, or something, grunted loudly as a thick pale hand with long dirty fingernails engulfed Tinkerbell and lifted her away.

"Now look what you've gone and done, Jimmy," said Sam. "You woke Tink. You need to act right, or go back to your camper and don't come back." Sam pointed to a rusty camper with a collapsed roof covered by a blue tarp in the bed of an old Chevy pickup with two flat tires. "Have you heard of guilty by association, Jimmy? I don't want to be friends with a pedophile."

"But it's true," said Jimmy, at a half-whisper. "I like boys." He popped the apple core in his mouth and laughed so hard that the veins in his neck and forehead popped at the skin. "I like young boys," he said. "Hey everybody, I am a pedophile!"

"Shut your trap," said Sam, as he struck Jim in the knee with the poker stick.

"Ouch!"

Richard used one part cane and two parts grit to stand and walk away while dragging a foot.

"You gonna eat, Richard?" asked Sam.

"I'm making a smoothie," said Richard. "And I need to get the hell away from that creep or I'll kill him."

Richard slowly dragged one foot to the trailer beside mine where he opened a squeaky door and stepped inside without looking back. Sam handed me a paper plate with two fried corn tortillas full of scrambled eggs, sausage, and diced ancho chilies. I thanked him. He did the same for Jimmy, who did not thank him, before making a plate for himself. We ate to the sound of Jim exclaiming the goodness of the food, like Bill Murray in the scene at his psychiatrist's dinner table in 'What About Bob?'. We could hear a family of deer eat fallen apples beside Jim's camper. We watched them as they watched us. It was a peaceful moment; the most peaceful moment I had since leaving Alaska three weeks prior. Hell, probably the most peaceful moment since buying land in Happy Valley, Alaska in 2012, with the hopes of starting a farm and pursuing an author career. Come to think of it, it may have been the most peaceful moment since parachuting into Iraq on March 26th, 2003. It was peaceful because all I was doing was listening to birds chirp, deer chomp, and a fire crackle while breathing in warm New Mexico air.

The peaceful moment came to an end when I realized that the strange man who claimed to be a pedophile was staring at me with a bloodshot eye. I tried to ignore it, but I could feel it—the way you can feel a dog stare when it needs to go pee. It felt awkward, and since I was used to feeling awkward around people—it didn't bother me too much, until a few days later, when I watched through the window as he stood in different parts of the park staring at my trailer, or a week later when he pounded on the trailer door at midnight begging to come inside to confess his secrets to a Jesuit Priest, and then tried to push it open. Then, and only then, as I stood by the door with my 7 3/8" Buck knife in my hand, did I want to kill Jim Hiller and bury his body under an apple tree.

2

It was nine-thirty in the morning on Monday, November 9, when I entered the campfire circle for the second time. The only reason I knew the time was because when I refused whiskey from Jim, Sam said, "Why not, Jimmy? Because it's nine-thirty in the morning."

The three men were drinking coffee while Sam cooked ground beef with diced onions, Hatch chiles, garlic, and "seven super secret special spices" that he sprinkled on everything. The smell seemed to make my entire body salivate. We ate sausage links as appetizers. Sam held the handle-less cast iron pan with pliers from a multi-tool and stirred with a hand-carved wooden spoon. Hot oil popped onto his thick hand and wrist and he did not flinch or grimace or make any mention of the pain.

"What, do you not drink or something?" Jim asked, too loud for such an early hour. He peered at me with one eye from beneath a ball cap while the other eye was sealed shut. "You probably need an entire bottle to get a buzz." He laughed hoarsely, coughed, and spat in the fire. He was the only person laughing.

"I drink," I said, "a little too much."

"Let me guess," he said. "Your dad is an alcoholic and your mother is an alcoholic. You've got it in your blood, so you try to stay away. Am I right?" His left eye opened slightly.

"We are a family of drinkers," I said. "No doubt, it is in

our blood. That is why I smoke bud instead." I should have said, 'That is why I *try* to smoke bud instead.'

"Good," he said, laughing. "That's real good. Stay away from booze, kid. It will make life a heck of a lot easier if you know that you have to."

"My grandfather died from alcoholism after Vietnam," I said. "His wife, my grandma, drinks Natural Ice Light all day in a frosty mug with ice cubes."

"Is that right?" he said.

"Yes sir."

"And why not?" he asked. "Can you tell me, why not?"

I shrugged, I could think of a few reasons.

"I would sure like to meet her," he said. "We would have a hell of a time!"

"I bet you would," said Sam. "You old dog. Speaking of dog, who is ready for breakfast tacos?" He held up a paper plate with two tacos.

"Right here," said Jim, raising a hand. "Give 'em here!"

"Here ya go, Jimmy," said Sam, handing him the plate. "But only if you promise to keep it down. I don't want you to wake the neighborhood, especially Moose and Tinkerbell."

Jim ate the first taco like he hadn't eaten since the prior morning.

"Who's next?" asked Sam.

"I just ate," said Richard, patting his extended stomach and leaning back. "I made some organic refried beans with organic meat from the Co-op and rolled them up in an organic tortilla."

"Sounds like an organic breakfast burrito," said Sam.

"Good stuff, too," continued Richard, "and some darn fine women working down there at the Co-op."

"We all know you don't go there for the overpriced meat," said Sam.

"It's not a secret," said Richard. "Me and every other lonely guy in the valley."

"I'm good, thanks," I said, always one to have coffee before breakfast.

"Here," said Sam, handing me a plate with two tacos. "You are young and growing, you need to eat."

"Yeah, he is," said Jim, with bits of sausage in his beard. "Feed the kid! He could use some meat on his bones."

I didn't want to think about Jim looking at my body after his comments the previous day.

"Don't you backtalk me now, Jimmy," said Sam, standing to stoke the fire with wood from a pallet. "I am the camp chief here, and if you backtalk me now I will take you out later."

Jim laughed so loud that a flock of birds flew out of the tree near his camper.

I ate slowly, trying to appreciate every bite. I was happy not to be home alone in the cold Alaskan countryside, or alone on a beach somewhere in Mexico. I needed company more than I realized.

"These are some good tacos," I said. "Thank you."

Sam made no notice of the compliment. "I have to fry up some more tortillas inside," he said. "Dick, watch the food, would ya?" Sam handed Richard the wooden spoon and smiled as his face turned red and his cheeks swelled with laughter.

"It ain't Dick," said Richard. "Like I told you last time."

"Oh yeah, that's right," said Sam, holding back the laughter. "Sorry about that... Richard."

"Shut up, saggy tits," Jim said to Richard. "You take life too seriously. Lighten up and have some fun."

Richard's face turned red and his lips moved like he was whispering to himself.

"I'm done with this," said Jim, handing a plate with a half-finished taco to Sam.

"Finish your food, Jimmy," said Sam, holding the screen door open to walk inside the school-bus-converted-motor-home. "Starving kids could live on your food waste."

"There ain't no starving kids around here," said Jim. "If there were, I'd give 'em my food. But I ain't going to put it in a box and mail it to 'em, it'd be spoiled by the time it got there." He took a swill of coffee and made a face that said, 'That was strong,' before finishing his taco in a single bite.

Sam stepped inside the bus to fry tortillas leaving Richard in charge.

"Stir that up," said Jim, moving his thick fingers with his elbows tight against his ribs. It looked like he was moving his arms by leverage alone.

"God dammit, Jimmy, I know how to cook," said Richard, stirring the food. "You don't even cook for yourself, you pathetic drunk."

"Oh now, be nice," said Jim.

"I do not see how a man can live to your age without cooking," said Richard. "Handouts—that's it. Handouts

71

have kept you alive. Ha! You couldn't cook if you wanted to because you cannot stand straight longer than a few seconds."

I laughed at their bantering and removed my Red Sox hat to scratch my head. Jim turned his attention to me.

"Why in the hell do you have an afro?" he asked.

"It is not an afro, you idiot," said Richard, "it is a mohawk."

"Oh..." said Jim, stroking his gray beard. "A mohawk, huh? Are you a damned Indian or something?"

"Yes, sir—I am," I said. "My grandma prides herself on our Seminole heritage. Nobody knows if it's real or not, but she claims that it is."

"I am one-sixteenth Apache," said Richard, stirring the meat. "And proud of it."

"Who gives a shit, Dick," said Jim. "Nobody cares if you are one-sixteenth dead!"

"I would rather be one-sixteenth dead than one-hundred percent drunk asshole."

"Now, now boys," said Sam, stepping down from the bus with a plate of hot tortillas. "Let's not get our panties in a wad, ladies." He took the spoon from Richard. "Anybody want more coffee? I am brewing another pot."

"Coffee," said Jim. "Give me some more!"

Richard shook his head in disgust while Sam and I laughed so hard that leaves fell.

"You have to wait until I am finished eating, Jimmy Boy," said Sam.

"Coffee!" Jim yelled again, followed by coughing and spitting.

"Hey now, buck," said Sam, with kind eyes that showed anger, "calm down or get back to your camper. I will pour more coffee when I am done. Besides, it is still brewing."

"Fine," said Jim. His shoulders sank and face drooped as he pulled a poncho to his chin and pouted.

Sam made himself two tacos and set the plate on his lawn chair before pushing one onto Richard and two more onto me. Jim asked for another but Sam ignored him. We ate to the sound of songbirds from a distant apple tree and a crackling fire. The New Mexico sky was full of red as the sun rose over the hills.

Sam finished his tacos and grabbed our mugs to go inside.

"Booze?" asked Jim, smiling mischievously.

"Do not order me around, old man," said Sam. "I'll make you the same thing as before."

"Good," said Jim, sighing. "Because it was so good. Man, it was good! Are you going to drink booze with me, young man?"

"Not now," I said.

Although it sounded good, once I started I could not stop, and my entire day would disappear like too many days before.

"He doesn't drink," Jim said to Richard, "but I do."

"I know you do," said Richard. "And it's disgusting."

Richard had been scowling at Jim ever since he called him saggy tits. Hell, I would be, too. I laughed while thinking about the insult and the way the old timers bickered.

"Oh now, Richard," said Jim, with a delicate voice. "If I didn't drink, what would I live for? I have no kids, no spouse, no job, and no purpose. What would I do with myself?"

"That is just pathetic," said Richard. "There is an infinite number of things to do with one's day, but your tires are axle-deep in mud and you can't get out."

"Do you think that I want to sit around watching television all day like you?" said Jim.

Sam stepped out of the bus and handed Jim and I a hot mug. We thanked him. He split one by fours with a kukuri to stoke the fire. The heat was comforting. Jim held his breath, closed his eyes, and drank.

"Any good, Jimmy?" Sam asked.

"It's really something. You know that?" Jim opened his left eye and looked at Sam with a straight-face. "You truly amaze me by the way you run a kitchen."

"I'm glad you like it, Jimmy. What do you guys think, do aliens from outer space live among us?"

"They have to," said Richard. "Without a doubt."

"I don't like that," shouted Jim. "I don't like it at all!"

"Damn it, Jimmy, quiet down," said Sam. "Richard, Rob—you boys need earplugs?"

"I turn down my hearing aid every time I come over," said Richard, fidgeting behind his ear.

"Oh, come on," said Jim, whispering. "I ain't that loud."

"You're going to wake Moose," said Sam, "and you know he doesn't like you already."

"I don't give a hoot," said Jim. "If I cared what other people thought, I would be a different man. All Moose does is sleep in that moldy old trailer anyway. He should get outside every once in a while. In the six months that he's been here, I have

74

seen Tinkerbell outside once. Once! Where does that poor dog poop and pee? I'd hate to smell the inside of that trailer!"

As if Tinkerbell was listening for her cue, she scratched at the window and barked. A thick and chapped red hand with long fingers and uncut dirty nails picked her up. She stared with bulging eyes.

"It is a real shame about my riding partner, Juan," said Sam, splitting weathered strips of plywood that he scavenged from a vacant lot.

"What happened, again?" asked Richard, who was deeply ashamed to have forgotten the story. Losing memories upset Richard more than anything else about growing old.

"Juan and a buddy down in Big Bend went out on the town in Juan's '57 Charger."

"Oh no," said Jim. His left eye closed and he stared at Sam.

"They ended up drinking too much and driving around like crazy Texans all over town and country until Juan ran that Dodge Charger into a cement barrier at one hundred and thirty miles per hour."

"Did they die?" Jim asked.

Richard shook his head.

"Yep," said Sam, hanging his head while standing in smoke, "they died alright."

I shook my head and thought about losing my friend in a recent plane crash.

"That's horrible," said Richard, shaking his head. "It's too bad."

"The funny thing is," said Sam, "they were going so fast

that their bodies went right through the concrete barrier and disintegrated. They were never found, which is why I ask about aliens."

Jim and Sam burst into laughter.

"Good," said Jim, gulping the last of the coffee and holding out the mug for more. "He deserved to die."

"Jesus Jim," said Richard, "you are going overboard now. You insensitive prick."

"No, no—you are right Jimmy," said Sam. "We all die at some point. It was Juan's time is all. God willed it, my friends—there is no escape from death."

A wind gust blew from the south and a handful of apples fell from the tree onto the ground. One bonked Jim on the head and we all laughed.

"My point exactly," said Sam. "There is no escape."

Jim picked up the apple and examined it before chewing loudly and spitting out pieces of skin.

"I keep wondering if my death will be in three days or three years," asked Richard.

We laughed quietly like we knew how he felt. I woke up in a warm trailer in the southwest corner of New Mexico, truly happy to be alive for the first time in years and looking forward to the day. For once, I didn't want to think about dying.

"In three days," said Jim. "Dick, you'll be dead in three days. I can guarantee you that."

3

Richard slowly turned to face me with great strain.

"Do you partake in the cannabis?" he asked.

"Yes sir."

"I am known around here for my baked goods," he said. "I will grab you one."

"Make that two," said Sam.

Jim coughed loudly, "Three…"

"I will grab one for Sam and one for Rob," said Richard, using his cane to stand. "But you need nothing more than pure H2O in your body, young man."

Jim laughed, "You aren't known by anybody for your baked goods because you don't share. You are cheap, cheap, cheap!" He held his mug upside down over the fire with a shaky swollen hand. "Sam, more coffee… please."

"Oh yeah," said Richard, turning to look down at Jim from a few feet away. "That's why I pay $5 for a dozen eggs and $7.99 a pound for grass-fed beef while you buy $1 dozens and expired meat from Albertsons. If you even buy your own food, you bum."

Richard turned to walk away without looking back.

"They taste the exact same," shouted Jim. "Sam, more coffee… please."

"I just poured you that one, buckaroo." Sam stood to look in my mug. "How you doing on coffee, Rob?"

"I'm good," I said, swirling the grounds. "Thanks."

A spark leaped from the fire onto Jim's overalls. He

jumped out of the lawn chair and brushed himself off as Sam and I full-belly laughed.

"Go Jimmy go," said Sam. "Dance Jimmy dance."

When Jim was in the clear, he sat and sighed then slouched in the chair. Sam took our mugs for another round.

"About time," whispered Jim.

"I'm sorry for the delay, captain, there was heavy action on the poop deck." Sam laughed. "We need all hands on poop deck."

I drank black coffee, Jim drank coffee with whiskey, creamer, and honey, and Sam drank coffee with cream and sugar.

"So how long you sticking around P.A?" asked Sam.

"P.A?" I asked.

"Pinos Altos."

"Oh… I'm not sure. I rented the trailer for a week, so we'll just see how it goes."

"He's leaving," said Jim. "He's going to leave us like everybody else!"

"Keep it down, Jimmy," said Sam. "Moose is trying to sleep."

"I don't give a shit!"

"Well, that's too bad, because I do. Now you're either going to keep it down or get on back to your camper."

We turned to look at the old beater with flat tires as Richard sat in the lawn chair.

"At some point, we are all leaving," said Richard. "Where we're going, nobody knows."

"I want to explore the countryside first," I said. "I'm not sure how long it will be, though. I like Silver City, and it seems like an easy place to find work if I decide to stick around."

"Silver City is a fine town," said Richard.

"And it's full of fine women," said Sam.

"That's a good thing," I said. "There seem to be some good people around, too. So I don't see why I should leave anytime soon, but you all know how it goes."

They nodded in understanding.

"Why?" asked Jim, with a blank look. "Why would you stay here? Once you get out in the forest, among the rocks and snakes, all it will take is a couple of times and you will never want to see them again. That's the way life works. People strive so hard to achieve great things and then realize instantly that the achievement is nothing compared to the expectation. So why not stop the cycle altogether?"

"Get out of here, Socrates," said Sam. "You're depressing. This is beautiful country—full of hidden gems, ancient spirits, and energy vortexes—especially the hot springs. The hot springs are God's waters. You have to soak in the springs."

"I will, I will," I said. "But first, I got to ask… What's the deal with the apples?"

"They're for the public," said Jim. "My tree is loaded."

He pointed to the tree between his camper and a school bus where Boyd sat on the stairs cleaning his pistol. The tree was over twenty feet tall and weighed down with hundreds of apples.

"It's true," said Richard. "Sam and I juice them. They are

tasty, and healthy, too. I brought a box down to the ladies at the Co-op and they were tickled pink."

"You want to try some juice?" asked Sam, standing and reaching for my mug. I swallowed the last of the coffee and handed it to him. "We have apples by the baskets here." He pointed to an overflowing basket under the bus. "The hardest thing is to keep the deer from taking bites out of them." A few apples on the ground by the basket were missing chunks.

"Sure is," said Richard. "They want to taste every one of them, it is just like candy to a child."

"The cute creatures are just like humans," said Jim. "They want a taste of everything."

"It's the perfect time of year for them, too," said Sam. "Perfectly sweet and juicy, you can't help but eat two or more."

Jim shook his head and made a disgusted face. "I don't like that!" he said.

"What's that Jimmy?" asked Sam.

"I don't like sweet apples. I like green apples, I like sour apples without juice."

"Whatever you say, Jimmy," said Sam. "You sure you don't want any juice or coffee, Richard?"

"I have to watch my blood pressure and glucose levels," said Richard. "Not to mention my unbalanced HDL and LDL levels."

I drank fresh squeezed apple juice to the sound of a crackling fire as the warm sun stretched its bright hands over the land with golden rays of warmth. I promised the creator to plant apple trees on my land in Alaska when I returned.

When I return? I wondered. *Have I begun to look forward to living instead of being stuck in self-pity?*

"You know what they say?" said Sam.

"What's that?"

"An apple a day keeps herpes away."

We laughed, and a banging sound came from Moose's trailer.

"An apple a day keeps the gays away," said Jim.

Nobody laughed. Richard shook his head.

"Whoa now, Jimmy," said Sam. "Let's not go so far as to speak poorly of our beloved countrymen. Just because a man likes another man doesn't mean he should be disrespected."

"Amen," I said.

"Like the two that lived in the trailer over there," Jim said, pointing to my trailer. "I almost went inside and took a fat dump on the floor and left a note that said, 'Pack that you homos!'"

"You're a real prick," said Richard. "Undoubtedly."

Jim stared at the clouds. "To be honest," he said. "I was in awe of them. I have never seen anything like it. The way they were so madly in love, out in the open, was mesmerizing."

"Yeah," said Richard, "it was romantic in its own way, no doubt, but they hated each other, too. They fought harder than me and my third wife." Sam's face turned red as he laughed quietly. "I finally called the Sheriff that night when one tried to kill the other with a baseball bat."

They laughed in recollection.

"Oh yeah," said Sam, "they fought alright. But what couple

doesn't? The hardest thing about being in a relationship is learning how to argue without fighting. If it's possible at all?"

"My Uncle Joe gave me advice one time," I said, "and he's been married over thirty-five years."

"What's that?" they asked.

"He surprised me, you see—because he's a very respectful man. He retired from the Army as a sergeant major—then went into corrections. He doesn't drink alcohol, and has always been a family man who everybody respects. He told me that he and his wife have never had a fight in their entire marriage."

"That's a lie," said Richard.

"Don't believe it," said Sam.

"That's what he said," I said. "And you know the secret?"

"What is it?" they asked.

"My Uncle Joe said, 'Bobby Joe, the secret is this, I always get the last word.' And I looked at him puzzled, 'What do you mean, Uncle Joe, you always get the last word?' 'You know what I mean,' he said. 'I always get the last word, and the last word—is 'yes ma'am.'"

We laughed.

"That's good," said Jim. "Wow! That is good."

"I wish I would have learned that with my first wife," said Richard. "The snub-nosed bitch ordered me around like an eight-year corporal. As the years passed by—over fifty years ago now—I realized that she was exactly what I needed but I was too proud to see it."

"Pride is the deadliest sin," said Sam. "It ruins more families than anything else."

"They were just so damn cute it was unbearable," said Jim. "Two grown men madly in love out in the open. Ha! They would've been strung up back in my time."

"Still today in some countries," said Sam.

"He almost killed the poor son-of-a-bitch with that bat," said Richard. "I was impressed how fast the Sheriff showed up, and how fast Jack came out of the house in his jammies to see what the commotion was all about."

"The sheriff was lucky that Jack didn't run him out of here," said Sam. "He does not like the cops." Sam turned to me. "The owner of the place does everything in his power to keep from dealing with police. He is a good Christian man who does not believe that government control is necessary. Instead, he believes that men can be taught and disciplined to do the right thing by their community members and by God."

I nodded while remembering two years prior as I sat outside a coffee shop in Olympia, Washington as a cop appeared around the corner yelling at a man without a shirt. The cop used a taser on the man, and as the barefoot man convulsed on the ground the angry crowd yelled at the officer to stop. "What are you going to do?" the officer shouted at the growing crowd. "Nothing! Who else wants some?"

"Some people use power to the extreme," I said. "And they don't know when to stop."

"Amen."

"The owners seem like kind folks," I said.

"Every day I am impressed by their kindness," said Sam.

"They're like Joseph and his rainbow coat," said Jim. "Done

wrong over and over by people who travel through here, yet still—they give everybody a clean slate and a fair chance."

Richard glanced at Jim in a look of surprise.

"I can't believe that you would know the story of Joseph," said Richard.

"Doesn't everybody?" said Jim.

"You know you're about done with that bottle in there, right, Jimmy?" said Sam.

Jim stood and removed his hat before frantically running his hands through his hair.

"We need to go to town," Jim said. "Right now. Let's go, let's go, let's go. Who's driving? Richard? Sam? Rob?"

"I don't know if it's a crisis, now, Jimmy," said Sam.

"Then you don't know me," said Jim. "I need more Crystal or I will die!"

Sam put his hand on Jim's shoulder and looked in his eyes.

"I believe you just might," said Sam. "But slow your roll, buckaroo, I will make you the last drink and then we will figure it out."

Jim sank into the lawn chair and let out a deep sigh of relief. Richard gave Sam and I two brownies each before slowly dragging his foot back to his trailer. I thanked Sam for breakfast and coffee then said goodbye. I picked up two apples from the ground while walking to the trailer where I set the brownies on the counter and laid in bed reading *The Treasure of the Sierra Madre* before taking a nap.

4

The three men were seated around the campfire the next morning.

"I would rather have a bottle in front of me than a frontal lobotomy," said Sam, preparing a breakfast of steamed then fried potatoes with cheese-stuffed bratwursts cooked over the fire on whittled sticks.

"You're right about that," said Jim, his right eye was bright red and the other was shut.

"Sit and eat," said Sam, handing me a plate with two sticks of meat, potatoes, and tortillas. "Eat it how you please."

"Thanks." I sat in a lawn chair and ate. I hadn't eaten anything but snacks since breakfast the previous day and I was hungry.

"Richard?" Sam offered, holding out a plate.

"I should stop making breakfast altogether and come here to eat," said Richard.

"If you bring it, I will cook it," said Sam.

"Well, that is good to know," said Jim. "That is really good to know!"

"Richard," said Sam. "Don't insult me. I made enough food for the four of us and if you don't eat it, Tinkerbell will."

Richard took the plate and the four of us ate in shared silence.

"There's something special about shared silence," I said, and they nodded.

Few cars drove on the Trail of the Mountain Spirits that

morning. Tiny birds sang from apple trees and an occasional "thump" was made from a fallen apple.

"You know what they say?" asked Sam, tossing his paper plate in the fire.

"What's that?" I asked.

"'After good taco—good tobacco.'" He went inside for a light blue pouch of American Spirit rolling tobacco, and when he came outside, he rolled a cigarette for each man. We sat and smoked with full bellies, all but Jim, who kept asking: "Why?" without further explanation.

They joked about the Kennedys, Clintons, Bob Hope, Ford vehicles, Bing Crosby, and others I had not heard of.

"What year were you born, Jimmy?" asked Sam.

"I was never born."

"Well, then what year did you climb out from under the cabbage leaf?"

"I was never born and I will never die," he said. "Let's just say that I am a fierce dragon, and we will leave it at that."

Sam smoked in silence for a minute. "You were born in 1940 then—weren't ya, Jimmy?"

Jim's red eyes opened wider than I had seen them.

"How did you figure that out?"

"You told me that you were a dragon, and I am a dragon, too. Since I was born in 1952, and I know that the Chinese calendar returns in full circle every twelve years, I figured that you were born in 1940." Sam inhaled from the perfectly rolled cigarette and blew a perfectly formed smoke ring.

"I'll be hot-damned," said Jim. "You really are from another planet aren't you?"

"That is impressive," said Richard. "Hell, I would rather be a dragon than a rat." He hung his head in shame as we all laughed.

"We already knew you were a rat, Dick," said Jim. "Everybody knows that."

"Don't call me…"

"I am a rat, too," I said. "A wood rat. I was born in 1984. What year were you born, Richard?"

"I was born in the summer of 1932 in Miami Beach, Florida."

"So that makes you… 82 years old?" I said.

"That's right," he said. "Sometimes I feel like I am still your age, a young man—until I go to bed at night and have to drag my old ass to the toilet every hour just to tinkle."

We laughed.

"Well, Jimmy," said Sam, "at least we know that we have a couple of rats to eat when times get hard. Ain't that right?"

"Have you guys eaten human?" asked Jim, out of nowhere.

"Hell no, Jimmy," said Sam, shaking his head. "That is disgusting."

"No way," said Richard. "I would rather die."

"Never," I said.

"Why not?" he asked. "It is delicious!"

"That's like the other day," said Sam. "A young guy, about Rob's age, told me that he never goes to the hot springs because there are just a bunch of old naked men there and he doesn't want to see that. He asked if I had ever been and I says, 'Yes sir, I go all the time. The first time I went, I walked on up there to the steaming pool enjoying the beauty and bliss of the area, and when I got there all I could see were five bald, grey heads that were obviously men, and right beside their faces were five pairs of floating testicles.'"

We laughed.

"The kid laughed and said, 'That is exactly why I don't go,' and I told him that I didn't mind because I am one of the old guys with floating testicles."

We laughed for the hundredth time in two days. I wondered if the old men were ever serious, and if so, about what?

Sam continued: "We don't need perverts going to the springs anyway trying to get a peep of a naked girl. They can find a bar or a café to meet a woman and leave the springs to those who appreciate them for what they are—a sacred pool to heal the body and soul."

"Blah blah blah," said Jim. "We all know that you just go for the gay orgies."

Sam's face turned red. I didn't know if he was mad or not, until he started laughing.

"And for the meth," said Richard.

"You guys know me well," said Sam.

"I love meth," said Jim. "The only problem with meth is that it is so hard to find around here."

"I highly doubt that," said Richard, shaking his head.

"I love crack, too," said Jim.

"You need serious help," said Richard.

"We are smack-dab in the middle of Drug Runner's

Alley, Jimmy," said Sam. "There should be no problem finding crack or meth here."

"If you want it, you can find it," said Richard.

"I want some meth," said Jim. "And crack."

"Then go on and find some," said Sam. "But you're going to need money first, and we all know you ain't got no money."

"Oh yeah," said Jim. "About that... I guess I won't be getting any meth or crack."

Jim stood and walked to his camper.

I could not remember the last time I had laughed so hard or spent so much time hanging out around a fire. It felt good—like all of my problems had disappeared and all I had to do was eat, drink, sleep, and laugh.

When Jim returned from the camper with a full bottle of vodka, I stood to walk away. I wanted booze so bad that I felt it in my dry mouth and shaky hands. I tasted it on my tongue and smelled it on my skin. It had been too long since I drank and I was craving. But I had learned as a teenager that when I drink early, I drink all day. I had to fight the demons.

As if Jim could read my mind, he staggered toward me and raised the bottle to my face.

"Want a nip, kid?"

"I'm good, thanks."

He stared at me with an open eye and a look of despair

and loneliness, I saw myself in his face. I saw my father, my brother, my grandfathers, and grandmothers on both sides. I saw a long line of alcoholics and addicts who shared my DNA.

"Not the vodka," said Sam. "It's nine o'clock in the morning, Jimmy."

"Who's keeping track?"

Jim carefully turned around and stumbled back home.

"You have to watch that guy," said Sam. "He will trip and fall and not be able to get up. We all have to watch out for him."

Sam stood and looked around his bus to make sure Jim got home.

"It's good to know that people are looking out for each other around here," I said.

"That poor boy would receive a gold medal in drinking if it were an Olympic event," said Richard. "It is a sad thing to watch."

"It sure is," said Sam.

"Does anybody know why he drinks so much?" I asked.

"Does anybody know why any alcoholic drinks so much?" asked Sam.

"That is the question people have been trying to discover ever since man first crushed grapes," said Richard.

I thanked Sam for breakfast and then excused myself from their company to do laundry and other chores. I had to resist the temptations or I would be on a two or three day bender. But I could not stop thinking about how fun it would be to drink whiskey in coffee all day while chain smoking cigarettes."

Fight the urge, Bobby. Fight the craving! You have to stay busy.

With dirty clothes in a grocery bag, I walked a hundred feet to a brick shower house with a single washer and two showers. A pair of black Carhartts, five pairs of black socks, two black tee-shirts, a blue and yellow tank top that I bought in Bangkok six years prior, a red handkerchief, and a worn out pair of black Adidas Sambas. I loaded the washer and noticed the extra space before walking barefooted back to the fire to see if the guys wanted to add anything to the load.

Richard shook his head. "No thanks."

"We don't want any complications separating Jim and Richard's panties," said Sam.

We laughed, and I went back to the washhouse to start a load. I stood in the sunshine with my back to the bricks basking in the warmth. A dry, dark brown, and green forest covered rolling hills to my front. I stared at the two-tone green and white trailer, and I realized that I lived further from my neighbors than if I were in an apartment building.

"Where the hell is Rob?" I heard Jim yell from the campfire.

"He's over there looking around," said Richard.

"What the hell is he looking at?" asked Jim. "There ain't a damn thing to look at around here."

"Probably just taking it all in," said Sam.

I took the silence in conversation as a cue to walk back to the fire.

"What the hell are you doing over there?" asked Jim, tilting his head sideways to look at me under the bill of his cap.

"Doing laundry and checking out the area," I said. "What's it to ya?"

"Why?" he said, shaking his head. "What is there to check out?"

"I'm doing laundry because my clothes smell like sour milk."

"Huh?"

"Because I stink," I said.

"Why?"

"Oh hell, Jimmy," said Sam, "just let the kid do his laundry. You are the one who desperately needs to wash his clothes. You smell like someone coming off a month-long elk hunt."

"Huh?" said Jim, before bursting into drunken laughter followed by hoarse coughing. "Actually, I never stink," he said. "It's quite amazing really. And it's the honest-to-God truth, I never stink."

"Okay Jimmy," said Sam, "whatever you say."

Richard rolled his eyes.

"I'm going to start picking apples," I said. "To dehydrate for the road."

"Then quit talking about it, and get on with it," said Richard.

"You just love to work don't you?" said Jim. "You are like Sam. You guys just love to work. I don't understand it. I hate work! I just don't see the point in any of it."

"It's called being self-sustaining," said Sam, "and eating good, healthy food."

"Oh, what's the point?" said Jim. "Nobody gives a shit anyway."

"I do," said Sam.

"Me, too," said Richard.

"Same here," I said.

The one-eyed drunk let out a deep sigh and stared at the sky. His full grey beard covered the lower half of his face and hung past the middle of his chest. He picked out food from his beard and flicked them away. Sam, Richard, and I smoked a joint that was followed by a cigarette while watching the fire. It helped take the edge off. I climbed the tree by Richard's trailer and shook a single branch with all of my might until dozens of apples fell to the ground. It was the first time I had harvested apples directly from an apple tree, and the first time I had heard so many apples hit the ground. I smiled in satisfaction at the sound and action.

I rested on the largest branch and thought about the tale of two Alaskans who left the village to reunite with childhood friends in the city. One man was a heavy alcoholic and the other was sober. When they arrived to the city, the alcoholic spent time with his best friend, a sober man, and the sober man spent time with his best friend, an alcoholic. A month later, when they returned to the village, the alcoholic was sober and the sober man was an alcoholic.

Who will I be when I return home?

S

Oh, how the apples fell! They thumped on the ground, bonked off Richard's trailer and truck, and rolled in every direction. The guys came over to watch. They stopped the apples with their feet, chased the apples while laughing like boys, and gathered them into five-gallon buckets.

"I've been watering this tree twice a week since early spring," said Richard. "Pickers came out last week and used tall ladders to try to get those high ones up there," he pointed to where I was in the tree, "but they couldn't reach them. Ha! Looks like they are S-O-L now."

"A ladder, ay?" I asked, barefoot and shirtless.

I was eating an apple while taking a break.

"Yep, none of them would climb them," said Richard. "They said they were too tall."

"Well… that's good for us," I said, tossing the apple core aside to shake the tree.

When I was finished, we had three five-gallon buckets and two stock pots full of light red apples.

"What are you going to do with all of them?" asked Richard.

"Dry them," I said. "And eat a dozen a day while I'm here."

"I like them steamed, cut up in salads, added to beans, pressed into juice, and turned into applesauce," said Richard. "And, of course, there is always apple pie."

"I haven't had steamed apples," I said. "Do you guys want any of these apples?"

"I have plenty inside," said Richard, "but if I need more—I know who to ask."

"I hate apples!" said Jim, taking a bite of one. "I absolutely hate them."

"I already have a full basket," said Sam, "but thanks."

I carried two buckets to the fire. Sam grabbed the third. Jim and Richard carried pots.

"What are you going to do with all of them apples?" asked Jim.

"He already told ya, Jimmy," said Sam. "He is going to slice them and dehydrate them."

"Oh…" said Jim. "Will they dry out? They have so much moisture."

"I sure hope so," I said. "What do you guys think is the best way to keep varmints and birds from eating them?"

"The roof," said Sam. "Put them on the roof or the deer will have them gone by morning."

Jim and Richard nodded.

"Good idea, thanks," I said. "That's what people did in Nepal. They sliced them thin and put them in small baskets to dry on their thatch roofs."

"You guys are nuts," said Jim, taking a drink from his plastic cup. "Absolutely nuts."

I walked to the trailer to grab the Buck knife and a cutting board, and then sat by the fire and sliced a full pot's worth on a TV tray, keeping cores for stock while handing thin slices to Jim.

"I don't eat the things," said Jim. "I can't stand 'em! I just suck the juice out of them. Here, like this..." He bit into a slice and sucked so hard his face reddened and the veins on his neck and forehead turned thick and swollen. He spat what was left of the slice into his hand and threw it in the fire. "See!"

"So you do like apples, then," said Sam.

"Nope, I hate 'em," said Jim, shaking his head so vigorously he nearly lost his hat. "It is just the juice that I like."

It took three hours to slice the apples. I took breaks by finishing laundry in the washhouse and hanging the wet clothes on a line I tied to the porch. When the apples were sliced, I carried the buckets to the trailer to figure out what I could use to dry them on.

"Let's go check out an abandoned lot across the street," said Sam, walking beside me to the trailer. "It's just over there." He pointed across the highway. "Maybe we can find some screen or other useful material."

"Let me put some shoes on."

We crossed the street and entered the abandoned lot where I found two sea shells hundreds of miles from the shore and Sam found a 3-foot by 10-foot section of metal screen.

"We can use my hose to rinse this off," he said. "We will cover the apples with it so the birds don't get them. There aren't many around this time of year, but it can't hurt."

We sprayed off the screen and left it out in the sun to dry. With a large piece of tinfoil and the tent's rainfly, I used the deck railing to climb on the trailer roof and kept my weight on the edges while laying out the tin and tarp. Sam handed up the buckets, and in no time the sliced apples were baking on a sheet of tin foil in the sun.

"It's not even noon yet and you've already done your laundry, harvested apples, and processed them," said Sam. "I'd say that you're a highly productive young man."

"Thanks."

A red Chevy Suburban with a large ladder hanging out of the back showed up.

"Good timing kid!" yelled Richard, from the front of his trailer. "You beat them to it!"

"Yes, sir—I did." I smiled from the rooftop.

Sam handed up the screen, and I covered the apples and nodded as a way to tell myself, "You've done good, Robert. You've done good." The driver of the Suburban reversed to a different apple tree on the other side of the park where two women unloaded the ladder and propped it against the tree. One woman climbed the ladder to grab an apple at a time to gently place in a bucket while the other lady held the ladder. I hung from the edge of the trailer's roof until my feet touched the deck railing, and I let go and jumped down.

"What are you going to do with the rest of your day?" asked Sam.

"Not sure," I replied. "I need to eat and I need to write. I want to go for a ride, or maybe a hike. What about you?"

"I haven't left the park in five days and I am starting to get stir-crazy."

"Then let's ride!"

"Let's do it. How does thirty minutes sound?"

"Perfect. I will be outside on the bike in thirty minutes."

I watched the thick, bear of a man walk barefooted across the gravel road, and I wondered when the last time he had a steady woman in his life. He removed a black cover from a black and yellow BMW road bike before inspecting the tires, oil level, fuel level, lights, and blinkers.

I should probably start doing the same thing, I told myself.

He went inside to grab his gear and I inspected my bike just like he did.

b

"First things first," I said, swinging my leg over the motorcycle to sit. "I haven't ridden with anybody, so I am a rookie." Sam straddled his bike in matching black and silver riding pants and jacket. He wore a red handkerchief over his neck and mouth. "So I'll probably be going slow."

"It's a good thing," he said. "We all have to go slow on this road. Don't worry about things that don't matter. Let's ride."

I followed him across the highway and down the street to the corner where we took a left and crossed a small bridge until turning right on Main Street. We passed an old fort and the Buckhorn Saloon and the museum until intersecting with the highway and continuing our journey on the slow and windy road toward the cliff dwellings. We swerved through a piñon forest while admiring towers of gigantic rocks. He turned down a dirt road and we rode for miles into the hills until parking at an open area with a hitching post and a long flat grassy area perfect for camping. We stepped off the bikes and removed our helmets to lean on the hitching post inside a shadowy forest where ancient stories went untold.

"Do you know Ben Tilly?" he asked.

"Never heard of him."

"Nothing?"

"Nothing."

"What about Mangas Coloradas?"

"Doesn't ring a bell."

"I'll be damned," he said. "What do they teach kids in school nowadays?"

He walked over to the flat grassy area where I imagined thousands had slept over the centuries, and he knelt down, breathed deeply, and prayed. I could not believe my eyes. The black bear himself—the trailer park chef, the jokester, the Winter Hawk—on his knees with his palms pressed together and pointer fingers touching his third eye. He whispered words that I could not hear as I tried to provide privacy by turning away to roll a cigarette while watching beams of light shimmer in the forest. When I looked back, he was pressing his forehead to the Earth and then he kissed the ground. His prayer style reminded me of the Muslims in Iraq, the Buddhists in Nepal, and the Hindus in India. Watching a tough man humble himself before his creator made me want to do the same.

He stood and walked toward me with a slight upturn of his lips before removing the helmet from the seat.

"You ready to ride?"

"Yes sir."

"Follow me."

We rode the Trail of Lost Spirits Highway for another dozen miles before stopping to admire two vast valleys to the east and northwest. To the east were the charred Black Hills and to the northwest was the seemingly endless tan of the Gila Wilderness range.

"I have traveled much of this land on foot," he said. "Bushwhacking through it. I built a stone house down there by a creek," he pointed to a break in the forest a few miles down. "It is near a spring and tucked away in the rocks, unobservable by planes."

"Sounds like a lot of work," I said. "How'd you get materials down there?"

"I hiked them in and hid them in separate caches," he said. "I am building another one now in a different part of the forest."

"That's so cool," I said, unsure if he was telling the truth. "When I was nineteen and fresh back from Iraq, I went to Ireland with an army buddy named, John Sullivan. Of all the things I loved about Ireland, the one that stands out the most was the endless rock walls. Somebody built those walls centuries prior, and they still stood. I left Ireland hoping to one day build a rock wall myself. After visiting the Gila Cliff Dwellings, now I want to build a stone dwelling to go along with my wall."

Sam laughed and stared into the distance with his sky-blue eyes under bushy gray eyebrows.

"Ancient traditions and techniques are in desperate need of being passed on and carried forward," he said. "No matter what race of man carries them onward. Old Ben Tilly has caves dug by hand, and stone homes all along this here countryside. I have found them myself and slept in them for a time. He hunted and walked all over this land, just him and his hounds, like no other man has done."

"Why did he walk and hunt so much?" I asked.

"He was paid by government officials and farmers," he said. "Wildlife were seen as a nuisance that needed to be removed for man's survival."

What else was seen as a nuisance to Western expansion? I wondered. *What animals do I see as a nuisance to my farm in Alaska?*

We smoked in silence for a few minutes.

"I can't imagine walking thousands of miles out here alone," I said. "I would probably die."

"Ben Tilly was a real mountain man," he said. "There aren't many like him anymore."

"The terrain in Alaska is more daunting than this, though," I said. "With alpine mountains, devil's club, bears, mosquitoes, and the cold."

"Don't forget the rushing rivers and streams," he said. "Out here, it is a completely different place than back in Alaska. It is like comparing Venus to Uranus. The biggest worry here is fresh water, which is hard to come by, especially during the dry months." We rolled and smoked another cigarette as a flock of birds left one pine tree for another. "It was a tradition in these areas to share smoke with new friends, and as a way for old friends to grow closer. We will have to smoke one when we get back and I can show you my place."

"Sounds good."

"We should probably head out," he said. "I have to put those short ribs of Jim's on the grill."

"Jim has short ribs?" I said. "How did he acquire them?"

"Not sure," he said, "but I'll cook 'em up."

The sixty-two-year-old led the twenty-nine-year-old down a highway surrounded by boulders and pine trees. A truck pulled out in front of us with two teens in back with rifles pointed out each side. I saw myself as a teenager in Iraq in the back of a Humvee with my rifle and grenade launcher pointed out. I hoped they were not hunting the same thing I was.

When we arrived to the park, Sam invited me inside the bus for a joint. I put my gear away, climbed on the roof to stir around the apples, and then went to his place. His retired school bus was fully equipped with a four-burner propane stove, hardwood cabinets, a toilet, a shower, a queen-sized bed, two single recliners in the living room, a flat-screen television, and the internet. A crystal dangled above the television. A small collection of books on herbalism, Native American culture, Celtic folklore, American history, nutrition, and poetry were neatly shelved in alphabetical order by the recliner. He had dozens of crystals, stones, and feathers, as well as leather pouches, knives, drums, jackets, belts, and other handicrafts that he made.

"It's kind of a hobby," he said, shrugging. He held out a knife handle he made out of dried cholla and a handful of mushrooms he planned to use after he completed the next stone sweat house. "This is a picture of me sending off the ashes and spirit of my friend, Juan," he said, holding a framed 3 x 5 picture of himself on a mountaintop shooting a longbow with a medicine pouch tied to an arrow. "That is how he wanted to go," he said, "and how I also want to go."

"It's important to fulfill a loved one's wishes regarding their remains," I said.

He told me about living off-and-on for thirty years in a stone house he built with his bare hands in the Big Bend area of West Texas along the Rio Grande. He claimed to have toured the area between British Columbia and Mexico by motorcycle more than anyone else. He camped under the moon and stars, hunted with a knife and a bow, studied Native and American cultures, and learned the lifestyles and philosophies of the original inhabitants. He told me the story of Wounded Knee and the massacre of two hundred Indians by white men with Gatling guns like he was there. He spoke of Mangas Coloradas, an Apache tribal chief and warrior, who was burnt with a bayonet, tortured, and beheaded in Pinos Altos in 1863.

"He knew the day would come when he would be captured because there was no way to stop the invading armies," he said. "But that did not stop him from fighting. He fought to the death to protect his people and their way of life. In my humble opinion, Mangas Coloradas should be revered like Saint Francis of Assisi or Saint Terese de Avila, instead—he is forgotten by most and viewed as an extremist by others."

I imagined frontiersmen like Ben Tilly hunting bears, mountain lions, elk, deer, wolves, coyotes, and javelina to protect crops and livestock, and to eat. Animals that fed the Natives were poached and skinned with meat left to rot in the dry forest, skins stretched tight on cracked walls. After gold was found in the area in 1860, it was goodbye to the Apache and time to make money for white businessmen. Thousands of settlers seeking gold moved west.

"What do you think of cultural appropriation?" I asked.

"What is that?"

"It is a fancy term being thrown around intellectual circles referring to people who take practices from other cultures and use them as their own."

He sat in his recliner with his foot propped up in an open window.

"Many white men believe the land is ours," he said. "We build cement roads over the forest, grocery stores, skyscrapers, box stores, and bars for every lonely, obese American to fulfill their heart's desire. The countryside is littered with millions of acres of barbed wire fences with "No Trespassing" signs to keep out the original inhabitants and anybody else who wants to travel through on foot or horseback. This is all God's land, though, all of it. It is not the native's land or the white's land or your land or my land, it is God's land. Our planet is a melting pot of cultures. Some stay, others go. I believe it is important to find traditions that are right for you, no matter which culture they come from. Because what people so often forget is that we are not only made up of our bodies but also our spirits, and who knows what color our spirits are. Do I think it's okay for museums to steal artifacts to exhibit for high paying clientele? No. Do I think it's okay for a cornfed white boy from Kansas to spend a decade studying Tibetan Buddhism in Nepal only to return to Kansas and open a Buddhist temple? Yes."

I stared out the windows of Sam's bus at the little green trailer I had rented and I wondered how long I would be there and how much money I had tucked away in my backpack. And for a brief moment, I wondered about my dogs, my mother, my brother, my nephew, and my property. I missed my brother terribly.

Two months prior, when I was seated at the bar drinking beers with a guy from Detroit who is considered a master conversationalist, a weathered sailor named Mike Britton sat beside us and began to speak about sea-related subjects that I knew nothing about. I sat on the stool listening to Mike and the Detroit guy banter for an hour without saying a word, until the Detroit man excused himself to use the restroom. Mike and I shared a moment of silence as I tried to digest what he had said. Just when I started to feel self-conscious about being a turd of a conversationalist, he leaned over and put his hand on my shoulder.

"You know Bob, I haven't learned a thing in my life while I was talking, but I learned a whole hell of a lot while I was listening."

And he winked.

2

THE COLONOSCOPY CAPITAL OF THE UNITED STATES

Fascist State | The War on Drugs | Drinking & Writing Alone | Keep It Simple | Hungover and Hungry | Jim Keeps Staring | Double Jameson on the Rocks | Mountain Lion Urine | Buckhorn Saloon & Opera House | $28 Macaroni & Cheese | Hair Stands Up | Hungover in Reflection | Buying Land in Alaska | Sour Deal | Clearing Land | Planting the First Garden | Forgiveness Meditations | Lost Hope | Casting Blame | Debt, Depression, & Despair | A Farmer in the Fertile Crescent | A Seed Grows | Study Agriculture | Canned Red Salmon | Man's Best Friend | Accomplice to Murder | No Solutions | Nala Saves the Day | Cranes & Puppies | From Warrior to Busboy | Chasing an Escape in Women | $10,000 Withdrawal | Closed Account | Goodbye Alaska, Hello America | Dazed & Confused in Portland, Oregon | Seattle to Victoria, BC | Robert Service's Old Worksite | Instead of Worrying | Coffee and Jim Beam | Hungry People | Grilled Cheese Sandwiches | North Country | "Want to Watch Some Television?" | Wheel of Fortune | A Love Story | Eerie Feeling | Happy Veteran's Day

1

"Welcome to Silver City, 'The Colonoscopy Capital of the United States,'" said a guy in a ball cap, sunglasses, and a thick neck beard. His brown hair was pulled back in a ponytail and he had a short, stubby nose. His name was Woody, and he was in his sixties or seventies. "They pulled a poor bastard over yesterday driving to work at five in the morning," he said. "He was stripped naked on the side of the road before they shoved him in a cop car butt naked and took him to the station for a colonoscopy."

"Motherfuckers," said Richard, wearing the same tie-dye shirt with a hole in the belly as the previous two days. "It is a goddamned fascist police state, I tell you!"

"Yes, it is," said Sam. "Martial law over the entire nation."

Woody smiled, like he enjoyed riling men up. Jim was silent. "The police station didn't want to be involved with the search, so they sent the poor bastard to the Silver City hospital where an Indian Doctor was happy to make him spread his legs."

"I'd sue the bastards!" shouted Richard.

"He will," said Woody, "you bet your ass he will. For at least..."

"The police station," said Richard, "sue the officer and the hospital, and the god damned Indian Doctor. I'd sue everybody!"

"He will," said Woody, "and he'll get at least a couple million."

"He should get ten million," said Richard. "After being sodomized by his own government."

"He needs the most crooked lawyer around," said Sam, leaning back in the lawn chair with his shirt off, shorts on, and bare feet propped on a wood round. "To seriously take advantage of the situation, he needs the nastiest, no-good lawyer around who wants nothing but money, money, and more money."

"Well, that shouldn't be hard to find," said Richard, and everybody laughed "Sounds like my second wife."

"And let me tell you boys something else," said Woody, pulling a joint out from behind his ear to show the group before lighting it, "the same thing happened to another poor guy down in Deming."

"That is why we need to build a stone dwelling near a water source," said Sam. "A place to hunker down when things get worse—because they will get worse. We cannot trust the federal government. Any day now they are going to lock us down and ration out our food and water. You boys just wait. We need a place where the government cannot find us from the air. Where we can store enough food, water, and fuel to last. Where we can live off the land without the government's permission."

"'If you build it, they will come,'" said Richard, quoting *Field of Dreams*.

"I second that," said Jim.

"It's all because of Nixon's war on drugs," said Sam. "It brought harder drugs into the country with more cartels, more drug-related violence, more wasted taxpayer dollars, and more crimes against innocent civilians. Our government needs to admit their mistakes and open the door to legalization."

———

I slept in until 10 that morning. After Sam and I returned from our motorcycle ride, I went to Silver City for a bottle of Jameson and groceries. I made a pot of vegetable beef soup with onion, garlic, potatoes, celery, and carrots. I ate two bowls full with Hatch Chili sauce and three slices of bread and butter. After supper, I sat at the table writing and drinking until half of the bottle was gone and it was past 3 am. I fell asleep and woke up the next morning feeling like shit.

After an hour of visiting by the fire, I returned to the trailer to write until evening. Soup simmered on the stove and created a comfortable feeling of being at home. While writing the first draft of a long story, I have to keep it simple because so much of my energy is used on the story. So I ate small bowls of soup with bread and butter and smoked a half dozen cigarettes on the porch to take breaks. I climbed on the roof to take another break and to check on the apples. They were free from flies and drying nicely.

I finished the whiskey while smoking on the porch and watching gray clouds and the setting sun. I noticed that my trailer was the only one with open drapes, which were pink, thin, and see-through with tacky orange borders. My world was revealed whether the drapes were open or closed. At night, with the lights on, a person could see my silhouette inside without me ever knowing. But hell, I had nothing to hide and nothing to steal, so I didn't worry.

An hour later, I saw Jim on the other side of Sam's bus with his hands tucked deep in his overalls swaying like an old tree in a light breeze. And while I could not see his eyes, I could feel them. So I closed the drapes, turned off the soup, and read through the entire handwritten story wondering why the hell the one-eyed drunk was staring at me and if something had to be done about it.

2

It was after 8 pm, I was exhausted and drunk but I wanted to continue the party. So I walked the dark roads towards the old western Buckhorn Saloon comforted by silence. As I opened the door, a wave of sound hit me and I almost turned around. I stumbled past smiling people in a jolly conversation and found a corner stool at the bar directly in front of a four-piece band. A bearded man in his thirties wearing a Red Sox cap played an upright bass while a skinny guy with feather earrings and a Stetson played the fiddle; a goateed man in his early twenties with brown dreadlocks and a driver's cap played the mandolin and a curly haired, full-bodied thirty something-year-old woman played guitar and sang. The band played with passion, however the sound system was turned down so low that I could barely hear them over the loud conversations.

I felt a tap on the shoulder and a female bartender asked: "How's it going tonight?"

"Good," I said. "And you?"

"Good," she said. "What do you want to drink?"

"A double Jameson, please, on the rocks."

She gave a thumbs up and walked away. I noticed a wall full of paintings with naked women holding umbrellas, a naked female mannequin, and hundreds of liquor bottles behind the bar. I was in the right place. I spun around to watch the band. When the song ended and I turned to face the bar, the Jameson was in front of me with floating ice cubes that resembled tiny glaciers in a golden lake. I had entered a magical world. I stirred the ice with a tiny black straw and smiled at the sound of ice clinking off the glass.

The more I drank, the more I noticed the pretty girls—and the more I wanted to snuggle up with one. One girl in particular caught my attention. She was strong in shoulders and thick in arms with full breasts and a round butt. Her eyes were big and blue and she had sandy blonde dreadlocks in a high crown on top of her head like Marge Simpson. She was a white Egyptian goddess who probably had a pet sphinx at home. She wore a long, tight turquoise dress that covered her knees but not her form. She was at a table with five well-dressed people, all of whom I had seen around in Silver City, nursing a glass of red wine and eating the macaroni and cheese that everybody talked about but I was unwilling to buy. My mother would roll her eyes if I paid $28 for a bowl of macaroni and cheese. I wanted to talk with her but didn't know how to start a conversation.

Another woman had long, straight black hair and square, red-rimmed glasses with green eyes. She was like a sleek and graceful cat or a beautiful witch, I wanted her to sit on my chest and purr. She was tall and lean with a red and black flannel shirt and baggy blue jeans. The dress of a simple, hard-working country girl. Her frame was wiry and strong and I knew darn well that there was a sexy body hiding under her clothes. Her and another woman watched the band and quietly spoke between songs. I liked how quiet and reserved she seemed. But she was wearing a ring, and even though it was a small ring, it was still a ring. However, I was advised by guys in Silver City that many of the single women wore rings to ward off miners, contractors, old artists, lesbians, hobos, hippies, and other hounds like me.

"Just like a farmer who puts the scent of a mountain lion on the edges of his field to keep out deer and other varmints," said one man.

I showed interest to both women with my eyes. Not in a perverted way, but in the "Hey you look interesting, maybe we should talk sometime" way. They seemed like women who wouldn't go home with someone after meeting for the first time, and I liked that.

I bounced between groups of people like I had lived there all my life, before stepping outside to smoke two cigarettes to steady my nerves. It was cool and quiet outside, a relief to the heat and sound inside. When the band ended, I paid my tab, thanked the bartender, and made eye contact with both girls before stumbling down dark roads, over a narrow bridge, and up a slight incline to the trailer park. Where Jim was standing by the park's entrance sign with a shawl over his shoulders watching the road.

"Where'd you go and run off to?" he said.

"What's it to ya?"

"I noticed you left," he said. "Just wanting to make sure everything's alright."

"I went to the Buckhorn for drinks," I said, walking past him. "Goodnight."

I could feel his eyes on me as I walked to the trailer. I went inside and turned on the hood fan light before peering out the drapes. The hair on my body stood when I saw Jim standing by Sam's bus facing my trailer.

3

My head pounded and my eyes hurt when I awoke the next morning. I wasn't up for conversation, and I wanted to steer clear of Jim, so I tidied the trailer, made a pot of beans, and spent time reflecting on what led me to the park in the first place.

On March 26, 2012, exactly ten years since the day I parachuted into Northern Iraq, I cashed in a Roth IRA and a 401k to buy twenty acres and a seven hundred square foot house in Happy Valley, Alaska with my brother, James. I wanted a family farm, he wanted a home to raise his son. It seemed like a good opportunity to grow closer as a family while achieving our dreams together. The house was off-grid and unfinished, with heaps of potential for somebody with skills and time. I had tons of time, but hardly any skills that would be useful in the new endeavor. I would learn them along the way. An $80,000 mortgage with a downpayment of $16,400 left a $540.17 monthly payment. Divided by two, and we each owed roughly $270 per month, which was totally doable. We left Seward on May 1, 2012, to move to the property while his girlfriend and son stayed in Seward waiting for us to install a wood stove. Two weeks later, after the stove was heating the home, she confessed to not having plans to move out. James returned to Seward to work as a longshoreman and to camp a mile away from his girlfriend's family home, where she had moved back in with her parents. I was alone in the country with surging memories of my time in Iraq, a lack of confidence and skills, and a growing resentment toward my brother.

After our second mortgage payment, James asked if we could reduce his share to an acre of raw land. We did the math, and cut his payment to less than a hundred dollars a month. A month later, he wanted to sell the place entirely. Since I had cashed out every dime I had in pursuit of an early retirement as a farmer and writer, I was unwilling to sell the place and I took over the mortgage and property. And just like that, what started as a family adventure to bring us closer became a solo journey that divided us. To make matters worse, James drunkenly accused me of trying to steal his girlfriend and told me to stay away from his family entirely, thus alienating me from my nephew and namesake. I toiled on the land obsessively to escape the violence of the past, the pain of the present, and the hopelessness of the future.

Before buying and moving to the land, I had never used a chainsaw or a splitting maul, yet my only heat source had become a wood stove—so I had to learn. I bought a chainsaw and watched some YouTube videos on felling trees and then started doing it. I knew nothing about mechanics, carpentry, and the intricacies of off-grid life, but the responsibilities of generator, truck, and house were mine alone. So I focused my efforts on what I knew—manual labor—while using the house as a place to cook, eat, and sleep. I designated a fifty foot by fifty foot section of land as the first garden space to be cleared and cultivated. I cleared dead standing trees and carried logs to a pile to buck and stack. I built fires under stumps and used a pry bar, a shovel, and a pick to dig them out. A smoking pile of debris burned for weeks. Azalea, horsetail, and fireweed sprouted where spruce trees once towered before a spruce beetle infestation killed them and they were logged. I used a hand saw to cut azaleas at the roots and a shovel to dig them out. Nobody patted me on the back for a job well done or criticized my work. To labor on my own land without anybody to validate or direct me felt good. My short-term goal of having a garden and my long-term goal of having a family farm kept me going. It took three hard weeks to clear a large enough space to plant thirty pounds of potatoes and a decent patch of radishes, kale, cabbage, carrots, and lettuce. My goal of clearing a fifty by fifty garden space was not going to happen in one season, and that was okay. There was always next year.

After planting the vegetables, I cleared a space near the

house for a perennial garden to plant rhubarb, raspberries, strawberries, and chives that were gifted by friends in Seward. I was beginning to feel like a Demi-God of the Agricultural Realm. When I hand dug a hundred thirty-five-foot trench six feet deep to insulate and bury a water line from the well to the house, I felt like a Master of the Water Clan. Now, I could have water inside all winter!

When I was not obsessively laboring to escape my thoughts, I did forgiveness meditations I had learned at a Buddhist Retreat Center in Northern India. I tried to forgive myself for terrorizing the innocent Iraqi people asleep in their homes in the middle of the night. I tried to forgive Darryl Foran for shooting an innocent Iraqi man in the throat and smiling as he died in the arm's of his wailing brother. I tried to forgive my father for not calling or writing or being there for me. I tried to forgive my mother for choosing a murderer doing a life sentence over me and my brother. I tried to forgive my brother for accusing me of trying to steal his girlfriend and family. And I tried to forgive my former baseball coach, who groomed me for months before trying to rape me as a twelve year old boy. I tried to love and understand them. To recognize that they were the way they were because of the events that had happened to them. I would only be free from hatred and despair when I stopped hating and started forgiving. Despite my best intentions, the resentments raged and the forgiveness meditations did not seem to work. After three weeks of regularly meditating, I gave up the hope of ever finding peace. I tried to pray, but I didn't know what to say and who to say it to, so I gave up on that, too.

To numb the rage, I used my monthly Veterans Affairs disability compensation on intoxicants. I smoked weed all day every day and spent hundreds each month on pot alone. Because marijuana was illegal, I bought everything besides pot with a credit card to make sure I had enough cash for the dealer. I clicked the "Minimum Amount" button every month to pay the credit card bill as spending money I did not have became another habit I had to quit.

Every morning, I woke up thinking, 'Today I will not smoke, drink, or spend money that I do not have.' But by the end of the day, I had usually done all three, and I felt pathetic because of it. I thought about ending my life but I wondered, *How will it impact my namesake, my mother, my friends?* I was hesitant to talk to anybody about what I was going through because I did not want to bring them down. I was too angry and ashamed to make a friend, and too drunk, stoned, and anxious to get a job. I blamed my brother, mother, and father—the recruiters who coerced me into joining the army, the movies for misleading me to the infantry, and the American people who supported a useless war that caused me to wreak terror on thousands of people inside their homes while they were safe and sound thousand of miles away. I blamed everybody—but the person I blamed more than anybody was myself. When nighttime arrived, and I was done chain-smoking cigarettes on the back porch while swatting mosquitoes, I laid in bed telling myself that tomorrow would be a new and brighter day. But as tomorrow came and went, I dove deeper into debt, depression, and despair.

4

I have no background as a farmer. In fact, the largest garden I ever kept was a small community garden plot at my college campus in Olympia, Washington where I grew food to donate to the local food pantry for college credit. I was raised in houses with small yards, apartments, and barracks. The only landscaping I ever did was mow lawns and rake leaves. My first step-father, Dan Silver, loved to come out of his office after I was finished only to rake the leaves and cut the grass I had somehow missed. I never did things right.

Shortly after parachuting into Iraq in March of 2003, I was riding in the back of a Humvee chasing a man carrying an AK-47 through a farmer's field. We could not find the gunman, so we returned to the farmer's mud hut to provide his kids with small American flags and toothbrushes in exchange for driving over his crops in a four vehicle convoy. The simplicity of the farmer's lifestyle, the look of hard work and determination on his face and body, the kids playing outside in the sand without plastic toys, and the way he leaned on his hoe with a look of resilience made me feel in awe of him. I wanted a similar version of his life back home in Alaska. Of course, I had no idea how his life really was—it was merely a teenage hopefulness that enveloped me mixed with an escape from the harsh realities of how my actions were actually impacting his people and country. I was unable to comprehend or imagine the challenges of being a father raising a family and a farm in an arid, war zone. The kids accepted our gifts and waved goodbye. The farmer and his wife did wave. I respected him for that.

The seed to have a family farm was sown in the ancient fields of the Fertile Crescent and watered in the Mayan temples of Guatemala. The seed was fertilized while eating dried apples grown outside of a stone built town in the snow-capped Himalayas, and later watered while riding a bicycle on a dirt road in Thailand surrounded by flooded rice paddies. In 2009, the agricultural pull was too powerful, so I used my Montgomery GI Bill to study sustainable agriculture at The Evergreen State College where I fermented in farming for a year.

Now a year is certainly not long enough to learn how to farm, but it was a solid introduction to soil science, seed starting, plant varieties and needs, business plans, market gardening, the ethics of small scale agriculture, tractor and tool maintenance, harvest and preservation, and field chores and tasks. I learned a lot *about* farming in school, but I did not learn *how* to farm. When I returned home to Alaska and bought the property to start my own farm, I quickly realized that I didn't know squat about how to start a farm.

It is going to take years, I told myself. *A labor of love that will last a lifetime. Think about the work that you can do now to pass down to future generations.*

In the meantime, I caught and canned salmon, traded stories with a neighbor for moose, and lived without electricity for the first time since the war. I wrote and read by candlelight, cooked on a two-burner Coleman camp stove, and bathed outside with the moss and mosquitoes.

My new friends were characters in books. My mentors were dead homesteaders whose black-and-white pictures I had photocopied at the library to hang on the wall. At the end of the day, I hand-rolled a dozen smokes and two joints to sit on the porch smoking while listening to birds and bugs and chainsaws in the distance.

I was lonely and desperate for a friend. And as I have come to learn, what we want is often right in front of us—if we would only open our eyes to look around. My future best friend was lying at my feet slobbering, twitching, and snoring.

Nala entered my life as many friends do, by mistake. She was a three-year-old Saint Bernard on the verge of being euthanized due to hyper-aggressive behavior. Kept inside a kennel or outside on a short chain, she eventually broke the chain and snarled at a guest with hackles up and jaws wide. Her owners were tired of feeling guilty about her kennel-based life and did not have the time or energy to train her. And since Nala's mother was euthanized due to hyper-aggressive behavior, they believed that the trait was hereditary and so they planned to kill Nala. Most people from my generation know the story of *Cujo,* Nala was on the brink of being the rabid beast in real life.

A week before moving to the property, my big brother, James, asked the owners if he could adopt her instead of putting her to death, they agreed. The first time I met her, she was walking on a leash beside James, and when I leaned down to pet her head she lunged at my face with jaws wide.

"This is the dog we're adopting?" I said.

James laughed, "She's just like us, brother. Tough on the outside, sweet on the inside. Just wait until you get to know her."

I did not want to get to know her and I sure as hell did not trust his decision. Nonetheless, I agreed—I could not bear the thought of being an accomplice in the murder of Beethoven. Besides, it gave James an opportunity to bond, and take care of, another life. Something he really needed. But when James returned to Seward to be with his son and girlfriend, Nala stayed with me on the property, and I was left with the responsibility of taking care of an attack dog with big jaws and a quick temper.

During our first week alone, she tried to back me into a corner of the house with her hackles up and head low and I kicked her in the jaw so hard she ran away yelping. She approached me outside a few days later in the same manner and I swung a shovel at her head only stopping inches away. And finally, after she snapped at a neighbor's leg when he stepped out of his truck, I punched her in the thick head as hard I could. My dominance and aggressiveness were matched with table scraps, belly rubs, and time together outside where she curled up on the grass chomping at mosquitoes or roaming about the forest in freedom. It is no surprise that when a living being is kept inside a cage both day and night they may become aggressive. I would be pissed. On the property, Nala was encouraged to bark at the many foreign smells and sounds of the wilderness. She chased squirrels up trees, ran moose out of the garden, and rolled in bear poop every time she found a pile. I believe that it was just as beneficial for Nala to channel her innate aggressiveness as it was for me. After a month, she stayed by my side at all times, and if she growled at somebody without a good cause or thought that it was funny to eat my smoked salmon from the counter or to beg while I ate, I changed my tone, pointed at her, and stared with angry eyes. If she kept doing it, I stood over her and she eventually dropped her head, tucked her tail, and rolled onto her back.

There are less aggressive ways to train a dominant dog that are probably more effective, but I don't know the first thing about training dogs—so I did what came natural. I protected myself from a hundred and thirty pound beast while establishing dominance, and I made a best friend along the way. No matter what dark feeling I had at the time, whether guilt, pity, shame, or anger—Nala needed food, water, and shelter. To provide the essentials for another being gave me a feeling of purpose I had never known, and it made me feel good about myself. While I thought that my brother needed to learn how to take care of somebody other than himself, in reality—I was the one who needed to learn how to be depended on. After three months together, Nala helped me when I needed it most, when nobody else was around.

I was over ten-thousand dollars in credit card debt with a minimum payment and a mortgage that nearly exceeded my disability. I did not have a job, and I was too anxious to leave home to find a job or to make friends. I didn't want to lose the house and property but I didn't want to be there alone.

The embarrassment and shame of losing the house haunted me. My dream of being a family farmer would never work out because I failed at everything. My dream of being an author was pointless because I wasn't smart enough. I had shit for brains. I couldn't buy a plane ticket to try a new life elsewhere because I didn't have the money and I had a dog to take care of. I felt trapped under a mountain of problems without any real solutions. I grabbed my rifle and walked into the woods to lean against a spruce tree and end the never-ending circle of chaos. As I spun the barrel toward my face and took a deep breath, I remembered Private Loveall turning the barrel of his rifle toward his own face on the drop zone in Iraq, and how I had yelled at him for being pathetic. And there I was, doing the same damn thing nine years later. Just as I put pressure on the trigger with the muzzle pressed against my forehead, Nala whined from behind the tree.

"What?" I shouted. "What the fuck do you want?"

She whined again.

"I can't take care of you!" I yelled. "I can't even take care of myself!"

She peered around the tree with soft brown eyes, stepping closer with her head down.

"What the hell do you want from me?"

She started to whine so loud that I could not focus on my own thoughts. She took another step toward me and cried even louder while lying down and resting her head on my lap.

Who would feed her if I died? I wondered. *What the fuck am I thinking? Like this is really the only solution to my problems. Quit being a fucking coward, Robert, and face your problems like a man.*

I discharged the round from the chamber, laid the rifle down over tree roots, and curled into a fetal position and wept.

S

Happy Valley, Alaska is a haven for sandhill cranes. Every spring they arrive to live, breed, and train their colts before flocking in fall to fly south. When the cranes flocked together to fly south for the winter of 2012, I left the homestead for a rental cabin in Seward. I thought it would be good for my mental health to be closer to friends and family, and I knew that I could find work no problem. I was confident after sticking out the summer on the land and paying my first mortgage for six months.

Despite moving back to Seward for community relationships and to make money, I spent the winter writing a book and playing music. I isolated and sunk deeper into guilt, regret, and thoughts of suicide. I rarely spoke with anybody besides grocery store clerks and librarians, and I refused all invitations to social gatherings. Nala became pregnant by a wandering nomad German Shepard and she had a litter of fourteen puppies. After eight weeks of hearing them whine, pee, and poop in a 16 x 16 cabin, I sold every pup but one, who I named because he was determined to charge up mountains. Charger calmed Nala down tremendously and brought out the loving mother in her.

I was tired all day and unable to sleep at night. I barely ate anything besides Top Ramen and egg and potato burritos, because I spent all of my money and energy on smoke and drink. I resisted thinking about my time at war unless I was working on the book because what I remembered made me feel guilty. But when I fell asleep, I had two recurring dreams. In one dream, I was seated in the back of a Humvee pointing an M4 at an old Iraqi farmer as he dragged sheet metal behind a tractor. In another, I was standing in a dusty yard outside a mud hut staring at a child covered in elephantiasis. The child wore a thick chain around its neck that was staked to the ground beside a dog house with a bowl of mush on the ground. It stared at me with human eyes of terror while I did the same to it. I regularly woke up covered in sweat. It was a mystery why I did not dream about firefights or IED attacks, but instead—I continued to chase a farmer and to see a creature after all these years. So I started the mornings with strong black coffee and a shot of guilt. Why did I point my rifle at the farmer's face and want to kill him so badly? Just because he was stealing a piece of sheet metal. Why was the creature kept outside tied to a stake? And why did we leave it there to search other houses for weapons? These thoughts turned to guilt as I recalled kicking down doors to wake up sleeping families where we flex-cuffed innocent men and put sandbags over their heads in front of their wailing wives and children.

To prevent thinking, I drank and smoked. To prevent dreaming, I drank and smoked. The VA offered high blood pressure medication to stop dreaming but I didn't want to add pills to my daily concoction. And, I knew that I wasn't ready to stop smoking pot or drinking. Potty training Charger led me outside multiple times a day, where a five-minute stroll put me in a hemlock forest with expansive views of Resurrection Bay, snowy mountains, and the hamlet of Seward nestled in at the base of the mountains. I smoked cigarettes on a stump listening to hemlocks crack in the wind, admiring the landscape as a puppy wrestled its mom. The quiet moments reminded me of the goodness of life by providing brief moments of peace. When spring equinox arrived, I laughed and fist-pumped the gods for my survival. Although we still had months until the snow melted, the end was in sight. When the snow was finally gone and the tourist season started, I was offered a job bussing tables at a busy restaurant, and while I wanted to return to Happy Valley to work the land, I needed to get out of debt. So the house in Happy Valley stayed empty during the summer of 2013, the land unworked, and I bussed tables as I did when I was a teenager.

While being a busboy was humbling for a former combat infantryman in his mid-twenties, I like fast-paced work and I enjoy being around people without having to talk. I worked six days a week earning around a hundred and fifty dollars a night in tips plus eleven dollars an hour. So at roughly five-thousand dollars a month on top of my disability income, I paid off my debt in two months. With restaurant work came restaurant life, and when work ended the party started.

I pursued and dated a virgin Bulgarian artist in her early twenties with a thick British accent she'd learned from television, full lips, and long blonde bangs. She was gorgeous and hilarious and she said she loved me before we slept together. It baffled me, and since I was closed off emotionally, I refused to love and be loved by her. So when a friend told me about a nineteen-year-old local girl who had a crush on me, I broke up with the Bulgarian artist at the Alaska Zoo while watching brown bears.

"Why are you crying?" I asked her while driving one-hundred and twenty miles back to Seward. "You don't even know me."

I could not comprehend that such a beautiful and innocent woman would love a depressed, murdering asshole like me. I saw myself a former employee of a global militia sent to the Middle East to find weapons of mass destruction. When they weren't found—we hunted Saddam—and when he was found—we stayed to extract oil and feed billions of dollars to the war machine economy while young, terrified American soldiers harassed and killed innocent Iraqis every day. She would find out that I was a violent piece of shit hiding behind a peaceful façade. A coward who traveled thousands of miles to fight strangers with a big gun but could not stay and fight bad guys in his own state and country. So I did what I always did, I escaped before becoming attached. A few days later, I asked the local girl on a hike and she showed up in short shorts and a tank top. I assumed she wanted my attention, and it worked. So I asked her on another outdoor date the following day and she arrived at the beach wearing a bikini that revealed more of her body than I had seen of a woman in years. I was hooked. We dated for the remainder of the summer, and I became distracted of my own self-loathing by a combination of sensuality and the feeling of being validated for my life experience. Since she was nineteen and I was twenty-seven, I often felt like an innocent young man around her, which was a great break from feeling like a guilty old man.

When the tourist season came to a halt, the local girl broke up with me and left Alaska promising to always love me. The same thing people always say when they leave. I went to the bank to withdraw every dollar, leaving the dogs with my mother in her tiny apartment, while waving goodbye to the house in Happy Valley for the second winter in a row.

b

October, 2013:

One Month Prior to Arriving in Pinos Altos:

"Are you sure you want to take out that much cash?" asked a bank teller at First National Bank of Alaska in Seward. "You can always use a debit card to take out money along the way."

"I plan to be in Mexico by the end of the year," I said, "and I don't want to deal with banks. Besides, they say that cash is king for a reason."

The manager was called out of her office. She whispered with the teller as they looked me up and down before she turned around to enter the vault. I didn't realize that withdrawing ten thousand dollars would turn so many heads.

"Come with me please, Mr. Stark."

I followed the manager into an office where she counted out one hundred, hundred dollar bills.

"Are you sure you want to carry this much cash around?" she asked. "A lot can happen to money in paper form. Anything from water damage to fire to being lost or stolen. You could be robbed outside as you walk to your car! It is much safer in the bank with us."

"I rode a bike," I said. "Thanks for the concern, but I'll take my chances."

"Okay," she said, pausing. "The teller said you want to close your account, too."

"Yes, ma'am."

"I can help with that."

What the curly-haired lady with the plum-shaped body did not know is that I was on a one-way trip to buy a motorcycle in the Pacific Northwest and to ride that bad boy south until I found an oasis in Mexico to hide away for a while. A long while. I closed the account and left the bank with every dollar left to my name in a sealed envelope inside my backpack.

After leaving Alaska, I spent two weeks in a daze at a friend's apartment in Portland, Oregon where I smoked pot and cigarettes for an hour while drinking coffee before skating around the city all day while listening to Bikini Kill, Operation Ivy, and Elliot Smith. Two guys from Seward lived there, one was in college and the other was a cook, they did not seem to mind having me around. I ate at food trucks, smoked, read, and wrote by the river, skated Burnside Park, watched a man foam from the mouth on the concrete outside a corner store in Chinatown, and attended an apple harvest festival on Stark Street. Time flew, and every red-eyed day blended with the next. It was exactly what I needed at the time—relaxation without responsibilities.

I caught a ferry from Seattle to Victoria to visit friends who had recently moved there for college. I exchanged emails with a tall, skinny woman with nerdy glasses, long, straight brown hair, and a nice round butt who I met on the ferry. She sent an email later that day to see if I wanted to go sailing at sunset with her and her friend, I declined. I was afraid that she would get to know me and not like me.

My friend Buddy and I quit drinking five years prior on a handshake, a week before he met the love of his life, Fiona. He stayed sober, I did not. Being around him while still smoking, drinking, and smoking bud all day was torture. A pendulum between really great and really difficult. Feeling inspired by him and his happiness and feeling bad about myself for failing to find a sustainable foothold on a positive life. Fiona is tough, brilliant, artistic, and beautiful, inside and out. Buddy is mathematical, philosophical, confident, and calm. They are a perfect match. And while it was great to see them, it was painfully awkward to be around two people so healthy and in love while I was a wreck. Since I could not find any marijuana in Canada, I smoked cigars all day and resisted the urge to drink until night. I skated around Victoria listening to Nick Drake and Tom Waits while Buddy was at school and Fiona was shopping to decorate their Victorian studio. I stayed out of their way the best that I could to not bring them down. Ever since I was a teenager, skateboarding has been a way to forget about life by focusing on the present moment. So I skated all day, every day—meeting up with them when they were done with their daily tasks to eat dinner and chat.

Victoria is gorgeous in the fall. Multi-colored leaves cover clean sidewalks; world-class architecture based on English royalty; warm coffee shops with gorgeous red-haired baristas and tidy bookstores with endless titles; tons of restaurants and bars where intellectuals debate; sailors jib and tack off the coastline; a Burger King near the wharf served an excellent poutine; and a thrift store that was larger than all of the thrift stores in Alaska combined. Victoria was a great place, despite my melancholy.

One afternoon as Buddy, Fiona and I were strolling around the downtown district, we popped into a restaurant for lunch. After being seated and ordering a sampler of five local beers, I discovered that my favorite poet, Robert Service, used to work and live in the same building a century prior where he was a banker by day, a writer by night. I could not believe the coincidence! *It is a sign from God,* I told myself. *I am on the right path. If I keep working on my writing, I will soon be a published author.* Being in the same space where a literary hero used to sleep, work, and write was a jolt of inspiration. I could not stop smiling as I wandered around the restaurant looking at the framed pictures and poems of one of my heroes. But once we left the restaurant and I had four or five beers in me and my friends walked hand in hand, I skated away to find a solitary place to smoke, drink, and write. No matter what I did, I could not shake the feeling of not being good enough for anybody or anything.

Despite Buddy and Fiona's outpouring of love, I avoided them as much as possible to keep from influencing them negatively or feeling jealous for their happiness and love. I was proud of them for all that they were accomplishing, and I tried to show and tell them, but after five nights in a studio apartment I was ready to isolate. Since it was mid-October, I had to buy a motorcycle and start my journey before snowfall. So I smoked the last of my cigars, wrote the last of my melancholy Canadian poems, and said goodbye to my dear friends, probably my best friends—to return to the United States to buy a motorcycle.

7

"What would you want from a woman anyway?" asked Jim.

"I could think of a few things," said Sam, raising his eyebrows and puckering his lips.

"I haven't been with a woman since 1989," said Richard. "It was twenty-four years ago, yet I remember it like it was yesterday."

"It's been awhile for me, too," said Sam. "I love listening to a woman talk. Hearing their voice and watching their body language. I love the company of a woman, and I sure miss it."

I sat back and listened to them talk for hours that morning. Sam had lived a rambler's life. He never married or had children, but had been dealt more than his share of heartbreaks. Jim had spent many years "living on the streets." Richard said, "You mean you were homeless. Don't church it up!" Jim did not mention any previous relationships. Richard dodged the Army draft in 1949 and joined the Navy in 1950. He was "the luckiest man in America" at the time because he was not sent to die in the Korean War, instead, he spent his enlisted time safely in Michigan, California, and the Philippines. After the Navy, he lived in Silicon Valley before it was Silicon Valley, "doing coke and being a big shot." He left his first wife and son in Silicon Valley and moved to Florida, and then to Mexico, where he lived for three years. He spoke passionately about Mexican culture and cuisine, from Puerto Vallarta to San Miguel de Allende, Oaxaca to Los

Cabos, and east to Playa del Carmen—if he could still live in Mexico, he would.

I stirred and flipped the drying apples while checking for mold and bugs. They were drying, just not as quickly as I had hoped. So I sliced the larger ones into smaller pieces before adding ten more gallons to the batch. I made another pot of beans with garlic, jalapeño, ginger, onion, carrot, and sausage, which I hoped to share with the guys. I stirred the beans throughout the day, adding more water and salt. I moved between apples, beans, writing, and fire chats all day. It was a good day—a fully present day—I forgot about the summer flings that had dominated my emotions and the war that had dominated my spirit; I was finally focused on people other than myself.

The next few days were quite the same. I holed away to drink Jameson and write before going to the Buckhorn for live music. I pulled out a hundred dollar bill from the envelope without counting the total. I knew that there wasn't much money left based on how thinness of the stack of bills, but I did not want to count it because I felt fully present at the moment without any cares or plans and it felt damn good. And while I felt like hell physically all day, I felt better mentally than I had in years. I accepted the drinking and writing routine, even though I had plans of hiking, I couldn't pull myself away from the stories. For less than $11 a day, I had shelter, a propane stove, a refrigerator, a toilet, a sink, some lights, an electric heater, a couch, a table, a chair, and a mattress with a comforter and two pillows to keep warm. The natural light that came in the large windows was better than in most places I had lived, besides my home in Happy Valley, which was alone and cold and trying to reenter my thoughts. When I wasn't writing or talking with the guys, I sat on the front deck in the sun reading with my feet on the railing.

One morning while on the porch, I heard Sam's voice reading the poem, "A Rolling Stone" from the Robert Service book of poetry I had lent him.

"To make my body a temple pure
Wherein I dwell serene;
To care for the things that shall endure,
The simple, sweet and clean.
To oust out envy and hate and rage,
To breathe with no alarm;
For Nature shall be my anchorage,
And none shall do me harm."
"That was good!" Jim yelled. "Wow! That was really good!"
Sam continued,
"To scorn all strife, and to view all life
With the curious eyes of a child;
From the plangent sea to the prairie,
From the slum to the heart of the Wild.
From the red-rimmed star to the speck of sand,
From the vast to the greatly small;
For I know that the whole for good is planned,
And I want to see it all."

I wondered, *Am I going to keep running forever? What will I tell my mother if I don't return for Christmas? Would my brother even want to see me? I sure miss him. What about my dogs, my belongings, and my house? What about my plan to finish writing the first book? I am always writing new stories and books instead of finishing the first one and putting it out there for people to read.*

I caught myself thinking and I stood and walked inside to stir the beans. I climbed on the roof to check the apples before I sat on the front porch in the sun to finish reading *The Treasure of the Sierra Madre* and to start reading *Star Rover*.

Sam whistled at me and I walked over.

"We are eating grilled cheeses in a couple of minutes," he said. "You want one?"

"No thanks." It was probably the first time I had turned down a grilled cheese.

"What, you don't like grilled cheese sandwiches or something?"

"I love them," I said. "I'm just not hungry."

"You are a young and growing man," he said. "You need to eat. I will let you know when it's ready."

"Roger."

It was no use to argue with the chef, no matter what I said I was always fed. It was a good thing I had given up an eight and a half year vegetarian diet only two months prior, I would have missed out on a lot of campfire meals.

"It's actually quite impressive," said Jim. "My feet really do not stink… Never! I hardly take these cowboy boots off, but still—they never stink."

"Right," said Sam, shaking his head and rolling his eyes.

"Do you take them off when you sleep?" I asked.

"Hardly," said Jim. "I don't get out of my clothes either. I just lay right down and pass right out and then wake right up and keep on going. But for some reason—God knows—I do not stink."

"I can smell you from here, Buck," said Sam. "You smell like rotten meat in a garbage can."

Jim laughed so loud that the resident spirits stirred in their graves.

"You are good," he said. "You are real good."

"I have always been a smart ass," said Sam. "When I was in school, my teachers did not like me. Do you know why, Jimmy?"

"Why?" said Jim.

"Why do ya think, Jimmy? Because I was a smart ass!"

We laughed and Sam leaned forward in his chair to flip two grilled cheese sandwiches inside a cast iron skillet on a grate over the fire. They were perfectly golden.

"Those are ready!" said Jim.

"I don't know how many times I have to tell ya, Buck, but I am camp boss," said Sam. "I will tell you when they're ready. Some people just can't stand being hungry, like my friend Arthur over there in Montana, every time I cook for the guy he never stops asking if it's ready. I tell him, 'I know when it's ready, and it will be ready when I say it's ready,' and he sits there whining like a little pup just taken from its mother. 'I'm so hungry,' he says, 'so hungry.' One night he ate raw elk that we had killed a few hours prior because he couldn't wait to build a fire and cook it. Some guys just cannot stand being hungry. They are the ones you don't spend much time with in the woods because they always talk about food and they complain about being hungry. Arthur would eat me, without a doubt, if he was hungry enough."

"Is that right?" said Jim.

"That's right," said Sam. "Most people do not realize what little amount of food our bodies need to survive, and they need to learn it—fast—because things are only going to get worse."

"Just put the sandwich on a plate and let me eat it," said Jim.

Sam gave Jim a serious look, before smiling and plating the sandwich.

"Here you go, sir," he said. "And for you, young man."

He handed me a paper plate with a golden grilled cheese steaming on top. I stared at the sandwich and then the fire as Sam smoked and Jim ate. I was filled with a desire to pray, so I did. It was the first time I had prayed before a meal since I could remember.

Thank you God, for putting these men in my life to teach me the ways of growing older as a man in America. Thank you for this sandwich, the trailer, and my many blessings. Amen.

Sam slathered butter on four slices of bread for two more cheddar and provolone sandwiches.

"Young Apache warriors used to fill their mouths with water before traveling fifty miles on foot over these here mountains," said Sam. "When they made it back to camp, they were expected to spit out the water in front of their chief and fellow warriors. If they did not spit out the full amount, they were not expected to make true warriors."

"Why?" asked Jim. "Many men make fine soldiers without having to endure such ridiculous tests."

"I miss my mother," said Sam. "What a woman. She will make a pot of soup and a loaf of bread better than anything you ever tasted, all without a recipe. She always makes enough to feed the neighborhood, and people come from all around to eat her cooking."

"Is that right?" asked Jim.

"It sure is," said Sam. "She is eighty-six years old and still keeps an expansive garden of corn, taters, garlic, peppers, onions, and other things. She grows flowers and herbs, too, to use for teas and medicine. She always has."

"That's impressive," I said. "It takes a lot of work to grow your own food. She must be a hardy woman to be able to do all of that at her age."

"Where does she live, this mother of yours?" asked Jim.

"Up in the north country."

"Where?"

"The north country. Up there in Washington State."

"What do you do with her?" asked Jim.

"I'll call her on occasion, but that's about it," said Sam. "It's hard to do more when I live a thousand miles away."

"Do you have any brothers or sisters?" I asked.

"My older brother Mike lives up there with her. He is a retired cabinet maker, a fine woodworker. It's good for Ma to have him around, it really is."

Sam put a sandwich on his plate and then gave me one. I cut it in half to share with Jim but Sam grabbed my wrist as I was handing it over.

"He never finishes a meal," he said, as Jim tossed his crust in the fire. "I'm tired of him wasting food."

I returned to the trailer to continue writing in cursive until 3 pm before opening a bottle of whiskey and pouring a three finger drink. Around supper time, I brought a bowl of beans to Jim in his camper where he pulled back a blanket from the doorway to welcome me in.

"I've got to be getting back to work," I said, staying outside. "I hope you enjoy the meal."

"Thank you, thank you, thank you," he said, while watching Wheel of Fortune on a small black and white television inside a tidy room with a single chair and a small bed with folded blankets. "Thank you so much! This is my meal for tomorrow." He was wearing his cowboy boots. "Where you going?"

"Back to the trailer to work," I said. "I'm on a roll with this story that I'm writing and I have to keep the momentum."

"You boys and your work," he said. "It is like our entire nation is focused on one thing and one thing only. Work! Whatever happened to loving God, family, and neighbors?"

"You tell me."

"I don't know," he said. "That's why I'm asking. What are you working on?"

"I'm writing a book."

He perked up and looked at me with eyes of wonder.

"A book… *You* are writing a book?"

"Yes sir," I said.

"So you are creating something out of nothing? Poof! What was once an empty page is now an entire book full of your ideas."

"I guess so," I said. "I've never thought of it like that."

"You must be brilliant! However, it seems to me that a handsome young man like you should be out meeting women and working with your hands instead of holing away inside a trailer in the mountains of New Mexico writing a book. Ha! Now why would you go and do something so solitary like that?"

"I don't really know," I said. "I guess it's because I have to. Every day that I don't write, I feel like I am slipping deeper into insanity. I haven't found a better way to make sense of the world around me than by writing. Why do you drink every day?"

He laughed and nodded.

"Because I have to."

"Exactly."

He paused and watched Vanna White dance on the TV.

"I have a story to tell you that you need to write down," he said. "A story that I haven't told anybody.

He turned and looked at me with both eyes.

"Is that right?" I asked.

"That's right."

"What's it about?"

"The only thing that really matters," he said. "Love."

I thought about the bottle of whiskey in the trailer and how I was having so much fun drinking and writing alone, but I wondered what kind of love story Jim would tell.

"Come over in a few days and tell me your story," I said. "I will write it down for you."

"I will be looking forward to that," he said. "Geronimo!" He yelled at the TV. "It is goddamn Geronimo!" He let go of the blanket separating us. "Thank you and goodbye."

I walked back to the trailer to continue my mission. Veteran's Day was the following day, and I had to try everything not to relive my two tours. The guilt made me want to wallow in a lifetime of intoxication. I ate a bowl of beans with bread and butter and then laid in bed reading until falling asleep. I woke up when it was still dark and I had an eerie feeling that something wasn't right, so I stepped onto the back porch to smoke and piss and I noticed Jim standing on the far side of Sam's bus. He quickly turned around and walked back to his camper.

Had he been looking in my windows? I wondered. *No way... Why the hell would he do that?*

I flicked the cigarette and went inside where I grabbed the Buck knife from the counter to sleep with in my hands like I used to sleep with my rifle.

"Happy Veteran's Day," I whispered, falling asleep with an all-too-comfortable smile.

3

THREE PIZZAS AND A TWELVE PACK

Leaning and Smoking | Fast Shower | A Visit With the Baseball Coach | Roustabout Problems | The Crystal Palace First Motorcycle | Three Nights at Diamond Lake Resort | No Map, Compass, or Phone | South Along the Sierra Nevadas | Ambushed in Al-Hawija | Visiting a War Brother in Phoenix | Tortured in Santa Fe | Drunk at a Buddhist Temple | Abducted in Rowell | A Watermelon to the Head | Recuperating in a Hotel Room | Take a Walk and Grab a Bite | Two Bald Men and a Fat Lady | Free Coffee and Donuts | Meet a Veteran Event | The Comforts of Pizza, Beer, and Tobacco | Atlantis Rising | "No Baksheesh!" | Persian Cat | Indians Take Arrows | A New York Hitchhiker | Moose and Tinkerbell | Pizza for Jim | Preparing for the Open Mic | Indian Mannequin | Perverted Photographer | A Lone Vietnam Veteran | Patchouli and Fresh Air | Confident Welsh Bastard | Stir the Cubes | Erupt on Dale | Boring Ballads | Close Down the Buckhorn | A Buck Knife and a Pillow

1

I woke up on Veteran's Day morning grateful to be alive. I thanked God for surviving the war, and for a warm, dry, wind-free, soft bed. I made coffee and rolled three cigarettes then went out on the porch to drink and smoke while leaning against the trailer and reading Robert Service. It was chilly, and the crisp air felt good as it tightened my skin. I had mastered the lean-to at a young age. I had leaned against The Fish House in the Seward boat harbor as a teenage smoker; against the Empire State building in New York City; against Saddam Hussein's palace in Baghdad; against a stone restaurant in the mountains of Slovenia; against the Gran Jaguar temple in Tikal; against the cabin of a boat while drift netting in Bristol Bay; against a Buddhist temple in Thailand; against a dumpster surrounded by monkeys in India. I leaned against my buddies in Iraq to stay warm and smoke, and against my brother, James, when we were drinking too hard. I had leaned too hard on my ex-girlfriends and their parents, not allowing them the chance to lean on me. And then, at the age of twenty-nine, I leaned against a 1956 trailer at an elevation of 7,080 feet to smoke three American Spirit cigarettes while trying to memorize the poem, "The Men Who Don't Fit In."

I had wondered at a young age if there was a profession that allowed a person to lean and smoke and drink coffee while observing the world, and all arrows pointed toward a professional writer. So there I was, trying to be a professional.

"Shut the fuck up, hoe!" A man with a southern accent yelled from fifty meters south. "Give me the keys, bitch! I told you to shut up. So why the hell are you still talking?"

The sun was cresting over the rolling mountains as shades of gold illuminated red apples. I took a long drag while trying to decide if I should intervene or mind my own business. I swallowed a drink of coffee with smoke in my mouth.

"Waterfall," I whispered, remembering my high school buddy, Bruce Rockefeller, who always drank his smoke and said 'waterfall.'

"Why are you still talking, bitch?" he yelled.

I could hear a female voice but I could not make out the words.

"Shut up!" he yelled.

I took another drink.

What can I say? I wondered. *What can I do? I can tell him to quit talking to a woman like that, but that will lead to a fight, and I don't know if I am fully prepared for that or if it's my fight to fight.*

Every solution I could muster led to violence, so I did nothing. I assumed it was the forty-three-year-old roustabout from Alabama named Eli, who lived with his thirty-six-year-old girlfriend, Anna. I had met them the day prior, and the moment I shook the man's hand and tried to meet his wandering eyes, I disliked him. There was just something about him.

As I listened to him yell at her, I understood why. He was an abusive asshole who took out his insecurities and anger on women and probably children. Since I was not in the right mindset to be a peacemaker, I grabbed my toiletries and walked to the shower house to shit, shower, and shave before the big Veteran's Day ceremony on the Western New Mexico University campus in Silver City. I hoped that meeting other veterans and seeing a crowd of civilians gathered to honor us would make me feel better about my time in Iraq.

After running the shower for a minute with nothing but cold water, I tried the other stall and was rewarded with heat.

"Thank God!" I said.

I quickly moved my belongings from one stall to the other.

I suddenly recalled the times I had seen Jim watching me and I had a surge of paranoia wash over me.

What if he comes in here while I'm showering? I thought. *And he stands outside of the shower listening to me shower. Or even worse, he tries to threaten me to do something with a gun or some shit? What if he pulls back the curtain and he's standing out there naked? I will kill that old fucker like I should have killed my baseball coach when I was a kid. Bob Mann, you sick fuck. I can't believe that sick fucker used to make me go to the gym after private coaching lessons and make me take a steam bath with him before taking a shower. There are sick, perverted people among us and I am not about to have some shit like that happen again.*

I finished showering and brushing my teeth in less than two minutes, and I was fully dressed within seconds. When back inside the trailer heating up the pot of beans for a warm start to the day, I opened the pink drapes and almost jumped at the sight of Jim standing under the apple tree by Sam's bus with his shoulders covered in a shawl and his hands tucked in his overalls staring at my trailer.

I stepped onto the deck and then walked down to my motorcycle to confront him on the other side of the road.

"You need something?" I said. "Or are you just over there staring at my trailer for nothing?"

"You ready to go to town?" he asked, slurring his words and barely able to stand.

"I'm about to head in myself," I said. "Why do I keep seeing you staring at my trailer? You some kinda sicko or something?"

"Why are you going to town?" He could barely open his eye to look at me.

"It's Veterans Day, and there's a ceremony at the college."

"Is that right?" He swayed for a few moments before speaking. "You a veteran?"

"Yeah," I said. "A combat infantryman."

"Well, if you ask me, every day is Veteran's Day in my book."

I nodded and felt my entire body well up with shameful tears for wanting to beat the shit out of the drunk old man.

"Drive me to town for vodka," he said. "Please."

Did he give that compliment just to get more vodka, I wondered.

"How about you give me the money and I will pick you up some," I said.

He searched his pockets with shaky hands and pulled out a crumpled ball of wrinkled bills.

"The beans were so good," he said. "I still have the flavor in my mouth."

"Good."

"What were the little explosions of flavor?"

"I don't know," I said. "Either garbanzo beans or apple, probably the apple. Speaking of apples, I need to climb on the roof to check them out before this damp air causes them to mold."

"You put apple in beans?" he asked, slowly and shakily straightening the money.

"Yes sir," I said, reminding myself that continuing the confrontation with a drunk man will go nowhere.

Jim looked at me with a bloodshot, tired eye.

"It was the apple... without a doubt," he said. "I have ten bucks here..." He held out the money from the other side of the road. "So..."

"What do you want?"

"Vodka."

"What kind?"

"The biggest bottle you can get for ten dollars." He staggered to where I was standing by the bike. "The Crystal. Get the Crystal Palace." He handed me the money and turned around to carefully walk to his camper. He stopped to turn around and yell, "Thanks!"

"What a strange man," I whispered.

At least he can own up to his money situation rather than acting like it doesn't exist, I thought. *He even lets everybody know how much money he has, while you won't even tell yourself what you have. Tomorrow, you have to count your money to see how much longer you can fund this trip before finding work.*

I climbed on the roof to check the apples and an old blue and white Ford Bronco flew past with the roustabout's girlfriend behind the wheel. Dust covered the apples and I could hear the tires screech when she hit pavement. The apples were drying out nicely. I went inside to eat a bowl of beans with bread and butter in peace before the anticipated crowds at the event, until Jim knocked on the door with a bowl and a spoon.

"More beans, please."

"Wait here." I closed the door and filled his bowl to the brim, lathering up two slices of bread with a thick layer of butter to rest on the edge of the bowl. His eyes lit up when I handed him the food.

"This is breakfast, lunch, and dinner all in one bowl."

I watched him walk away while performing a circus level balancing act. I grabbed a hundred dollar bill from the skinny envelope and started the motorcycle to ride to town.

2

My first and only motorcycle was a 1983 Honda CB500 that I bought in 2009 from a cop forty-five minutes outside of Bend, Oregon. It broke down on the ride back to Bend, and when I called him to tell him what happened he swore that the bike had no problems and the sale was "as is." I rode it for a year with a faulty alternator, never trying to fix it. I was a twenty-five-year-old college freshman who went to school all day and hid in an unfurnished studio apartment playing guitar at night. I had quit drinking two months prior and was finding new ways to stay busy. But still, I didn't have patience when it came to fixing things, so I didn't even try. Since the alternator did not work well, every time I rode it, I carried a battery charger in a pack and if the battery died, I removed it and hitchhiked to the nearest place with electricity to charge the battery long enough to go back and bring the bike home. It was a pain, but I got a surge of adrenaline every time I rode it because I did not know if I would make it home. When I transferred colleges from Bend to Olympia, Washington—I left the motorcycle at the rental house with keys in the ignition.

I did not want that to happen again.

After a few days of studying online forums at my friend's apartment in Portland while looking for dual sport bikes for sale in the area, I caught a bus to Eugene to meet a man in a mall parking lot to test ride a green 2003 Kawasaki KLR-650. Riders agreed that the KLR is basically indestructible, and with the ability to ride on and off-road, I did not foresee any problems riding in Mexico or Alaska. I paid three thousand dollars cash and then strapped my pack on the back with bungee cords. I stopped at a motorcycle shop to buy a helmet and gloves, before finding a Fred Meyer for food and camping supplies. With a few hours before nightfall and snow in the forecast, I decided to ride east over the mountains to visit Crater Lake instead of riding south along the coast. I wanted a less populated route that I had not traveled.

The windy mountain road was slow and relatively free of vehicles. It was the perfect way to practice shifting gears, weight distribution, and feathering the brake and clutch. After two hours, the sun began to set behind me and drivers started flashing their lights. My headlight was out, and I didn't have anything to fix it with so I kept riding intent on reaching Crater Lake by dark.

When I finally reached the plateau where the towns of Bend and Sisters were established, I raced through the darkness while feeling the cold wind on my body and the power of the bike between my legs. I filled up on gas and stretched my legs outside of Bend, continuing south for forty-five minutes until turning right on the road to Crater Lake. I lifted my helmet visor to exhale a breath of air I had been holding since realizing my headlight was out. It was dark by the time I rode past the turnoff to Crater Lake toward the Diamond Lake Resort. I set up the tent beside the lake and smoked two cigarettes while thanking God for my survival before walking to the hotel restaurant. I sat alone at the corner of the bar and ate a cheeseburger with a double shot of Jameson on the rocks. By the time I had five or more doubles, a local guy was telling me about his brother, a returning infantryman from Afghanistan, who was a completely different man after the war.

"The poor kids that we send to war get addicted to adrenaline and have to run, run, run just to keep high."

I listened, without disclosing anything about my two tours in Iraq.

"My brother was the happiest kid in town before he went to Afghanistan," he said. "Such a funny, handsome little shit—all of the girls wanted to marry him. Now, the poor kid won't even lift his eyes to the world around him."

"Sorry to hear that," I said. "It seems pretty common."

"It sure is. Unfortunately, our family has tried hard to get him the help that he needs but nobody seems to know how to help him. The government gives him a paycheck every month and a shit ton of pills and they think it's a good fix."

"I hope he gets better," I said. "Do you know where I can find a mechanic around here?" I asked, changing the subject to avoid talking about myself. "I have a headlight out on my motorcycle that needs fixed."

He laughed, "Good luck with that one!" The bartender laughed with him. "The mechanic is a damn drunk. He hasn't showed up for work in three days. No call, no show. The thing is, he's the best mechanic this town has—so he can't be fired."

"Where would I find him?"

"Stop by his work tomorrow, maybe he'll be there."

I was unprepared for the cold nights in Oregon, so I shivered all night in a thin sleeping bag and paid for a room in the hotel for two nights. Without trying to fix the problem myself, I stopped by the mechanic's shop each day but he was nowhere in sight. I spent the days riding dirt roads between Crater and Diamond Lakes, hanging my feet over the rim of Crater Lake in admiration of Wizard Island, and writing in my journal by Diamond Lake. Because I did not have any bud, I fought the urge to buy a bottle from the liquor store because I knew where that would end up. I snacked all day and went to the restaurant at night for dinner and double shots.

I awoke restless on the fourth morning determined to continue riding south, so before paying for another night I found the mechanic half-drunk and reeking of booze underneath a plow truck. He looked at me like I was the first person he had seen in weeks before graciously spending five minutes to remove my seat and replace a fuse. I could not believe the simple fix, and I felt like an idiot for not even trying. He gave me a pack of fuses and refused my money. Instead—he sent me to the store for a case of beer and a pack of Camels, which I happily picked up for him.

I was grateful for my time at Diamond Lake Resort, for the kind bartender who over-served me and for the local guy who openly expressed his worries about his brother. But I was most thankful to the mechanic, who reminded me to look for the most simple solutions to life's problems first. The first step is being willing to try.

I rode south in high desert country through Fort Klamath and Klamath Falls before crossing into California at Tulelake. Since my phone did not work and I did not carry a map, I could not tell where I was and where I was going. I studied a map in a gas station after filling up and using the restroom, and decided to continue south on 395 toward Bieber and Susanville with the sun as my guide.

As long as I ride south, I told myself, *I am headed in the right direction.*

Highway 395 was a perfect road for a small-town Alaskan who wanted to travel slowly without traffic. Not too busy, and well maintained, with epic mountain views and fresh mountain air. Forested foothills, country towns, friendly folks, and pretty ladies. I was happy to have left the densely populated coast to pass through small mountain towns along the eastern cascades.

I stopped at a small fair in a small town where the only language I heard spoken was Spanish. It was like I was already in Mexico. It was uplifting to see so many kids laughing and running around and having fun. I set my helmet, jacket, and chaps on a picnic table to eat an elephant ear and a corn on the cob while watching Americans be free. My eyes welled with tears as I felt proud to have defended such a diverse and free nation. After an hour of meandering around the fair watching friendly people chat and happy kids play, I kept riding. Through farmland and hillsides, winds and turns, dips and bumps—I rode, and rode, and rode until nearly dark. When I pulled off on a random dirt road and rode a mile or more back to pitch camp. I hoped that a day's ride south and a descent in elevation would make for a warmer night, and I was right. I stuffed every article of clothing into the sleeping bag and used my riding jacket to cover up, and I slept warm and well with my foot long buck knife within arm's reach. It was the first time I had seen the Sierra Madre mountains and I was in awe. They were not as tall and rocky as the

Alaskan mountains, not the ones that I had seen so far, but they were bigger than I had imagined. I rode on their eastern flank for hundreds of miles with a feeling of freedom and excitement that I had not felt in years. I followed the sun south without a map, compass, or phone—and the feeling of freedom, faith, and bravery were indescribably powerful. It was not about the destination—it was about the ride. It was not about the past, it was about the ride. I continued to pitch camp before dark so I did not miss the sights. I packed up the frosty tent as water boiled on a single-burner camp stove. I held a hot mug of instant coffee close to my face to enjoy the smell and close to my heart to warm up before hitting the road after the frost melted. I stopped in small towns for breakfast and dinner and took breaks to smoke cigarettes and admire picture perfect countryside in the shadow of snowy peaks.

I hit a crossroads gas station in Southern California where I decided to travel east to visit a military buddy in Phoenix before going to Mexico. I filled up the tank, checked a map, and bought a can of beans and a loaf of bread before riding through Death Valley into Arizona where I pulled over somewhere in the desert to build a small fire and feel grateful for what I had. The motorcycle was running well, my mortgage was paid, my mother was helping me out by watching the dogs, and I had money in an envelope. It was the first time in years that I had not used alcohol or pot, and I felt pretty good about it. I opened the can of beans and poured them into a pot to cook on the camp stove, spooning the beans over bread under a black sky full of sparkling silver stars. It was the best meal I had eaten in years.

I laughed out loud while remembering the multiple-day mission in Iraq, where we searched houses and villages for weapons without finding any. The last night of the mission, we pulled out our sleeping bags to sleep on the desert ground out in the countryside and I shivered all night and could not get comfortable. I was exhausted the next morning, and when I climbed out of my sleeping bag, I found an AK-47 just below the surface of the sand directly under my bed. The platoon got a kick out of the fact that I found the only weapon during our multiple-day mission, and it was right under my ass.

When I entered the traffic of Phoenix the next day, I found a public library to use the internet and print directions to my friend's house. I was surprised to see that the local girl from Seward had sent me an email. I took a deep breath and started to read.

3

"Dear Robert,

How can I give you my heart when it is fully in the hands of another? That is not fair to you or me. May your journey be wild and safe, your heart open and full. I will always cherish the moments we had together. Please remember, I will always love you."

That's it? I thought. *From the girl who said she would marry me under a full moon.*

I left the library and found a liquor store where I bought a bottle to stash in my backpack. I found my friend's rental house without much difficulty, and since nobody was home and I didn't have a phone, I sat in the yard reflecting on my relationship with Whitelow.

Thomas Whitelow III is a half-black, half-white guy from Hammond, Indiana who grew up with the feeling of not being white enough or black enough. He was 18 and I was 17 when we met, and despite his youth—he sent money back to Indiana every month to help out his father and siblings. In basic training, our bunks were side by side, we went to Airborne school together, and then to Vicenza, Italy where we served in different companies yet were still around each other. When I was transferred and stationed in a small specialized unit as part of the 101st Airborne Division in Fort Campbell, Kentucky, I was surprised when Whitelow showed up a month later and even more surprised when he married his wife, Lashauna, shortly after. They have been married ever since. We spent every day together during our next year-long deployment to Iraq, and while we were not on the front lines like during our first tour, we still dealt with stressful situations that brought us closer together. Of all the men I served with, Whitelow is the only one I stay in touch with.

Whitelow was a family man and a jokester. He would tease me about coming to Moose Pass, Alaska to meet the girl named Willow, and I would tease him about going to

Hammond, Indiana to marry his beautiful sister. I loved the quiet outdoors while he loved watching sports on a loud television. I loved country music while he loved rap. During our first overnight bivouac in basic training, he so was afraid to sleep in the woods with bugs and snakes that he tightened every drawstring on his BDUs and stayed up all night on bug guard. It was his first time sleeping outside.

After the service, he did what many of us do, he bounced around. He went to a trade school for mechanics, a culinary school, and college. He worked on the side to provide for his wife and four sons. Whitelow is like many of us combat veterans, just below the surface of his jokes and smile are the hidden effects of war that he works hard to suppress.

At one point during my first tour in Iraq in 2003, my company, Alpha Company, was living in an abandoned school house in the middle of Al-Ḥawīja, while Whitelow's company, Charlie Company, was living in a safe house a few miles outside of town. Being in Al-Ḥawīja was like being in Hell, every hour was lived in fear. The city was pro-Saddam and covered in paintings and murals. We consistently underwent mortar attacks, small arms fire, and ambushes.

My platoon had been given a tip by an interpreter about a weapons cache and terrorist cell outside of town that we planned to ambush and search. As night fell and we left our safe-house in a convoy of Humvees, an eerie feeling came over us soldiers riding in back—something wasn't right. Despite the feeling, we powered on, as sitting ducks in the backs of trucks in pitch black darkness. On the way to the suspected terrorist cell location, improvised explosive devices detonated simultaneously from both sides of the road as rocket propelled grenades and small arms tracer fire flew in our direction. We returned fire in the direction of the tracers with a fifty caliber machine gun, a Mark-19 grenade launcher, and small arms fire. The lead vehicle in our convoy had a blown tire and two casualties that needed immediate evacuation, so we turned around on the narrow dirt road under heavy fire and slowly rolled back to Charlie Company's safe-house for assistance.

When we pulled through the concertina wire gate, I could hear Whitelow yelling.

"Stark! Stark! Stark! Where the fuck is Stark?"

He ran to my truck as we parked.

"Right here, Whitelow—I'm here!"

We moved quickly to put the groaning, bloody wounded on litters to carry into the gym for medics to do their jobs before the guys were airlifted back to Kirkuk.We had our friends' blood on our hands and uniform.

"You hit?" he asked.

"No."

When back outside by the trucks, tough warriors quietly wept.

"We watched the firefight from the rooftop," he said. "Shit was crazy. How you doing on ammo?"

I checked my grenadier's vest and 5.56 magazines and realized that I was short.

"I'll be right back," he said, I watched his six-foot tall frame walk away quickly. He returned a few minutes later with a fully loaded grenadier's vest and a half dozen thirty round magazines. "Take these."

"I don't need them, Whitelow," I said. "We're not going back."

"You guys are going," he said. "Take the rounds."

"You sure?"

"That's the word."

I took the rounds.

The word began to echo around our platoon. Orders came down from higher, we had to return to the ambush site to find and kill the bastards that wounded our men. Tough men cried in fear of returning to the site and losing their lives. Because of Whitelow's strength and determination in that moment—I was able to set my fears aside and to rally our guys to take the fight to the enemy in vengeance of our wounded brothers.

"Kill those motherfuckers, Stark," he said as my truck was leaving the compound.

"I will."

The shooters were gone when we returned to the site. We searched the area until morning light finding only the tools used to detonate the improvised explosive devices. Whitelow was reprimanded for giving away ammunition without asking leadership, even though I returned it after the mission. He didn't care because he did what was right to help a brother in need. Like I said, Whitelow is a family man—and ever since we met in basic training, I have been included in his family.

I spent two days in Phoenix in a fog of blunts and television. Whitelow had a cousin staying with him and they went between watching sports and playing video games, and I was so high that I could barely function. Despite being unable to communicate verbally, it was good to visit the family and to get to know them a little better. I packed my bag early one morning while everybody was asleep and whispered, "goodbye."

I was off to visit a cousin in Santa Fe.

4

I rode east from Phoenix through long stretches of wind gusts in Arizona that almost knocked me off the bike, passing through Albuquerque without stopping. I filled up on gas twice, grabbed snacks, and stretched my legs until reaching the Buddhist center in Santa Fe where my cousin Michelle lived. She had returned to school in her mid to late forties to study acupuncture, and she was at school when I arrived. I parked the bike and emptied my pack and then rode to a store for a twelve-pack of Coronas and a pouch of rolling tobacco. I didn't care that she was living at a Buddhist center and one of the precepts of being a Buddhist practitioner is to refrain from alcohol. It didn't matter.

I sat outside the back door in the sunshine drinking a beer and smoking. An old white guy was quite surprised to find me drinking and smoking on the property. He hesitantly said, "Hello," and I returned the greeting as he quickly walked away. An hour later, with a row of five empty bottles by my chair, a resident Tibetan monk in a saffron robe informed me that I was not allowed to drink or smoke on the premises—so I walked across the street to sit under a sign in an empty lot to smoke and drink until Michelle arrived home from school. I was trying not to think about Iraq, about the local girl's email, and about the pain my brother caused by accusing me of trying to steal his ex. So I focused on the sensations of smoking and drinking while cars passed with people staring in wonder.

I won't be here long, I thought. *Not if I can't drink and smoke.*

I avoided the wonderful memories of spending a sober month at a Buddhist retreat center in Northern India. I avoided the feelings of peace I had while walking barefoot on grass as monkeys watched from nearby trees, or sitting on a meditation pillow as traumatic memories of war floated by like clouds in the sky. I avoided the feelings of confidence and well-being I had while living an alcohol free life for seven months at a Yoga studio in Guatemala where I practiced Yoga six days a week and ate healthy. Being sober and happy was possible, I had done it before—but it seemed impossible at that moment and not worth thinking about or trying again.

My cousin drove past and waved before parking in the driveway of the temple. She walked across the street to hug me and drink a beer with me before asking me to leave the alcohol under the sign and to come back to her place for a hot shower, dinner, and rest. I complied.

For the next week I stayed sober at the Buddhist Center where I received two acupuncture treatments meant to relieve symptoms of PTSD and to prevent nightmares. She occupied every waking hour with tours of the city and its surrounding areas. But the nightmares were worse than before, probably because I was going to bed sober. Being without intoxicants made me feel—and that was something I had tried not to do for many years—and I felt insane with guilt, self-loathing, and shame. When she was in school, I rode a public bus around Santa Fe to smoke cigarettes on different street corners. I visited the oldest Catholic Church in the United States where I felt nothing, and an open-air artist's bazaar in the downtown plaza where I didn't even see the art. Turquoise was all around yet I didn't even stop to look. I saw a roadrunner for the first time, and watched the original *Blade Runner*. I changed the oil and filter in the motorcycle, read *Atop an Underwood* by Kerouac, and tried to be happy while being around my upbeat cousin. I was proud of her for returning to school, it was very inspiring, but I still didn't see a future in my life that was worth living for. Michelle introduced me to a Vietnam Veteran who served with my same unit, the 173rd Airborne Brigade, and I could tell that she had told him about my struggles because he told me about his own struggles after Vietnam. When Michelle offered me to stay around for a while I knew that she was worried about me, so I packed my bag late one night and left town early the next morning without saying goodbye.

I rode south to Roswell at eighty-five miles per hour with the hopes of either being abducted by aliens or dying in an accident. I pushed the motorcycle to ninety, ninety-five, a hundred until a snake scurried off the road and I slowed down. I realized at that moment that I was running from the same things that I had been running from since I was fifteen. I was running from responsibility and relationships. When would I finally stop running?

I rode past countless hiking trails that led into rocky high desert country until reaching Roswell, New Mexico. A place I had wanted to visit ever since I was a child. I past funky alien themed museums and gift shops only stopping to eat lunch at a Chinese buffet, to buy a bottle of whiskey from a liquor store, and to fill up on gas. I pitched camp somewhere outside of town where I took the first drink before the tent was up. A wave of relief came over me that I had not felt since arriving in Santa Fe. I took a few deep breaths before taking another swill and feeling the burn in my belly that I loved so much. I drank the bottle and smoked by the fire as stars twinkled and embers flew and I stared at the sky wishing a UFO would take me away. I was cold, tired, hungover, sore, and lonely the next morning as I rolled a cigarette before packing up. Thick black clouds billowed and rolled like waves in the sky. Sand whipped my face as wind ripped across the desert. A storm was forming, I would follow it into Mexico with the hopes of finding a beach town where I could surf, be healthy, and eat street tacos and fresh fruit in the sun on the cheap.

I rode south and stopped at a diner to eat *huevos rancheros* before passing through Deming and filling the tank in Colombus. The gas station attendant wished me luck traveling into Mexico by bike. When I asked him why, he laughed and told me a story about two gringos who crossed the border on Harleys two weeks prior and had to walk back through after their bikes were stolen.

"Thankfully I am not riding a Harley," I said.

I entered Mexico without difficulty despite not having a motorcycle license, registration, and insurance. I cruised through the dusty town of Palomas as people stopped and stared. I became hyperaware and on guard and it felt good. My mental anguish receded into the past as I focused on my present surroundings. I rode southwest toward thick black storm clouds on a road with deep potholes as rain fell and I laughed and cried simultaneously. It was a similar laugh to the one that came out during a firefight. A combination of hysterical fear, adrenaline, and fun.

As I passed through a small town where school kids waved, I realized that the only money I had was in one-hundred-dollar bills tucked away in an envelope inside my backpack and I would eventually need to stop for gas. But it didn't matter, because I was in Mexico, where all of my problems would fade away. That is, until I noticed a traffic control point up ahead with Mexican soldiers armed with automatic weapons. I wondered if that was where the gringoes with Harleys had lost their bikes. I thought about turning around, but decided that it would look too suspicious. And besides, I wasn't doing anything illegal anyways. The soldier working the checkpoint provided two options: Return to the border and obtain a permit for the motorcycle, or leave it behind and continue on foot. I weighed the options, realizing for the first time that I would not make it to my dreamy beach town without legal registration and insurance. And that would require a motorcycle license. I turned the bike around to return to the border. I rode through the same town headed in an opposite direction as the sun sank behind me and school kids waved. I waved back. A small animal resembling a black bear cub crossed the road from one farmer's field into another. A ranchero wearing a big sombrero waved from horseback and I waved back. Rain fell as melancholy replaced adrenaline and hope.

People had advised me not to ride in Mexico at night, and not to stay overnight in the first hundred miles south of the border. So I held the throttle at seventy-five to try and beat the darkness as the gas gauge went below E. My concerns regarding women, family, shame, and unworthiness were replaced with survival. Melancholy disappeared, it felt good to be back in survival mode. Vehicles passed within inches as I dodged potholes of rain. Tiny crater lakes. When I reached the outskirts of Palomas, I turned left from the highway onto the border crossing road and a tall Mexican in sunglasses ran at me and tossed a watermelon that barely missed my head. He yelled something I could not understand as two guys sprinted at me from the curb. I yelled, "*Puto*" and sped by almost losing my balance. I glanced behind in the rearview to see them get in a car and start chasing. I revved the engine to ninety and flew down the straight stretch through Palomas until the bike sputtered and died without fuel.

"Oh God, oh God!" I said, pulling off to the side of the road. The small white car was approaching, and I knew it was the watermelon fucker and his friends. "Help me, God!"

Suddenly, I realized that I had a reserve tank, so I flipped the gas lever and fired the bike up and by the grace of God, Japanese engineering, and luck—I made it to the border crossing as darkness fell in Mexico. I passed through without a problem, and felt good to be safe on American soil. I took a deep breath as I filled up at the same gas station as before with shaky hands and a smile. When I went in to grab a snack, the same worker was surprised to see me.

"You still have *moto*," he said. "Good luck, you have *buena suerte*."

"Yes sir. *Yo tengo buena suerte*."

"Probably because *no es un* Harley," he said. We laughed. "*Donde vas?*"

I shrugged, "No idea."

I went north to Deming where I ate two cheeseburgers and two orders of fries with a large root beer from a fast-food joint I had never heard of while being grateful to be alive.

S

Since I had heard good things about Silver City, and I didn't feel like camping, I decided to ride fifty miles north to get a hotel room where I could wash clothes, write, eat, relax, and explore the Gila National Forest. It was dark by the time I left the restaurant. As I followed the tail lights on the car ahead, oncoming vehicles flashed their lights and I realized that my headlight had gone out again.

How did I not notice earlier? I wondered. *And why the hell does this keep happening?*

Instead of pulling off to check the fuses, I continued riding toward a warm hotel room and a break from the adrenaline. The rush from Mexico had receded while eating the cheeseburgers and I became exhausted, until it started pumping through me again as I rode within a few feet of the car ahead without a headlight. I feathered the throttle and breathed slowly, hoping for zero encounters with wildlife and police. Oncoming cars continued to flash their brights and honk. But what could I do? Thankfully my tail light worked, so the driver behind me gave me space. Images of my living room in Happy Valley flashed in my mind and I wished I could build a fire and lie down. I fought the thoughts and images while trying to stay focused on the tail lights in front. I pictured my three year old nephew, Robert Stark, seated beside me on a piano bench singing "Jolene" with all his might as I played the piano. I missed him so badly that it hurt. The lights of Silver City came into view and a breath of relief escaped my lungs. An O'Reilly's Auto Parts store appeared just outside of town and I pulled into the parking lot as a cop pulled out. I parked and stepped off the bike with a cold and shaky body and then watched the cop drive away until I was positive he would not turn around.

"Thank you, God," I said, raising a fist.

I paced for a few minutes and then shakily rolled a cigarette before removing the seat to replace a fuse. It did not fix the problem. So I went inside to buy a replacement bulb and a pack of fuses for backup. I installed the bulb and the headlight turned on and I fist-pumped the Heavens again and drove into town looking for a hotel.

I paid for three nights at the Copper Manor Motel. I emptied the contents of my backpack onto the floor of room 109. Sand and dirt fell on the carpet with garbage and cigarette butts. I apologized to the cleaners, turned on the TV, and flipped to the American Movie Channel to watch Chuck Norris kick bad guy ass. I looked in the mirror at a filthy guy who needed to clean up his act. I took a hot shower and brushed my teeth then took a hot bath while reflecting on my journey since Alaska. I had been reckless and depressed, I was lucky to be alive. I thought about the farmers on the eastern side of the Sierra Madres in California, and the farmer who waved at me on his horse in Mexico—and I knew that I needed to go home to Alaska to farm the land and write rather than evade all duties and responsibilities. I could not give up on my dreams just because they hadn't worked out as planned. Hell, I missed my brother, my mother, and my dogs—I was ready to forgive them and go home.

I changed out of my filthy black Carhartts for clean ones and put on a fresh tee shirt with a green and black checkered flannel. I looked in the mirror and kind of liked what I saw. I had fulfilled two lifelong dreams of visiting and camping outside of Roswell, New Mexico, and riding a motorcycle in Mexico.

"Good job, Robert," I said to the man in the mirror. "It wasn't like you had dreamed—but you did it."

I put on a worn-out Red Sox cap and walked across the parking lot to the Red Barn Steakhouse where I ate a bourbon burger with mashed potatoes and a salad. I took my time eating and journaling while washing the food down with four beers. I tipped the single mom waitress fifty percent and entered the lounge where I drank three double Jamesons while writing poetry at a corner table as a handful of locals laughed and talked. I felt good, damn good. I was thankful to be alive. By the time I stumbled back to the room, I was singing cadences from Airborne School under my breath. I propped up on two soft pillows on a soft warm bed watching television with a deep sense of gratitude I had not felt in years.

b

I woke up in the hotel room hungover and happy before walking a mile in the sunshine to downtown. I stopped in a coffee shop that was full of elderly artists with kind eyes and turquoise jewelry. People said "Hello," and I said "Hello" back. It felt good to be seen. I sat outside to drink coffee and write while smoking and watching people pass. I found an army surplus store where I bought a 173rd Airborne Brigade patch. Back at the hotel, I took a bath and washed my clothes with a bar of soap in the tub and hung-dried them on the curtain rod. I was sipping on Jameson with ice while writing with movies in the background without sound. I was writing another war story without realizing it, but this one was about the after effects of combat on a young man.

For three days in Silver City, I went to the same coffee shop in the morning to write and smoke followed by a stroll through town, a bath and a nap, and then a burger with drinks at the Red Barn Steakhouse. I was recharged by the third morning, ready to continue traveling. I wasn't sure how much money I still had in the envelope, but it was much thinner than when I left home. I knew that the responsible thing to do would be to count it, but I did not want to be disappointed by how much I had spent and how little I had left. So I put it off for another day...

As I packed my belongings into my backpack, I thought about the Bulgarian virgin with an English accent and bright white teeth. Her eyes were turquoise like a glacier fed river and she had full, red lips. She was pretty and funny yet terrifying in wit, intelligence, and talent. I was intimidated to open up with her in fear that she would discover how boring, unintelligent, and untalented I was.

Why do I let fear of people rule me all the time? She said she loved me and wanted to start a family with me and would be willing to live in Alaska with me. But what about in the meantime? Was I supposed to fly to Bulgaria every year or have a long-distance relationship over the phone? Ah hell, I am sure it would not have worked out anyway, once she really got to know me.

I tidied the room, stripped the sheets, and strapped the pack down on the back of the motorcycle with bungee cords. A former marine I met at the bar told me about a slow and windy road through Pinos Altos out to the Gila Cliff Dwellings that was worth checking out. The road was named, "the Trail of the Mountain Spirits," and with a name like that I could not pass it up. The further north I traveled the windier the road became, and as I gained elevation a view of a large open valley came into sight. The route was just like the marine had said, slow and curvy with stacks of red rocks on both sides like dominoes for giants. I passed a sign that read, "Continental Divide Trail," and I suddenly wanted to climb on the rocks and hike in the forest.

During my second tour in Iraq, I obsessed over three long hikes that span from north to south in the United States. The Pacific Crest Trail, the Appalachian Trail, and the Continental Divide Trail. To see a sign for one of the trails brought a long-forgotten dream back into view.

I continued the slow ride down through low forest and up into dry hills until the rolling Black Hills came into view. I pulled over and admired the mountains for the first time and felt happy to explore the country that I fought for. By the time I reached the Gila Cliff Dwellings an hour later, I was ready to rent a cabin to hang out for a while.

A park worker told me that I had to pay three dollars to enter and since I only had two singles and a five, I put the five in an envelope and started walking an ancient path below rocky cliffs comforted by silence. I imagined dozens of native families walking the same path thousands of years before. When I reached the dwellings, it felt like I was as close to being inside a real-life Jim Henson film as mentally possible. Half-built dirt walls inside a cave were reminders of America's past before it was invaded and named America. I imagined men, women, and children snuggled together laughing and singing in times of abundance and starving to death in times of despair. I sat cross-legged with eyes closed in the largest room feeling at peace and contented.

After two hours, I rode back toward Silver City in search of a place to rent. I found a cabin with a sign that read "Cabins for Let" and the owner told me he would give me a deal at

$89 a night before taxes for an extended stay. I did the math, and I did not want to pay $623 for a week or $2,670 for a month. He directed me to an R.V. park in Pinos Altos for the lowest rates around.

When I turned into the park, the first thing I noticed were hundreds of apple trees full of ripe fruit. I did not understand why the fruit had not been harvested, and I wanted to eat some. I parked the bike near a double-wide trailer, took off my pack, and pulled out the envelope of cash. I grabbed a hundred-dollar bill without looking inside, put the envelope back in the bag, and then walked up to the front door. A kind old Christian lady invited me inside an office full of family pictures and she offered me a trailer for $75 a week. I agreed, and when I went to pay her she said, "Wait, wait—you have to look inside first." I followed her to a lime green trailer across a narrow dirt road from a former school bus that was painted white with a red stripe around the center. "Winter Hawk" was painted above the windshield in the same red tint as the stripe with a bull skull by the W and two hawk feathers by the K.

When asked about the trees, she explained that her grandfather had planted them over a hundred years ago and had used the apples for cider, juice, and food.

"But nowadays they are mainly eaten by deer," she said. "Seventy-five dollars pays for electricity, propane, laundry, and showers."

"Sounds good," I said. "And what about the apples?"

"You can eat as many apples as you like, dear," she said.

"That is why my granddaddy planted them, so all God's children can be nourished."

I followed the sweet lady back to her double-wide to pay her. She asked if I was a follower of Jesus and I said that I was not sure. She handed me a Bible and told me to read the Gospels before expressing her deep love of Jesus.

"Only Jesus can heal our sick souls," she said. "And a lot of people who pass through here are sick."

I thanked her for caring about my health and my eternal salvation, and for giving me something to read. I moved the motorcycle in front of the trailer and removed everything from the saddlebags to bring inside. I removed my clean clothes and folded them to put near the bed in back. I set the remains of my instant oatmeal, instant coffee, and two cans of beans by the stove. And I placed my books and journal on a table by the window. I boiled water in a pot on a stove and then sat at a table in the warm trailer to drink coffee, write, and breathe.

"I could be here a while," I whispered. *A long while.*

7

On the ride to Silver City, I tried to focus on the road but I could not keep my mind from wandering.

Why does Jim drink so much? I wondered. *Has he always drank that much? What are the dark secrets that he is afraid to face? And why the hell do I keep catching him staring at me?*

Am I just being too damn harsh on the old man? Am I being over vigilant toward an innocent old man just because of my war experiences and my former baseball coach? Maybe you need to lighten up on him a little bit, Robert, and give him a break.

I glanced up from the road to view a sprawling valley to the south before fantasizing about the Veteran's Day ceremony in the same way I do every year. In fantasy land, hundreds of people show up wearing red, white, and blue in support of the service members who risked their lives for their freedom. A woman with big green eyes and long blonde hair wearing patriotic face paint and sparkles approaches me with full lips covered in red lipstick.

"Thank you so much for protecting our country and defending our freedom," she says. "How can I ever repay you?"

"How about we take a walk and grab a bite?"

She agrees, and we walk hand in hand on a forested trail as she asks questions about my time in the military. She listens for hours without judgment or interruption, and then she takes me to her favorite diner where we sit next to each other in a red booth and eat burgers with fries and drink milkshakes. She asks open-ended questions about the guys I served with, and then urges me to talk about my writing. When people enter and exit the restaurant, she doesn't even glance in their direction. After hours of talking about the things that are most impactful and important to me yet I never discuss…

"Oh shit." I skidded to a stop less than a foot away from the back of a car. "Back to reality, Robert. Focus on the road."

Unfortunately, fantasy land is never like reality. The only people who typically show up for Veteran's Day ceremonies are veterans, their families, and a handful of counselors. A few white-collar workers wearing dress shirts and slacks shake hands with the vets after the ceremony, and that is when I walk away. Most Americans are too busy to show up for Veteran's Day events.

In Silver City, a handful of Hispanic Vietnam veterans in uniforms and berets were Honor Guard while two vets from the middle east wars raised the flags. The hard, straight faces and lean bodies of the warriors were mirrored by two bald men with soft, pudgy faces and big belts and a lady who must have weighed over three hundred pounds wore baggy khakis and a wavy blouse.

I could've used her blouse as a parachute during the invasion, I laughed to myself at the image. *It probably would have worked better.*

I felt bad for teasing her in my mind. I was bitter about the small turnout and I should have been more kind toward her and the men for showing up, but I couldn't seem to help it.

After the ceremony, the veterans shook hands with each other and then with the two bald men and the fat lady. I watched from a hundred feet away while taking full advantage of the free coffee and donuts. Both of the younger vets wore the 173rd Airborne Brigade patch on their right shoulder as a combat patch, the same unit I parachuted into Iraq with.

I didn't recognize them and I wasn't ready to travel down memory lane, so I did not approach them. I waited in the college lobby for thirty minutes after the ceremony to see if anybody showed up for the "Meet a Veteran" event, but nobody arrived.

There goes my fantasy, you dipshit. Why the hell did you think that this year would be different? Make realistic expectations, Robert, and you won't be disappointed all of the time.

I went to the liquor store for Crystal, a twelve-pack of Indian Pale Ale, two pouches of American Spirit rolling tobacco, and a bottle of Jameson. I ordered three large pepperoni pizzas from Pizza Hut, and after picking them up and strapping them to the back of the bike, I rode twenty minutes to Pinos Altos with a smile.

I am going to drink, smoke, and eat pizza all day, I thought. *It will be a perfect Veteran's Day.* I smiled at the thought, while the question that would determine my future nagged at me.

How much money is left in the envelope?

8

When I arrived at the trailer park, I could hear the Alabama roustabout outside of Sam's bus talking about bow hunting and rig work, so I stayed at the trailer to unload the supplies. I carried them inside, closed the door, and felt a wave of relief at being behind a closed door away from everybody with food, smoke, and drink. I sat at the table to eat a slice and have a beer, and just before I bit into the pizza I pictured Sam praying on his knees in the field and I figured that I might as well give it a shot.

"God, I haven't been the best person... but I'm trying. Please help me to be the person that you want me to be. Amen."

I took a drink of beer and a bite of pizza and then let out a sigh of relief.

Knock, knock, knock...

Dammit, so much for my alone time.

"Anybody in there?" said Sam.

"Yeah, come in," I said.

The door swung open.

"After a good taco," said Sam with a grin, "good tobacco." He laughed. "Can I get my smoke?"

I tossed him a light blue pouch of tobacco.

"Thank you, sir," he said. "What do I owe ya?"

"Don't worry about it," I said. "Thanks for all the food."

"What are you doing inside?" he asked, removing the plastic to roll a cigarette. "While it's gorgeous outside."

"Not much," I said. He looked around the trailer and saw the whiskey, vodka, and beer on the counter. "Just writing." I motioned to the open notebook on the table. "I have three pizzas and some beers to share."

"You're a writer, huh?" He stepped over to the table and picked up the notebook. "You write in cursive..." he said, flipping through the pages. "I didn't know they still taught that in school. And you write... a hell of a lot."

"I enjoy the feeling of writing in cursive," I said. "It's an uninterrupted flow. Do you want a beer and a slice of pizza?"

"Would you want to take a ride to the springs today before you get plastered?" he asked. "It is a beautiful morning and it's supposed to stay nice the rest of the day. But a storm is rolling in that will hit us in two days, and we will probably be trailer-bound after that. It's supposed to snow."

"Snow… Holy shit… I didn't realize that it snowed here."

"Oh yeah," he said. "It's nothing like Alaska, but we get a little."

"Wow. I'll have to get them apples down before the storm comes."

"You have all day," he said. "No need to rush."

"I'm good on the offer to ride to the springs," I said. "I want to stay here and write."

"In that case," he said, "I'll take a beer."

I handed him one.

"No pizza?" I said. "Who turns down pizza?"

"Not now," he said, patting his belly. "I just ate. Maybe later."

"I bought the pizzas for all of us," I said. "Whenever you want some, let me know."

He put the bottle cap in his teeth and opened the beer. He had shaved his face that morning and he looked sharp with a silver goatee.

"Your arch nemesis is gone," he said. "I'll be hanging out by the fire when you want to come by."

"Good," I said. "Because I don't like him."

"Nobody does," he said. "Not even himself, and that's the problem."

"I'll finish this up, and be over."

I ate three slices of pizza and rolled three cigarettes while contemplating staying inside to start on the whiskey, but it was only noon and I didn't want to get wasted too early. Jim stopped by for his vodka while mumbling things that I could not understand. I grabbed three beers and went to the fire.

Sam's voice echoed from the apple trees and trailers as I approached the campfire.

"They say that God made the earth with all its splendors and beauty, and then with everything that was left over—he created southwest Texas; the area known as the Big Bend. There is no other place like it."

"I went over to Texas and joined a group called: 'The Atlantis Rising,'" said Richard.

"One hundred and fifteen people from our group went to Cairo, Egypt together. We were from all over the world. I ended up going over there with my girl at the time, the same one I later married, and I told her as we flew into Cairo: 'I have to spend the night on top of the tallest temple, or I will die unhappy,' and she told me: 'Well then, do it, but I bet you'll still die unhappy,' the snub-nosed bitch."

We laughed.

He continued, "It was just before sunset on the second day when a man of about seventy who sat at the lowest part of the temple offered me a way up and I said: 'No baksheesh!' And he agreed, and I followed him up the temple. Now, this was no place with tiny steps to take one by one with ease," said Richard, laughing in recollection. "You had to literally climb your ass onto one stone at a time because they were so damned big... Well, I followed this old timer up to the top of the temple, and when he said: 'Baksheesh?' I said, 'No!' and he went down all solemn like, just like a square peg.

"Well, then I was up there by myself, and I had about what you have on there, Rob, a tee-shirt and a pair of jeans, and I figured I would be okay, I was in Egypt for Christ's sake; until the goddamn wind started to blow from all angles and there was nothing I could do to escape it. I went to the north side of the pyramid where a Canadian couple were lying in their sleeping bags trying to get it on with what they said was: 'Pyramid Power,' so I left them alone and went back to my spot on the southern side of the pyramid.

"The wind hit me from all angles and I thought I was going to have to go back down to the hotel when all of a sudden a black Persian cat appeared to the left of me and posed for me in the way cats do... you know?" Richard stretched his body into a cat pose and looked back at us.

"The cat appeared to me just like that, all stretched out, and then it disappeared around the corner out of sight. So I sat there in the cold, just about to head down, when that damned cat come over to me out of nowhere and gave me the head nod like—'follow me.' So I looked around to make sure it was talking to me and it gave me the same look and head nod again, and I stood to follow it.

"That damn cat led me to an alcove in the rock where there was no wind at all. I mean none! So I sat there with that cat all night, hunkered out of the wind, and the next morning as the sun crested the ancient city, the cat took off and I followed it. The next thing I knew, I heard familiar voices from people in my group and I stood high on the pyramid and said: 'Welcome!' in the deepest voice that I could, and I have a deep voice, and they all turned white like I was a ghost of sorts until they saw me and they began to laugh hysterically.

"They told me that about six blocks down there were a couple of stones missing and they had spent the night in there doing a séance. I told them, 'If I would have known you were there, I would've been right there with you,' and then I realized that the cat had disappeared and I wondered: 'What the hell would my night have been like beside you bastards in the warmth instead of outside with that cat?' I never would know, but I sure was thankful for that Persian cat."

Sam and I nodded, laughed, and drank.

With shaky hands and two pairs of glasses, Richard lit a joint, took two puffs, and passed it my way. He told us about his twenty-five years as an ad salesman for hotels around the United States. His job was to sign on local businesses and create a booklet of their ads to be kept in hotel rooms for patrons to browse and buy. We have all seen them. He made a good living, he said, as well as in real-estate in Los Cabos and other parts of Mexico and the U.S. He married the woman he went to Egypt with and they had one son, who is older than me by twenty-five years. His son lives near his mother in California and unfortunately has not spoken to Richard in twenty years. Richard could not emphasize enough how grateful he was for being in the Navy between wars. I thanked him for his service, and he acted like he did not hear me.

"If I would have gone to war, I would either be dead or bat-shit-crazy," he said. "Just like them poor boys that went to Korea, Europe, and Asia during the wars. Hell, look at them poor boys in the Middle East. It doesn't matter where the war is fought and what it's called, a war is a war and the lasting effects stick with them poor boys."

They sure do, I thought.

Richard left our circle when the joint ended to sit in his trailer and laugh at the television. Sam and I stayed by the fire talking, drinking, smoking, and eating pizza reheated over the fire. I pulled out the whiskey around 3 pm and poured us both three finger drinks. I was grateful to have Sam to drink and shoot the shit with, it felt like I had a brother in arms.

Sam Hawk was born in British Columbia, and that was where he spent the first twenty-four years of his life. He met a guy named Xeno on a ranch as a teenage wrangler and they took an instant liking to one another. They ran wild all over the Northwest Territories on motorcycles and horseback, before Xeno hitchhiked the thousand-plus miles of dirt road to Fairbanks, Alaska where he landed a job on a drill rig working three weeks on, three weeks off. A few months later, Sam stood on the dirt road with his thumb out headed north himself. When he arrived in Alaska, he landed a roustabout job on an oil rig and he later became a truck driver. He drove trucks on the north slope for twenty-three years. For many years, he and Xeno kept matching schedules so they could take their motorcycles out of storage in El Paso for adventures around the Big Bend, Mexico, and the Western United States.

They once put their bikes on a small boat and crossed the Rio Grande, riding and camping in Copper Canyon and around the North Pacific Coast of Mexico for two months.

"That was back before 9/11," he said, "when things weren't so crazy at the border, and militaristic in our country. Back when a citizen was free to do what they wanted. Nowadays, you'd be locked away trying something like that."

Sam and Xeno once smuggled fifty pounds of Mexican dirt weed from Texas into British Columbia. Sam filled a backpack with bud and "cowboy cannons" and crossed the border on foot after nightfall. Xeno picked him up on the other side at a prearranged assembly area, and the two men spent a month on Prince Rupert Island trading dirt weed for hallucinogenic mushrooms with Haida Indians.

"We were camped across the road from Haida Land," he said. "Me, Xeno, and three beautiful granola crunchers we met earlier that day who had come up to pick mushrooms. So there we were, setting up our campsite, and you know, Xeno and I didn't think it could get any better than that. We had endless amounts of herb, mushrooms, and elk meat, and three fine women who wanted to spend weeks with us. Everything was peachy keen until nightfall, when we were sitting around the campfire listening to coyotes yelp in the distance and we heard the most god-awful scream.

"So Xeno grabs the twelve gauge with buckshot and I grab a longbow with three arrows that one of the girls was carrying, and we went to figure out what the hell was going on."

Sam stood by the fire with an imaginary bow in his hand, scanning the darkening horizon.

"We were walking at a low ready through tall grass when we saw a group of seven or eight big red-headed Haidas beating the hell out of a group of pickers who had set up camp on their land without knowing better. The Indians were all boozed up. The biggest one was easily over six feet tall and two-hundred and fifty pounds, and he was pouring a bottle of booze into one of the picker's mouth yelling, 'Drink it, white man! Drink it!' I whispered to Xeno, 'Step out with the shotgun and yell: 'Now I don't know what the hell is going on here, but I don't fucking like it!' and shoot two shells in the sky. I will creep around back with the bow and we will have them surrounded."

"Of course, Xeno agreed to the plan because he was a no-bullshit kind of guy, and seeing that poor granola cruncher guy treated like that caused our blood to boil. So I started to flank their left side, and when I was in position, Xeno hops out of the grass with that shotgun in his hands and yells, 'Now I don't know what the hell is going on here, but I don't fucking like it!' and he shot two rounds in the air and those Haida boys scattered like marbles on a cement floor."

He laughed at the memory while rubbing his belly and gazing in the distance.

"Two of them boys jumped behind an old cedar, one of them was the beast of a man who was pouring booze into that poor guy's mouth. That big fucker yelled with a heavy Indian accent, 'I have a fucking gun and I will kill you!' And the two Indians continued yelling threats while I crept closer to them without them knowing.

"When I was just about as close to them as we are to Jim's trailer, I stopped and watched them." Sam spread his legs and held his body like he was preparing to shoot a bow. "Now like I said, I only had three arrows on me because that's all the girl had. So I pull one of them flat-headed arrows out and put it in the bow and pull that draw back and tilt the son of a bitch upwards like this and then I fired.

"The arrow flew up like this... shhhhhhhhh," he used his hand and arm as if they were an arrow, "and it fell just short of them Indian bastards. But they didn't hear a thing because they were too busy yelling threats at Xeno. All the while, the granola crunchers were crying behind trees for God to save them. He, he, he..." He laughed and took a swill of beer chased with whiskey. "So I pulled out the second arrow and

I did the same thing, tilting the bow a little higher—I let it go and watched that arrow fly…

"Shhhhhh…" he did the same thing with his hand and arm to mimic the movement of the arrow in the sky. "'Thwap!' The arrow stuck straight in the left arm of that big bastard's friend."

Sam and I roared in laughter. I handed him a cigarette and we both smoked.

"The Indian with the arrow in his arm ran off without a word while the big bastard kept shouting threats and didn't even notice that his buddy was hit. So I pulled back that last arrow the same as before and I aimed just to the right of the last shot and I let that fucker fly and "Thwap!" it stuck that big son-of-a-bitch right in the back of the shoulder. He, he, he."

"Holy shit!"

"That big bastard stands up like a giant and lets out one hell of a roar when I come barreling in on him and tackle him to the ground. I beat the holy hell out of him until Xeno came in and grabbed me, and I picked up a good round stick about the size of a baseball bat and I hit his knees, shins, arms, and stomach… pretty much everywhere that I could without killing him… and I kept asking: 'Do you like to beat up people that are smaller than you, you big son-of-a-bitch?'"

"Holy hell," I said. "I wonder if he bullied any more pickers after that? And how the hell they got the arrows out?"

"We didn't stick around to find out," he said. "We ran back to our campsite and told the girls, 'We have to go. Now!'

They had already packed everything up, so we ran out of there and never went back. Xeno and I left Prince Rupert Island early the next day. About a month later, I received a letter at my address in the Big Bend from a Haida friend of mine who had cut out a newspaper clipping about the incident. I lost the darn thing by now, though. It was hilarious, the headline said something like: "Indian Men Take Arrows," or something like that. Xeno and I had some wild times, that's for sure."

"Where is Xeno now?" I asked.

"Oh hell," said Sam, walking over to his pickup to grab lumber scraps to stoke the fire. "He was busted for pot down in Texas and sentenced to twenty years."

"Jesus. Twenty years for pot, that's just wrong. How long ago was that?"

"Oh, probably…" Sam put his hand on his chin. "Sixteen years ago."

"That is a long ass time," I said. "At least he's almost done."

"It sure is," he said. "I'm willing to bet that it has been a much slower sixteen years for Xeno than it has been for me."

"I'd double your wager on that one," I said. "You ever write or visit?"

"Oh hell," said Sam, stoking the fire with the poker stick and adding the scraps of lumber. He looked up at the stars and took a deep breath. "I sent him a package with a satellite map of the Big Bend. You have to see this map, it is really something else. Anyway, my package was denied and sent back. I just don't have the heart to visit a man who loved the wilderness as much as he did stuck in a concrete hell."

"Hopefully you guys will get along when he gets out," I said. "I'm sure you'll both have stories to tell."

"You never know," he said. "People change in prison, especially after hard time. And it's not always for the better."

I know it, I thought. I watched my brother change from a teenage skateboarder with dyed hair seeking love and affection into a violent gangster in a matter of months.

"You ever hear about that city slicker from New York who hitchhiked across Alabama?" asked Sam.

"I don't think so."

"He was out in the middle of nowhere when a old rickety truck pulled up next to him and a redneck cowboy says: 'Hop in,' and the city slicker does just that, he tosses his bag in the back and jumps in.

"So they're riding down along the highway and the city slicker's eyes are closed and the warm wind is blowing back his shiny long hair, when the truck comes to a screeching halt that nearly throws him over the tailgate. The New Yorker looks up and around and notices a sheep with its head stuck in a fence neighing away. The redneck gets out of the truck and says: 'I'll be right back,' and he runs over to that poor sheep and he pulls down his britches and just starts going to town on that old sheep like it was his ol' lady.

"The city slicker wants to run away, ya know, but since

they were out in the middle of nowhere with no place to go, he decided it best to play cool and act like he wasn't seeing nothing. Well, after a few minutes, the redneck walks back over to the truck all bowlegged like and he says: 'Well boy, ain't you gonna get any?' and he walks around to the front of the truck to take a piss and smoke a cigarette.

"When the redneck turns back around, the city slicker is no longer in the back of the truck, but his head is stuck in the fence next to the sheep with his pants down around his ankles."

We erupted in laughter and Tinkerbell scratched the window and Moose pounded on the wall. Jim laughed from his camper and Richard laughed from his and shouting came from the Alabama roustabout's corner. Deer chewed apples as the guy with the 9mm sat on the steps of his school bus cleaning his pistol. The stars twinkled above as I watched something move that may have been a UFO. The shame, guilt, and regret that typically accompany Veteran's Day were relieved by listening to stories and focusing on people other than myself.

Sam hoped to return to Mexico to live out his retirement but had been refused a passport three times by Canada and America.

"I am a dual citizen but neither will let me leave because I have too many warrants."

"That doesn't make sense."

Jim coughed and yelled at the TV.

"A lot of things do not make any sense at all," he said. "Why is it you put up with us old, crazy bastards?"

"I have been here less than a week," I said. "I was raised to listen to the stories of my elders, so they will be passed on and remembered by future generations."

"That sounds like a Native American philosophy," he said.

"My mother raised us with various traditions, and I have explored others myself. Hey, do you want some more pizza?"

"Oh yeah," he said, "bring a whole pie over here and we will warm it up on the fire."

I jogged across the dirt road to grab a pizza as Richard dragged his leg to the fire to smoke a joint and bum a smoke. I thought about telling a war story but I didn't know how to tell one in a way that was fun and humorous, so I didn't. Sam reheated the entire pizza and the three of us ate every slice besides two, which I brought to Jim. I knocked on the side of the camper before entering.

"Come in!"

I pulled back the blanket and he looked at my hands with squinted eyes, until he realized what I had and he jumped out of his seat and grabbed the plate with both hands and shouted, "Pizza, pizza! Oh my God, it's pizza!" And he sat back down in a white plastic lawn chair and took a bite. "It's still hot! Wow!" He turned his attention back to *CSI Las Vegas* and acted like I didn't exist. As I walked back to the fire, I could hear him say, "Oh my god, pizza, pizza... I love pizza... Would you look at this... It's pizza."

"Well, guys," I said, trying to act less drunk than I was. "I'm headed to the Buckhorn to catch the open mic. You guys want to come?"

"You just want to see if that granola cruncher is down there," said Sam.

I smiled, I had told Sam about the girl with dreadlocks.

"Do you have eyes for a young lady, young man?" asked Richard.

I shrugged.

"Yes, he does," said Sam. "She has a head full of dreadlocks and a sexy body. He said they passed eyes the night before last."

"Is that right?" said Richard, smiling and turning to look at me in the dark through two pairs of glasses. "That a way kid. Be young, not like us old timers. Don't act older than you are, remember that. Just go on up to her and say..."

"Say, 'I've been wondering about you since I first saw you a week ago,'" interrupted Sam, "'and I think you are the best-looking woman in Silver City and Pinos Altos.' That should do the job."

"Oh yeah," said Richard, nodding in approval. "That would at least get you a ticket in to see the show. What happens after the one-liner, God only knows? You could be like my old friend back in Florida who says: 'Darling, you're an adult and I'm an adult, so let's get passed the bullshit and find a place to screw.'"

We laughed.

There is no way in hell I am going to say that, I thought.

I stood from the seat to be on my way.

"Thanks for the stories today," I said. "It's what I needed. Don't stay up too late watching TV. I'll let you both know how it goes with the girl in the morning."

I walked away from the fire and stopped to turn around.

"Happy Veteran's Day, you guys," I said.

"Happy Veteran's Day to you."

As I was just about to walk up the stairs to the trailer door, I heard Sam whisper.

"Yeah, he's a veteran alright. A combat veteran. I can tell."

9

I changed my shirt and socks and put on my worn-out Red Sox hat with a green beanie over the top. I wore a green and black checkered flannel, black Carhartts, and lace-up boots. I grabbed a hundred dollar bill out of the envelope and tucked it in my wallet before rolling two smokes to begin the journey. I sang quietly in preparation for the open mic.

"In the land that I fought for—I never feel free—
There's someone always watching, right over me.
Just in case I discover what they don't want me to see—
They'll lock me up forever without letters or TV—
Ever since the Patriot Act ruled the country.
I'm not free—not free—not free—in my country.

Maybe I will sing it, I thought. *If somebody lets me play their guitar, I'll play. Even though I haven't played in a few weeks, I still know the songs.*

I crossed the Trail of the Mountain Spirits and walked past small houses on a moonlit road with bright stars above. I crossed a small bridge and up a mellow hill to Main Street. I was happy that it was cool, and not freezing.

I could live here, I thought. *No doubt about it. I could live here for a long time.*

I stood on the opposite side of the road from an old fort wondering how many battles had taken place right where I stood.

"In the land that I cried for, I never feel free—

Police with wartime weapons

Keep peace inside the streets.

Those who object, end up with broken knees—

Or are never to be seen.

Those without money, we never hear their peeps.

I'm not free—not free—not free—in my country."

I leaned on a building across the street from the Buckhorn and felt intimidated by the number of vehicles outside and the deafening noise inside. I rolled and lit another smoke, and then continued to sing quietly in the shadows.

"In the land that I killed for, I never feel free—

Taxes on my own land, to work from nine 'til three.

You need to have insurance or disabled you will be,

You try to get some groceries but you can't afford the insurance fees—

If the coppers catch you driving, you'll be shuffling your feet.

You try to climb that ladder, but the damn thing don't reach.

I'm not free—not free—not free—in my country."

The granola cruncher stepped out of a white Toyota sedan with a tall redhead and they entered the bar in pure grace. I smiled at their beauty and elegance and thought that maybe, just maybe, she came out hoping to talk with me. Two more vehicles arrived and a group of well-dressed people walked into the bar laughing.

Why don't I laugh and joke with people my age? I wondered. *I feel so goddamn serious and awkward around them. And it seems like they don't have a care in the world.*

"In the land that I died for, I never feel free—

We fought to death for nothing, except the blood money.

Vanished are the traces of individuality.

Afraid to talk in public, accused of mutiny.

I've packed up my suitcase, to climb the tallest tree.

Into the storm clouds or I'll dive into the sea.

Maybe when I'm dead and gone I'll finally be free.

Cause I'm not free—not free—not free—in my country."

I crossed the street, removed my beanie, took a deep breath, and entered the bar.

The bar was packed with happy people laughing and talking loudly. Hands touched shoulders, glasses clinked glasses, and people looked at each other in the eyes and shared stories. I was out of place. Not only was I a serious guy who didn't spend time laughing and joking in groups of people, but I was stumbling drunk and did not realize how drunk I was until I was around normal drinkers. I zeroed my focus on the dreadlock girl and found her sitting with her redhead friend, another girl, and three clean-cut guys at a corner table.

She wore blue jeans with a checkered, button-up blue and white flannel. Her eyes were bright white and light blue. We made eye contact and I tipped my ball cap and smiled, she nodded and smiled back.

Oh shit, Bobby, I thought. *She likes you. Go ahead and talk to her.*

I nervously walked past her table without looking at her, through swinging doors, past a fake Indian mannequin, past a slot machine, and into the restroom where I hardly peed. A blonde girl in her thirties with an ivy tattoo on her left bicep played a small harp and sang a slow Irish ballad accompanied by a cellist with shoulder-length dark hair and a goatee. I sat on a corner stool directly in front of the band and took a deep breath.

Thank God, I found a seat, I thought. *This place is packed. I'll stay right here all night, until I get the courage to go up there and play a few songs.*

The guy next to me had a brown mullet with silver streaks, a trimmed goatee, and rectangle-framed glasses.

"How are you doing tonight?" asked the Hispanic bartender named Debbie. She had three kids from an ex-husband, a soft voice, dark eyes, and a thick chest.

"I'm alright, thanks. And you?" I said. It felt like I was yelling over the music, and I didn't like talking so loud that other people could hear me.

"Pretty good," she said, barely loud enough to hear. "Happy it's my Friday. It's been a long week."

It was a Tuesday.

"What are you doing with your weekend?" I shouted.

"What?" she said.

"Your weekend?" I said. "What are you doing?"

"Relax," she said, laughing. Her bangs fell over her eyes and she left them there. I hoped for details. "Apply for financial aid for next semester. Spend time with my kids. You know, the norm. You want a double Jameson on the rocks?"

"Yes, ma'am," I said. "Thank you. What are you studying?"

She either didn't hear me or she ignored my question as she went to make me a drink.

Must be hard to be a single mom going to college in the day and working the bar at night, I thought. *How the hell does she do it?*

Every stool was taken and every table was full, and it seemed like every person spoke at the same time as music blasted from the amplifiers.

A female bartender on the other side of Debbie smiled and waved, and I returned the gesture. Her name was Melanie and she had straight black hair down to the small of her back, dark eyes, curvy hips, and a full set of lips that formed into a pretty smile.

I'm sure they're just being friendly because I tip well, I thought. Maybe they just appreciate my manners. People can be snooty assholes in the bar and restaurant industry, and I am an easy customer.

An older man at the other end of the bar wore a Vietnam Veteran tee-shirt and hat. He had a cup of coffee in front of him. I walked over to him, thanked him for his service and shook his hand, and then asked Melanie to get him whatever he wanted. As I walked back to my stool, I glanced at the dreadlocked girl to see if she had witnessed my act of chivalry, but she was laughing with the company at her table.

Maybe I should talk to the guy about his time in Vietnam, and tell him about mine, I thought. Oh hell, what's the point anyway? Nobody gives a damn, it'll just be a one-up conversation and I would rather listen to the music and not think about the military.

The musicians that rotated on stage were talented, but the music was soulless and mathematical rather than passionate. So I chatted with my new drinking buddy, Dale, a fifty-one-year old recent divorcee who retired from the Bureau of Land Management two years prior. He was an avid photographer, quick to show me a dozen black and white photos of skinny pale naked girls half his age molding themselves around rocks.

"Nice," I said.

You fucking pervert, I thought.

We talked about Alaska, the inside passage, Pinos Altos, his crush on Debbie, and my crush on the granola girl. We talked about music, his three kids, and his ex-wife. He told me at least five times that the granola girl was looking at me and that if I waited any longer, I would miss my opportunity. But I played it cool like I always do, walking past her table three times to go smoke. She did not follow me, so I assumed she was a non-smoker and uninterested.

Just the girl I need to help kick these habits, I thought. *Or maybe she wouldn't go for me because every time she sees me, I'm drinking whiskey, smoking, and wearing the same damn clothes. Maybe I should focus on Melanie instead... She drinks while she works and seems to enjoy seeing me.*

I stirred the ice cubes of my third double Jameson with a cocktail straw while smiling at the sound of clinking icebergs on glass. A short Welsh guy with gelled hair, a trimmed beard, and a Goa fish tattoo on his left bicep took the stage and sang five or six boring cover ballads. The granola girl had stopped speaking with her table of friends and focused her attention on the performer. The entire restaurant and bar had quieted down while the calm singer sang. When he finished his set, he quietly walked off the stage and the entire place applauded him.

Now is the time to take the stage, I tried to coerce myself. *Ask the Welsh bastard if you can use his guitar and play four or five passionate songs to blow this fucking place away.*

The granola girl walked right up to him and said something to him and he held out his delicate hand and they shook.

The Welsh bastard, I thought. *With his clean clothes, trimmed hair, and confidence. I can't follow him up. Look at me, I am a fucking bum. A dirty hobo without any money... shit... I need to count the...*

"This is the worst open mic I've seen here in a long time," said the perverted photographer. "Do you play?"

"Yes sir."

"Then get up there," he said. "You can't be any worse than that guy."

We laughed as the granola cruncher invited the Welshman to sit between her and the pretty redhead. The three men at the table showed obvious discomfort and confusion as the Welshman sat down, but the trimmed musician showed no signs of missing a beat as he introduced himself to everybody and the table and began talking. The dreadlock girl stood and walked past a full-bearded man who said something to her, and she slowly walked towards me.

"Now's your chance," said Dale, nudging my arm. "Talk to her as she walks by."

She will cold shoulder me just like she did that other guy, I thought. *Besides, do I really need to focus on meeting another girl to try and make me feel better. I am a damn wreck.*

She passed within a foot of me and I could smell a mixture of patchouli, dirt, and fresh air.

"You wimped out," said Dale, nudging my shoulder. "You'll get another chance."

"Shut your fucking mouth," I said, and Dale looked at me with fear and surprise. "Don't you call me a fucking wimp, you perverted fuck. Why don't you go take some naked pictures of underage girls and leave me the fuck alone."

I stormed through the crowd to exit the bar and smoke on the other side of the street. I had to escape from the Welsh bastard charming people with a laid-back, no-worries accent and way of life. People smoked near the entrance while I stayed on the other side of the street. I felt like shit for erupting on Dale, and I felt like a coward for not talking to the girl or going on stage.

Back inside, Dale had moved to the other side of the bar and the two bartenders simultaneously looked at me with apprehension and wonder. The dreadlock girl was five feet from my stool admiring the rock work on a stone fireplace. She was within my reach and I didn't have the confidence to say anything. I admired her beauty while trying to think of something to say, but I had nothing. So I turned around to look at the colorful bottles behind the bar and to ignore her. She walked back to her table and leaned around the Welshman whispering to the redhead, they looked at me and shook their heads.

They know that I'm a coward and an asshole, I thought. *Better now than later.*

It was as if the cocky Welshman had no idea that the world was full of murder, injustice, starvation, desperation, and evil. He continued to smile and talk slowly and loudly with a table full of strangers and pretty women.

The music ended at 9:45 pm and by 10 pm sharp the bartenders were cashing out and kicking out. The dreadlocked girl and her redhead friend left with the bearded Welsh bastard and his fancy guitar case. I left a twenty dollar tip on the bar and mumbled some words to the bartenders before stumbling to the trailer to eat two slices of pizza.

I looked at the envelope on the floor and then got into the cold bed to snuggle with the Buck knife and the pillow.

"Happy Veteran's Day," I whispered, hugging the pillow tightly. "Happy Veteran's Day."

4

ONE POUND OF BUFFALO BURGER AND THREE DONUTS

1

"You'd better watch out there, kid," said Sam, spraying lighter fluid on wood to start a fire. "Or you're going to end up with the same thing the rest of us here have."

"What's that?"

"It is called *Polynormus Leadasstis*," he said, lighting

a match to throw into the fire ring. Flames erupted. "It is a serious disorder."

"Never heard of it," I replied.

"It is when tiny lead nodules grow inside the veins around the anus," he said. "They eventually become so heavy that a guy can hardly stand anymore, all you can do is sit around bullshitting and eating while being weighted down to a chair."

"I can feel the nodules growing," I said. "And I don't feel like doing shit today."

And so the day began.

The sky was clear blue and a cold breeze swept away the warmth. It was a perfect day to stay inside, be warm and write. But before hunkering down, I shook the apple tree by Jim's place and filled two more five-gallon buckets which I sliced by the fire to put on the roof. The drying apples had become tacky and shriveled like I wanted. I bit into one with great delight and gave another to Sam who thought they were done. He gifted me a cigarette holder he made the night prior by hollowing out an elk antler with a drill and sanding it down with a Dremel. I smoked a few with him before going inside mid-morning to eat beans with bread and butter and then read in bed. I felt like shit for yelling at Dale, but there wasn't much to do about it. I wasn't going to find him to apologize, I just didn't feel right being around people because I was afraid of being an asshole again. Even though I felt like shit, I felt better than I did a week prior.

Things were looking up.

I was learning a lot from the campfire trio, and I enjoyed getting to know them better while writing them into a story. And since I was feeling healthier and more purposeful than previously, I decided to extend my stay another week. Rent was due the next day, so I would finally look inside the envelope and count the money before paying.

Jim helped me to better understand the suffering that an active alcoholic faces, and while I was not willing to admit that I was an alcoholic, I knew that I needed to stop drinking or I could end up just like him. Sam taught me to be courageous, healthy, self-reliant, hard working, and spiritual, and that taking life, and ourselves, too seriously—isn't fun for anybody. Richard taught me that life is full of challenges, no matter who you are, and sometimes all we can do is move forward without dwelling and take time to sit back and laugh. I was finding hope through extraordinary folk.

Sam stopped by the trailer to see if I wanted to go to Albertsons with him and Jim, and I agreed. It would be good for a little bit. Sam drove Jim's little Honda and I sat in back. Sam talked and laughed in the driver's seat while Jim grumbled. I didn't say much. When we arrived, Jim reminded Sam to park in a place that did not require reverse, and we went our separate ways as we approached the store. Inside, Jim pushed a cart down every aisle until he was ready to pay for one pound of discounted buffalo burger and three donuts. I loaded up on fruits and veggies, and bought some candles to make the trailer smell good and to feel like being in my mother's home.

It was cool to see the guys in public. Jim wore dirty overalls, hole-filled cowboy boots, and a worn-out baseball cap. He had wild grey hair, a beard, and a closed eye. Sam wore a brand new pair of brown Carhartts with a crease, a button-up maroon shirt, leather boots, and a round Wrangler hat. He was quiet and reserved, saying only, "Yes sir, it's a fine day," to the cashier, whereas Jim didn't say anything to the cashier at all.

We stopped at a liquor store where Jim grabbed a liter of Crystal. I didn't want to think about drinking, maybe it was time to quit, maybe not. On the ride back, Jim shared the donuts and we ate while listening to him talk about how beautiful the area was, how beautiful the day was, and how beautiful life was. His attitude was completely different on the ride into town and the ride out of town, and I wondered if it was because he had booze. Or if it was because he claimed to have hamburger buns and cheese, and he was excited to provide and eat bison burgers by the fire. Despite my theories, I was growing fond of the old man and his childlike excitement for the simple things in life.

When we returned to the park, I went to the trailer to drink coffee, to put away the groceries, and to write. Jim brought me a hot cheeseburger with all the fixings on a paper plate with a handful of potato chips. I ate alone, feeling deeply grateful for their generosity. The fire was out and the four of us men were inside our homes before sunset as deer arrived to eat fallen apples.

.

2

A storm rolled in overnight and I awoke to a light rain on the trailer's roof. I climbed on the roof, folded the apples into the tent fly and dropped them on the porch. The apples were slightly damp, I hoped they would not mold. I dragged them into the corner of the living room and then went to brush my teeth. When I returned, Richard was leaning against his trailer smoking a cigarette and drinking a cup of coffee.

"Good morning, Richard."

"Morning," he said. "The storm rolled in just like Sam said it would."

"Yes, sir," I said. "Looks like we have our own personal trailer park meteorologist."

He laughed.

"Did you get those apples inside?" he asked.

"Yes sir," I said. "I just finished."

"Good thing, that could ruin a man's spirit—to do all that work for nothing."

"Amen."

"Is that restaurant open over there?" he asked, pointing with a shaky hand toward a building across the street. "Can you see it? I can't see that far."

"The sign is on."

"What's that?"

"It's open!" I yelled.

"Come over there with me to drink some coffee," he said.

"I spent eighty-one dollars on groceries yesterday," I said, suddenly feeling anxious about money. "And that includes coffee, so I can't afford to buy a cup."

"You don't need to buy anything," he said. "Just come over and drink a cup, it's on me."

"I'll be ready in a minute," I said.

I went inside to put on the same old black Carhartts and a flannel that I wore every day, and when I stepped outside Richard was leaning on my trailer waiting. We walked across the street at the pace of an 82-year-old with a cane and a bum leg. The wind blew against the trailer park sign and the sound of a swinging chain brought a smile to my face. Inside the restaurant, eight old-timers sat around a table with the final bites of their breakfast on plates in front of them. They quieted down when we entered and a cute waitress my age refilled their coffees and took plates.

"Morning, Richard," she said.

"Well, good morning, young lady," he said. "I'd like you to meet my new friend, Rob."

"Good morning, Rob," she said. "I am Rachel. It's a pleasure to meet you."

"It's nice to meet you," I said.

"Good morning, Richard," said a man at the table. "Where ya been?"

"Good morning, good morning, good morning," said Richard, spinning an unsteady circle to wave at everybody in the restaurant. "How many times do I need to say 'good morning' in a day? You all get the point."

We laughed.

"I've been married and divorced three times," said Richard. "I don't need another wife asking about my whereabouts, thank you very much."

I followed Richard past an acoustic guitar with nylon strings leaning against the wall into the back room where we sat at an empty booth.

"This is more like it," he said.

"We need a wall!" said one of the men at the table. "It needs to be a hundred feet high with four strands of razor wire. It's the only way to keep them out."

"It's true," said another. "If they were all Mexicans and Hispanics, it wouldn't be a problem. Hispanics are some of the best folks on the planet. Hardest working, too. The problem is—the damn Arabs are trying to overpopulate our country and terrorize us from within."

"And the Chinese," interjected another.

"Definitely the Chinese," continued the man. "They are literally buying our country and our natural resources right out from under us. And we are letting it happen."

"Blah, blah, blah," whispered Richard.

I tuned out the men's political discourse while wondering how to get my hands on the guitar. Rachel came over to take our order, and I asked for a cup of black coffee and a slice of apple pie *a la* mode.

"I said I would buy your coffee," said Richard. "I didn't mention pie. And besides, isn't it a little early for pie?"

"It's never too early for pie," I said. "And I'll pay my own bill, thank you very much."

Richard walked into the other room to engage in conversation without ordering. I read a local newspaper before looking through the Continental Divide R.V. Park's annual calendar. Sam and Jim entered the cafe and the entire restaurant seemed to echo 'Good morning' to both of them. They came to the back to sit with me in the booth. Sam was surprisingly quiet, yet he seemed to be listening to the conversation in the other room. While Jim looked around the restaurant like it was his first time inside.

"This is a fine place," said Jim. "A very fine establishment. They serve the best food in town."

A large man named Rex with a big red nose, thick fingers, and arms covered in tattoos came out of the kitchen in a white apron and walked up to our table. He stood over me and I felt a tad bit intimidated until he started laughing and patting Jim on the shoulder.

"Hi there, Jimmy boy," he said. "How's it been going, good friend? Long time no see."

"Oh, you know," said Jim. "I woke up on the right side of the ground, so I have no complaints."

"I can understand that," said Rex. "Well, it sure is good to see you. I wish you'd come in here more often, it's always good to see ya."

"Yeah, yeah."

"Do you want an omelet with all the fixings?" asked Rex.

"Oh yeah!" said Jim. "And some coffee… you guys have the best coffee. Just the good stuff in the omelet, please, just the good stuff… the meat… none of those little green and red things that you put in there sometimes."

Rex laughed, "I'm just trying to give you a daily dose of vegetables there, Jimmy."

"Oh heck," said Jim. "Look at me… I'm fit as a fiddle! You aren't sneaking anything past me today, Rex."

"The rest of you guys can put in your order with Rachel," said Rex, as he walked through the swinging door back into the kitchen.

How is it that the same man who was yelling, 'I am a pedophile,' a few days prior was being treated like a hero at the local diner? I wondered.

"How do you know Rex, Jimmy?" asked Sam.

"Oh, you know," said Jimmy. "From here and there."

The waitress set a round of steaming coffees in front of us.

"Thank you," said Jim. "I am treated like royalty in this palace."

"Anything for you Jim," she said, "you old softy." She touched his shoulder.

The tenderness she showed Jim made me want to know her on a more intimate level. I wanted her to be tender like that toward me. She was a beautiful, quiet, hard-working country girl with straight brown hair and matching brown eyes. She wasn't what modern society would deem "hot", but she was gorgeous in a down-home country kind of way. I imagined myself dating her, living in the trailer park while we courted, finding a part time job in the area that would provide me time to write and a money to pay for a nice place to rent. Rachel and I could live there for a year or two while saving our money to buy some land out near the springs to raise horses, kids, and crops.

Richard returned to our table, breaking my daydream.

"I have a personal request..." he said, talking to Rachel.

"What is it?" she asked, putting her fists on her hips.

"Can you keep my new friend, Rob, here warm?" he said. "With this storm rolling in, he might freeze to death without you."

Sam, Jim, and I shook our heads in perfect rhythm.

"Maybe if he stands a little closer to the heater," she said. "He can keep himself warm."

"What's up with the guitar in the corner?" I asked, changing the subject. "Can anybody play it?"

"You can go right ahead," she said. "And if you're staying at the park with the rest of these hoodlums, I'm sure you could take it over there to play. It needs a couple of strings is all, but other than that it's in good shape."

"Thanks," I said. "That's good to know."

"You play?" asked Sam.

"A little."

"Maybe you should play for us around the campfire," said Richard. "We could invite Rachel over."

"I'll be right back with your food," she said, walking away.

"Don't be scared to play in front of us," said Jim. "You young people today... You're so worried about what other people think about ya, it absolutely paralyzes you."

Our food arrived a few minutes later. The pie was made with fresh apples from the park and it was covered in three scoops of vanilla ice cream. I ate the pie with three cups of coffee, and it was easily the best apple pie I'd ever had. Jim devoured the omelet, potatoes, and toast while raging about how it was the best food he had ever eaten in all of his life. I swear I saw Rex blushing from the kitchen. Sam drank coffee in silence and did not eat, and Richard drank coffee that he brought over in a Thermos. I was beginning to understand why Jim had called him a cheap bastard.

"The good thing about having double vision," said Jim, opening and closing one eye after his plate was scraped clean, "is that I can see two things instead of one. Look here... Instead of having one waitress, there's two. Ha! Instead of one cup of coffee... There's two."

"You need to see an eye doctor," said Sam. "And get some prescription glasses."

"Yeah, yeah," said Jim. "I'm fine as it is."

"When I first met you," I said. "I thought you were missing an eye and never got a patch."

Jim broke into a wheezy, coughing fit.

"I get that all the time," he said. "Literally, all the time!"

I paid for my breakfast, Sam paid for his, and Jim did not get a bill. The four of us walked back to the trailer park in a light rain, where I borrowed a box fan from Jim to use on the apples. It was full of dust and lint and who knows what else, so I ran it outside for ten minutes, scrubbed it with soap and water, and then set it up inside the trailer.

I suddenly had an urge to hop on the motorcycle and ride someplace far, far away. I wanted to escape from the trailer, from my new friends, and from the newfound feeling of comfort. I wanted to escape from my anxieties about money, women, and not feeling good enough.

Rent is due, I told myself. *I need to open the envelope and check the money, but I really don't want to find out that I only have a few hundreds dollars left. That will determine everything about the near future...*

3

I turned my head to the side while reaching in the envelope to pull out two hundred dollars for pocket money.

Not today, I thought. *I don't need to count it right now. I can pay rent for a week, and use the libraries in Silver City to type the story. This story is going to be my breakthrough book, and I don't want my notebooks to get ruined on the road. I will continue to write the story in the trailer and then type it and send it to agents before leaving Pinos Altos. That way, I can return home to Happy Valley to work the land next summer while earning an income from writing. The dream life is to be a farmer and an author.*

I thought about riding down the windy road toward the cliff dwellings, stopping for a soak in the springs, and going for a hike, but instead, I went to Silver City to work on my writing.

It was chilly in November at 7,080 feet, so I wore a riding jacket, pants, and gloves for warmth, and a helmet for safety. I rode 55 mph during six miles of descent to Silver City while gazing at a sweeping valley to the south. I was thankful for the tans and browns of the New Mexican landscape instead of the blues and purples of back home. I rode with a smile of satisfaction at having made up my mind to stay another week, to finish the story, and to try and sell it. And while I tried to stay focused on the road, my mind drifted thousands of miles to Alaska as I wondered about my family.

———

When I reached Silver City, I turned right to ride up to the college. A police officer was talking with a campus security guard and they both glared at me as I rode by.

Mother fuckers, I thought. *I could take your fucking guns from you and kill you before you even knew it. Quit looking at me like a fucking terrorist.*

I parked, removed my gear and stuffed them in the saddlebags, and walked to the library with a notebook in hand. Of course, I was wearing the same thing I wore every day, black Carhartts, green and black checkered flannel, and a worn-out Boston Red Sox hat. My beard was growing in fairly well, too, and when I noticed the young and fresh people on campus I felt like an old, weathered man, and it felt good. The librarian assigned me to computer twenty-two in the back corner, which was perfect for watching both entrances, and I began the long and arduous task of deciphering and typing my hand-written cursive.

I took a break to think about what the hell I was doing typing a story in a college library in New Mexico instead of getting outside to explore the world.

The exploration of the world is what feeds my writing, I thought. *I need to make time for both. When people ask if I am a writer, I never know what to say. I am not currently making any money as a writer, yet I have worked thousands of hours on my trade while writing an unpublished book, hundreds of newspaper articles, poems, songs, short stories, essays, and letters. When I don't write regularly, I am overwhelmed, frustrated, short-tempered, and depressed.*

"I wrote for a small town newspaper in Seward, Alaska for a few years," I will say.

"What are you writing there?" they will ask.

"Oh, just a story."

"A memoir?"

"No," I will say. *"Who am I to write a memoir?"*

"A journal?"

"Something like that."

Despite not currently making money, I have made thousands of dollars as a journalist, and I can't blame editors and publishers for not publishing my work because I don't submit any stories. Hell, after being rejected over a hundred times by agents and publishers for my first book, I don't want to deal with any more rejections. Yet still, I hole away for hours, weeks, and months in a desperate attempt to dump my mind, and then I don't let anybody read my work. Hell, I am less of a writer and more of a self-indulged maniac who rejects the rest of the world by living inside my head.

I walked to the water fountain for a drink and when I returned to the computer to continue typing the third page, I was tapped on the shoulder by the librarian.

"We have a student waiting for a computer," she said. "And students have priority…Sorry about that, you can always use the public library."

"Understandable," I said.

I'm an old washed out bum that needs to give up my computer for hopeful young kids who will actually do something with their lives.

I was embarrassed, but tried not to show it. I walked out of the library while making eyes at a dark skinned girl with wavy hair. I rode down the hill to the public library in hopes of getting more work done.

"They should give me at least an hour," I said, parking on a side street.

An hour was exactly what they provided. Since the computers were full, I smoked outside while waiting and came in when it was my turn. I typed the first draft of the story from my notebook, while adding details and emotions to create a second draft. And in doing so, an hour was over and I had only typed three pages from my hand-written journal.

This is going to take a lot longer than I imagine, I told myself. *I need to rent a laptop to finish the job. First things first, though—I need a cup of coffee.*

I rode down College Street and took a right on Main. I followed Main Street past bars and shops until reaching Broadway where I took a right and parked next to a bike rack. I sat on a park bench and ate a ham sandwich with an apple and drank some water. I read to the sound of slow-moving cars, in awe of Jack London's ability to enter the minds of so many characters and to describe them and their settings so well that the reader actually becomes a character.

I finished the sandwich and the chapter and then walked around the neighborhood in search of a new composition notebook and a laptop. I was surprised to find a stationary store on the corner near the coffee shop where I bought a black pen and a composition notebook. It made my day, I felt like I was on the right path. I entered the coffee shop with my head on a swivel.

"One twelve-ounce black coffee for here, please," I said, paying and tipping a buck before sitting at a table in the back corner with a view of both entrances.

I had just sat to write with a new pen in a fresh pad when a soft, shaky female voice spoke.

"Hi," said a strange girl I had met a few days prior who looked like an elf. She was less than five feet tall with straight, greasy brown hair, slanted eyebrows, pointed ears, and an otherworldly awkwardness.

"How's it going?" I asked, looking at her and trying to be kind.

"You were writing in a different notebook the other day," she said, shifting her weight from leg to leg as she stood by my table. "So are you writing some kind of memoir or something?"

"No," I said. "I am just writing."

"Yeah," she said, shuffling her feet. "You are too young to write a memoir. You have to be old to write one. All of the great memoirists are old, and you're not old."

"Is that right?"

"That's right," she said. She leaned over and looked at the novel on the table. "Jack London, huh? I have only read part of "To Build a Fire" and it was too depressing. I couldn't read any of his other stories after that one."

"Oh yeah?" I asked, aware that I was talking to a critic. "That's too bad—he is an incredible storyteller."

"My life is depressing enough as it is," she said. "Being that I have Lyme's Disease and all... I lost my keys yesterday, too, both my car and apartment keys... I don't know how I'm going to find them... It's a side effect of Lyme's Disease."

"Losing keys?" I asked.

"Not necessarily losing keys," she said, "short term-memory loss."

"That sucks," I said, pulling out my tobacco to roll a cigarette and escape the conversation. "I'm sorry to hear that."

Would you just leave me alone so I can write? I thought.

"Yeah," she continued, "I was at the college and I found a really big cigarette butt next to where a guy was sitting, and he looked kind of something like you, you know, he looked like he smoked, so I asked him if it was his and he became defensive and I think that he stole my keys and threw them away or something."

"Oh, really," I said. "That sucks. Seems like an odd reason to steal your keys."

"Yeah, it was him," she said. "I don't know what else would have happened to them. He looked like a real sleazy guy... Really dirty... And he always wore the same things... He really looked like you... No offense."

"None taken," I said, laughing. "So where did you sleep last night if you didn't have your keys?"

"Excuse me?" she asked, with her hands on her hips.

"Can you get into your apartment and car now?" I said. "If not, where did you sleep?"

"Oh no, no, no, no," she said, shaking her head. "My car and apartment are both infested with mold and very toxic environments. I cannot be inside either one."

The terror on her face made me cringe.

What a poor life, I thought. *To be so afraid of people, places, and things.*

I stood from the corner table that had a view of both entrances, the entire room, and the barista, to excuse myself for a smoke. Strangely, the girl looked me up and down in a sexual way.

"I am going to smoke and write outside," I said, noticing that her nipples were showing through her shirt and she was not wearing a bra.

She caught me looking at her breasts and said, "Come chat when you're done."

221

"Sounds good."

I watched her walk to a table where two people I had watched stuff handfuls of honey packets into their pockets the day before were seated.

The first time I met her, just the other day, I thought that she had a nice butt and a cute elf look to her. But this time, after our brief conversation, the cuteness is gone. Will I ever actually like a woman after I get to know her?

I walked outside to sit on a chair, smoke, and read through my finished journal.

If only she knew what I did for this country, I thought, *sarcastically. And that I already have one finished, unpublished book and another that I'm trying to finish right now. Maybe then she would leave me the hell alone and take my writing time seriously.*

I went in for a refill and decided it was a tactical decision to further my relationships with people in town in case I stuck around. So I went to the girl's table where I was introduced to an older woman who had been sober for three years and was leading a healthy life. I didn't believe her; I didn't think that anybody who had been sober for three years would steal honey packets from a coffee shop. The man on the couch fixed his skirt and stood to leave the moment I arrived to the couch. The elf and the honey thief bantered and criticized writers, painters, and artists of all forms. When asked, neither of them made art themselves, besides photography. They spoke of their diagnosis' of post-traumatic stress disorder and how their minds were occupied by the harsh realities of life rather than art. I kept my own PTSD diagnosis a secret, because I was picking up on the vibes that if I mentioned my time in Iraq, they would tear me apart.

"I have online friends who die all the time," said the elf. "I am friends with thousands of people online through Lyme's Disease forums. Our people are dying every day because of the disease."

"I have friends die all the time, too," said the honey thief, "from another type of disease, called addiction."

The elf reached over and grabbed my notebook from my hand and started flipping through the pages.

"So what… are you writing some kind of *Motorcycle Diaries* meets *To Build a Fire* or something?" she asked.

"I'm just writing a story is all," I said. "I can't really say what it's about."

"Do you mind if I read something?" she asked.

"That's fine with me," I said. "But mind you, it's a first draft that requires editing."

She was quiet for a minute while reading and I thought about talking to her older friend, but decided against it.

"Wow," she said, "this entire notebook is filled with cursive."

"That's right," I said, hoping for feedback.

"Spectacular," said the honey thief, leaning closer to the elf to observe my cursive penmanship. "It is actually legible, too."

"I learned a hard lesson with my first book," I said. "Don't write the first draft too sloppy or it will be impossible to type."

"Your first book?" asked the honey thief. "Are you a published author?"

"No ma'am," I said. "Not yet."

"What's the holdup?"

"Good question," I said, thinking for a moment. "Maybe I'm not ready to put some of the material into the public's eye for fear of critics tearing me apart."

The elf flipped back to the first page of the notebook, and then onto the next page, and she flipped through the pages super fast trying to find an end. She closed the notebook and I let out a sigh of relief.

"That's a lot of detail," she said. "Where's the ending?"

"I don't have the ending yet," I said. "What did you think about the parts you read?"

"It's a little too much for me right now," she said. "I'm not much of a reader, anyway. I like it when people tell me about books because then I feel like I have read them and I can talk about them."

I took back my journal and felt the rage building inside. *You have to walk away,* I told myself. *Or change the subject.*

"Have you ladies been to the cliff dwellings?" I asked.

"Not yet," said the honey thief. "I moved here thinking that I would soak in the springs every weekend and explore the hills and trails, but then I started making friends and having social obligations. And now, here I am, four years later and I still haven't soaked in a hot spring or been to the cliff dwellings."

"It happens," I said.

"Somebody with a chronic illness like mine doesn't do much," said the elf, "but I have seen some very vivid pictures of the dwellings. So I feel like I have gone."

We awkwardly picked fingernails, scratched inseams,

yawned, and searched for something to say without finding anything. I thanked them for the conversation, refilled the coffee, and returned to the table to roll another cigarette.

"His problem is that he is too serious," whispered the elf, just loud enough that I could hear. "He shouldn't take life so seriously. All the guys who come through here are the same, they claim to be writers and artists yet they can't deal with criticism. How can you ever be an author and not be able to deal with criticism? He needs to toughen his hide and get over himself."

I was on the verge of walking over to her and exploding, but instead, I went outside to smoke and think while watching cars pass on Main Street.

Am I taking myself too seriously? I wondered. *Am I overly critical of myself to the point of being unable to share my work with others? Yes and yes. How the hell do I get over it?*

I walked back inside and sat down at my table just as the elf said, "I am going to email him and let him know how that made me feel."

Oh dear, I thought. *Just leave me the hell alone.*

I recalled the first time we had met. She ended our conversation by asking for my phone number, but since I did not have a phone, she asked for my full name and social media information. I had a friend request waiting when I logged in and she had a new friend to add to thousands.

I realized that being at the coffee shop would not provide a space to work, so I decided to leave in hopes of finding a laptop rental.

I walked over to their table to say goodbye and thank them for the conversation. I wished the elf luck in her search for the lost keys, and I wished the honey thief luck in her sober life. The elf apologized for any offense she may have caused regarding my writing and I acted like her lack of feedback about my writing and her mention of me resembling a dirty guy that may or may not have stolen her keys, did not bother me.

"Well, then," she said, red in the face. "I am deeply apologetic for the email I just sent you, I may have gotten a little carried away."

She smiled awkwardly and stood from the table. She stretched her arms back and I tried not to stare at her bare belly and perky breasts but I couldn't help myself.

"No worries," I said. "I won't take it personally." Although I was boiling inside.

I walked down Main Street past a couple of bars full of smoking, drinking people. I saw the guy who cleans his 9mm on the steps of his bus seated by himself on a bar stool, and I felt sorry for him.

Am I any different? I pondered.

I visited the Army Surplus Store where an old Vietnam Veteran gave me directions to a computer repair shop down the street where I could probably rent a laptop.

"You some kind of writer or something?" he asked, pointing at the notebook under my arm.

"I wouldn't go that far."

"Too bad," he said. "We need more combat veterans to tell their stories. I wish I could write, because I would. Maybe the stories could prevent history from repeating itself, or help some of these sad and guilty people to know that they're not alone. Hell, maybe it could help their spouses and family to better understand what the hell they're going through.."

"How do you know that I'm a combat veteran?" I asked, looking back while walking toward the exit as fast as possible.

"It takes one to know one," he said.

I nodded and opened the door to walk away.

"Stay alert, stay alive out there," he said. "Complacency kills!"

"Roger that," I said, closing the door.

"Tell your story!" he shouted to my back as I closed the door.

Yeah, yeah... Nobody gives a damn, I thought. The problem is that I'm only halfway good at two things, writing and digging ditches.

I found a computer repair shop where I rented a laptop for $50 for a week.

You know what, I told myself. Maybe that guy is right. Maybe telling my story will make a positive impact. To hell with the critics, I am going to keep writing this book until it's done, and then somebody will publish the first one. I will be an author, no matter what anybody says! But first, I have to stop at the liquor store for a bottle of whiskey and a twelve pack of beer.

S

AMERICAN MADE BOOTS

NOVEMBER 15, 2013

Week Two

1

I woke up with a splitting headache, crusty eyes, a dry mouth, and a stomachache. I rolled out of bed and stumbled into the living room to open the drapes.

"Thank God," I whispered to the clear blue sky. "I'll get the apples outside to dry so I can get the hell out of here."

I felt weak and sick but I had to keep moving, I was a writer with stories to tell and a laptop to type them on. I put the apples on the roof, took a shower, and dressed in the same dirty clothes as the day before. I grabbed the thin envelope of money and fought the urge to count it because of a potential disappointment, so I grabbed two hundred dollars and walked to the main house to pay for another week.

"The guitar is our grandson's," said the owner, still in a nightgown. "He has six or seven of them and doesn't play a single one. We tell him that he's spoiled, and he says that he's loved. Use it while you're here, he won't notice."

"Thanks," I said. "I will take good care of it."

I went to the fire to say hello to Sam and Jim, who were seated around drinking coffee and talking quietly. Sam had only slept a few hours, so he was quieter than normal. He awoke at 2:30 to listen to *Coast to Coast Radio* until 6:30 where guests talked about the power of the Ouija board, past life regression, reincarnation, and the use of crystals in healing and banishing evil forces. Jim laughed while eating Dinty Moore beef stew from a can. Richard's trailer door closed as he dragged a leg to the fire.

"A lot of people think booze is bad," said Jim, wiping bits of beef from his beard. "Booze this and booze that. Hell, there was always booze in my house growing up. Booze is a normal part of the American life. The first time I got drunk I was one year old. One! My godfather gave me moonshine and

I was crawling all over the yard, just as happy as a clam. Since that day, I was hooked."

"Are you drunk again, Jim?" asked Richard, sitting down to light a joint.

"Not yet," said Jim. "But I sure wish that I was."

"Have you ever gone without drinking?" I asked, taking two puffs from the joint.

Jim kicked his head back and laughed while holding his stomach.

"A few days in my teens," he said, setting the can on the ground and standing. "I am going to get coffee. Get off my case."

"I have coffee inside if you want some," said Sam, smoking from an elk antler.

Jim stopped walking, and without turning around, said, "With booze?"

"I have booze."

"Vodka?" asked Jim, turning around to face Sam. "Wait… you have my vodka! Make me a drink in that special way that you do."

"Hold on now, Buckaroo," said Sam. "Let me finish my cigarette first."

"Hurry up and smoke it," said Jim, sitting down in the lawn chair under the apple tree with yellowing leaves.

Sam reached over and grabbed the fire poker leaning against the tree and waved it at Jim's legs.

"Now you watch your mouth you dirty old man," he said. "I'll make your drink when I want to. If you keep ordering me around, I will lay a whooping on ya."

Jim laughed and lifted his legs to avoid the stick.

"Quit! Quit!" He laughed so hard that his forehead popped with veins.

"Burn his ass," said Richard.

Jim stopped smiling. Tinkerbell scratched the window and a pasty hand with long black nails grabbed the dog and grunted.

"You probably do want to burn me, don't you, Richard?" Jim crossed his arms over his blue overalls, leaned back, and raised his chin.

"That's right," said Richard. "Maybe it would teach you a lesson."

They stared at each other for a few seconds before Sam said, "Whoa now boys, let's not get our panties in a wad." He stood like a bear-in-the-woods and took a long puff of Richard's joint. "Let me make you a drink, Jimmy. Richard, Rob, you guys want coffee?"

"No thanks," I said.

"I just had a smoothie and brushed my teeth," said Richard.

Jim laughed, "Aren't you Mr. Perfect."

Sam went in to make drinks as the three of us sat in awkward silence.

"I rented a computer from town yesterday," I said. "I'm pretty excited about it."

"Why would you want a computer?" said Jim. "What could you possibly want a computer for?"

"To type the story that I'm writing," I said.

"You are writing a story?" said Richard. "Are you some kind of an author or something?"

"I wouldn't go that far," I said. "But yes, I am a writer."

"I wrote a few stories when I was younger that were published in various trade journals and hotel newsletters," said Richard. "It was fun to write words that people read. Are you a published author?"

"I wrote for my hometown newspaper for a few years," I said. "And I have two poems published in an Oregon Chapbook."

"Poetry, ay?" said Jim. "The language of love."

Richard rolled his eyes and shook his head.

"Speaking of love," said Richard. "I am headed to the Co-op today for a resupply."

"A resupply on pretty women," said Jim.

"That goes without saying," Richard laughed.

"Maybe I could ride with you," I said. "For something to do."

"That is fine with me," said Richard. "I have to put oil in the truck first. The damn thing leaks oil like an old man leaks from places he doesn't want to." He laughed, coughed, and made other phlegm-removing sounds while shakily standing upright. He did not spit. "I'll get things ready to go."

"Here ya go, Jimmy," said Sam, handing him a steaming mug.

"Oh yeah!" said Jim, who sat a little taller and had a brighter twinkle in his eyes. He stuck his nose over the cup and inhaled. "Mmm, now that smells good."

"Well, all right," said Richard, walking away. "I will see you boys later, then."

"See ya, Richard," said Sam. "Be safe out there on the road, we all know how you drive."

"Bye Dick," said Jim.

Richard shook his head and walked away.

"I'll be over in a minute," I said.

We sat in silence for a few moments enjoying the warm sun as a breeze blew yellow leaves to the ground and small birds flew from tree to tree.

Even though I am hungover, I should take advantage of the nice weather by going for a hike, I thought. *It would definitely make me feel better.*

"Do you guys know how to tell the difference between a McDonald and a McElroy?" Sam asked with a Scottish accent.

"How?"

He squatted and held his right arm in front of him like he was holding a bowling ball.

"You reach under their kilt and grab hold of their balls like this." He moved his fingers like he was squeezing something and his arm like he was weighing something. "And if it feels like a quarter pounder, then by god it's a McDonald."

Jim almost fell out of the lawn chair laughing while I snickered.

"You guys want anything from town?" I asked.

"I am all set, thanks," said Sam.

Jim stroked his beard with his right hand and held the drink with his left.

"Grab me some Folgers Decaffeinated Instant Coffee," he said. "Please and thank you."

I laughed at his taste in coffee.

"I didn't know they made such a thing."

"It is the best stuff," he said, "it really is."

"Whatever you say, Jimmy," Sam said, rolling his eyes and looking at me.

Richard closed the hood of his truck and started the engine.

"I'll do what I can," I said. "See you guys in a few hours."

I jogged to Richard's single cab red Mitsubishi where he sat behind the steering wheel. We started moving before I closed the door.

2

As we sped toward Silver City, Richard wore thick bifocals under a thick pair of sunglasses with side lenses that covered half of his face. He mentioned that he was blind in the left eye and nearly blind in the right and when I offered to drive, he said, "The only time a man should ever let another man drive him around in his own vehicle is on the way to the hospital or the funeral home."

He drove 55 around 45 corners and swerved over the yellow lines. I gripped the handle by the window and made sure my seat-belt was fastened securely. We made a side-trip to visit one of Richard's friends where he fills up five gallon containers with potable water.

"Just wait until you meet him," he said. "Jammin' Jeff is the real deal. And he will probably give you new strings for that guitar."

"He has one hell-of-a-nickname," I said.

When we pulled into his driveway, Jammin' Jeff Cerwinske was bent over working on a Harley Davidson motorcycle. He had a full beard down to his chest and a warm smile.

"Jeff saw some shit in Vietnam," said Richard, as we parked. "Then he toured all over the country as the lead guitarist for Bo Diddley when he got out."

Jammin' Jeff lived alone in an open, tidy, sunlit single story home on the outskirts of Silver City. The drapes were open to the sunlight that shone on a mahogany grand piano that was ten feet from a radiant Blaze King wood stove. A vast library stood six feet high and ten feet long and a small wooden table was in the center of the room with an open notepad and a pen.

"Richard tells me that you are a writer and a musician?" he asked.

"I write a little," I said, shrugging my shoulders. "But I am definitely not a musician."

"What do you write?" he asked.

"Poetry, songs, book length stories, and some short stories," I said. "I haven't had any luck with publishing, but I just enjoy writing."

"That is a hard row to hoe," he said. "It takes luck and determination to make it as a writer. If you keep trying, you will make it eventually."

"Thanks."

"Follow me out to the garage," he said. "Let me show you the studio."

"You are going to shit!" said Richard, patting my shoulder and coughing.

We followed him around the side of the house into the backyard where a homemade hot tub was heated by a wood stove below a large array of solar panels. Six raised raised garden boxes were filled with bolting plants and vibrant flowers. Three bee hives were surrounded by active bees. We entered the garage, where I quickly learned that a professional musician does not keep a garage for the same reasons a mechanic or a carpenter might. There was not a single hand tool or a drop of motor oil.

I slowly spun in a circle trying to take it all in. My hands were behind my back in parade rest, the way I do in museums, cathedrals, and temples. Baffling covered the walls and ceiling, and a large room kept the soundboards and other recording equipment. There were drums of all shapes and sizes, keyboards, guitars, amplifiers, a banjo, ukuleles, flutes, chimes, and horns with microphones galore. The walls were covered with signed photographs and posters of Led Zeppelin, Pink Floyd, Jim Croce, John Lee Hooker, and others. A life-size poster of Bo Diddley playing beside a much younger Jammin' Jeff was the centerpiece of the room. Hundreds of bar signs, bottles, paintings, photographs, ticket stubs, and trinkets from around the world were hung on the walls with the precision of a museum curator.

"Wow," I said. "This is your temple."

"It certainly is," he said. "It has taken a lifetime to get here, and I'm still not finished. But, it's good enough to record and practice."

"I'd say."

"I told him that you were a collector," said Richard, still wearing sunglasses.

"I am not a collector," he said. "I am a gatherer. A gatherer of good times."

"This place is phenomenal," I said, unable to act stoic any longer. "I could hunker down in here for days, weeks, years! This is fucking crazy, Jeff!"

He laughed, "That is exactly what happens. Especially during recording and writing sessions. After Vietnam, I needed to release the shit that I saw in a healthy way, or it would eat me alive. So I turned to music and writing, and they have been my saving grace ever since."

"Before I forget," said Richard. "Do you have the extra guitar strings I asked about?"

"What kind of guitar is it?" His hands were interlaced on his stomach.

"It's a classical acoustic," I said. "I don't know the model, but we only need the top and bottom E strings."

"I just took off some decent strings for my last show," he said. "Let me find them."

He left us alone in his temple. Richard followed shortly after, and despite my best wishes of staying there for the remainder of the day, I tagged along. Jeff was coming out of the front door as we were about to walk in. He held out a package of strings.

"Now go and jam," he said.

I thanked him twice, once for the strings and once for his time in Vietnam. He shrugged at both.

"I want you to remember, kid," he said. "Don't let your doubts hold you back. They are the artist's worst enemy."

"Roger that."

"Rob here did two tours in Iraq as an infantryman," said Richard, putting his hand on my shoulder for the second time that day.

"Is that right?" said Jeff, looking at me in a different way than before.

"Yes sir," I said, wondering how Richard knew.

It must have been in a blackout, I thought. *I had to have told one of them. The things that I say when I'm drunk.*

Jeff took a deep breath and said, "Then that makes playing music and writing not just a hobby or a career, but a necessity. Let me tell ya, brother—if I wouldn't have played music when I got back from 'Nam, I would've ended up like so many of my buddies, either dead on the streets or stuck in a bar. Don't let what you did over there define who you are. Leave it behind and move forward as a new man. Share your stories with the world, in whatever form they are released from your soul, and don't let your doubts, and guilt, take over."

"Yes sir," I said, fighting the surge of emotions welling up in my chest and throat.

"If I wouldn't have quit drinking and drugging back in '71," he said. "I wouldn't be here today, I can guarantee you that. I am thankful to have a Higher Power who loves and guides me, a program of recovery to keep me on track, and a fellowship of men and women who taught me how to live a sober life on life's terms."

"I'm not sure what you're talking about?" I said.

"You will know what I'm talking about when the time is right," he said. "If you ever think you have a drinking problem and you want help quitting, give me a call. Anyway, when I was six years old my mother took me to church and had me in the choir. I was given a drum set at eight, a keyboard at nine, and finally an old guitar from a guy named Louie when I was twelve. I have been playing ever since."

"That is some dedication."

"Music is a spiritual practice," he said. "Find your spiritual practice and you'll live a good life. Okay guys, I have to start practicing, I have a recording session in an hour." He and Richard shook hands. He and I did the bro-hug. "Thanks for coming over. It was great to meet you, Bob. And remember what I said, don't ever hesitate to call."

"Thanks for the strings."

"Oh, and Richard, you blind bat—don't kill the kid on the roads."

Richard laughed, as I loaded the full water containers into the back and we swerved on down the road.

3

Along the way, Richard spoke about his ex-wife, their son, and how they had split when the boy was seven.

"I wanted to get as far away from that crazy bitch as I could!" he said, gripping the steering wheel of his memory. "So I moved back to Florida, where I was born."

"How old is your boy?"

"Oh hell, let me think…" he paused for a moment in recollection. "He would be forty-three years old, now. I'll be damned, he is not a kid anymore, that's for sure. He is close with his mother and stepfather, but not me. It's okay, I guess that's what happens when you run away from your kids, they don't want much to do with ya."

"I'm sorry to hear that," I said. "It must be tough not being close with your son."

"It is what it is," he said. "He is a good man and that is what counts."

I wondered how he knew that his son was a good man.

"Where are we headed to now?" I asked, as we slowed down and turned right without a blinker into a parking lot with a few shops in a single building.

"I have to stop here to get some screens."

He came to an abrupt halt and my seatbelt kept me from hitting the dashboard.

"I'm going to check out boots at the store next door," I said. "See you in a few."

We went our separate ways.

A heavy man with a red face and a soldier's haircut was seated behind the cash register. He had a trimmed grey goatee and a pair of square rimmed black glasses.

"Can I help you find something?" he asked in a deep voice.

"No sir," I said. "I'm looking for a pair of boots to wear riding a motorcycle."

He pointed at a wall of boots behind me.

"Thanks," I said.

His hat read: "My Property Is My Property!" with a picture of two hands holding a rifle. His tee-shirt read: "N.R.A. Protecting Our Country from Foreign Dominance for 140 Years." I snickered at the seriousness of the guy, wondering if that was how the elf girl saw me.

I looked at the wall of boots and picked up a pair of Red Wings only to find a "Made in China" sticker on the bottom. I did the same with a pair of Danners, before picking up every pair that I liked to find the same thing.

"Do you have any boots that are not made in China?" I asked.

He nibbled on his mustache and crossed his arms.

"Unfortunately, they are all made in China," he said. "It is a damn shame, too. I wish it weren't the case, my friend, but it is."

"I wonder if military-issued Jungle Boots are made in China?" I said. "Do you have any?"

"I sure as hell hope they aren't," he said. "Either way, I don't have any. Check the surplus store downtown, it would be the only place around here where you could buy a pair."

"Thanks," I said.

"You a vet?" he asked.

"Yes sir."

"What detachment?"

"Army. Airborne Infantry. 173rd Airborne Brigade and 101st Airborne Division. You?"

"Hooah," he said, raising his large fist and pointing at a 101st Airborne Division flag behind the register. "I was with The Big Red One during Desert Storm. You see combat?"

"Yeah," I said. "I did two tours in Iraq. Not straight combat, for sure—but we fought." I didn't ask him the same question because I figured that the likelihood of him saying "yes" was slim and I didn't want to embarrass him.

"That will change a man," he said. "You getting help?"

"What kind of help are you talking about?"

"A good counselor," he said. "Some disability?"

"I get fifty percent," I said.

"Only fifty percent," he said. "Shit. I get more than you do and I didn't see anything more than a few suspected mortar attacks that never came. Do the work to increase your disability, and get yourself a counselor. You deserve both. And you sure as shit deserve to be happy. You gave for your country, now it's time to accept what your country will give to you."

What the hell is this place, the Veteran's Psychic Zone? I thought. *I feel like I am in an episode of Twilight Zone where everybody is a veteran and they all want to help me.*

"Thanks," I said, awkwardly backpedaling to the door. "If I can think of anything else that I need, I'll be back."

"I've lived here all my life and I've never seen you," he said. "Where are you from?"

"Alaska," I said. "Seward, Alaska."

"Well, I'll be," he said. "You're a long ways from home."

"Yes sir, I am."

"Some good fishing up there, I heard. I hope to get that way in the next couple years, but it's hard to leave a business in good hands."

"Good luck with that," I said. "I have a friend waiting outside. I have to run."

"Take care of yourself," he said to my back. "And remember what I said."

Yeah, yeah… I thought.

"You deserve it!"

I went to the smoke shop to look for Richard where a pale girl covered in tattoos and piercings worked behind the counter. She looked at me awkwardly without saying anything and I did the same to her. I walked around looking for Richard, noticing an open room with tall racks of porn videos and walls full of sex toys.

"That's quite a collection," I said.

The counter girl smiled, a piercing under her top lip dangled between her teeth.

A weathered woman in her fifties, sixties, seventies, or eighties walked out of the sex room with something hidden behind her back. She had a thin red mullet, thin pale lips, and was built like a college linebacker. She placed the item on the counter and looked back at me with paranoid eyes.

"He's in there," said the counter girl, pointing at the sex room.

"In there?" I asked.

She nodded.

I tip-toed into the sex room hoping to catch Richard looking at something horrendous, but to his great fortune, and my disappointment, he was nowhere to be found. I assumed all workers were required to provide customers with privacy, so I moseyed around looking at sex toys until the customer paid and left.

"In the other store," said the clerk, blowing a bubble with chewing gum. "Next door."

"I see," I said, embarrassed by the mistake. I backpedaled toward the exit, opened the door with my back, and said, "Fine store you have here, some wholesome items." And the serious woman smiled again and I thought she was beautiful when she smiled.

Maybe I'll come back here sometime and ask her on a date, I thought.

Richard was waiting in the truck when I arrived.

"How did we miss each other?" I said.

He shrugged, and put the truck in reverse.

I told him what happened and he laughed while lighting an American Spirit out of a blue box.

"What type of guy do you think I am?" he asked. "I want nothing to do with that nasty stuff. It is a pollutant to the soul of man and to the world at large. One of the many reasons our planet has gone to hell in a hand-basket."

"It is difficult to escape the bombardment of sexual advertisements," I said. "They are everywhere."

"That is the truth," he said. "Just wait until you are old like me, you won't even think about sex anymore. It's too much work."

We laughed, as I wondered how true the statement was.

Richard gave me five cigarettes for the ones he had bummed. I knew that he wanted to give some away to feel better about buying a pack, I had done it dozens of times while trying to quit. We smoked with our windows down on the way to the Co-op, where he stocked up on groceries before flirting with a grey-haired cashier. I searched the bulletin board for jobs, rentals, and other opportunities.

With a guitar to play, a laptop to write on, and a few friends in the area, I think I'll stick around for a while, I thought. *If I have enough money...*

4

Despite my intentions to isolate and write, I sat on the trailer's porch in the warm sunshine drinking coffee and listening to Jim.

"I was a businessman," he said, pronouncing *business* like *bidness*. "And being a businessman came with a lot of perks, you could say."

He had been in orgies, danced naked under the stars, managed several businesses in Nebraska, kept several heads of cattle on a large parcel of land, partied with the best people in the country, and had his own claim on a gold mine in Colorado. A car accident at the age of twenty-four left Jim in a coma for four months after dying four times on the operating table.

"A few months after I woke up, my business partners told me: 'Jimmy, you're not the same guy anymore', and I wasn't. I haven't been ever since."

I know the feeling, I thought. I returned home from Iraq to have friends and family tell me the same thing. I wasn't the same lighthearted, happy-go-lucky guy anymore. I never would be.

Jim continued, "A woman asked me one time: 'Did you see the light?' I laughed at her and said: 'Yeah honey, I saw a lot of lights. The bright lights on the ceiling in the operating room, and the lamps of the doctors as they worked to save my life.'"

"That must have impacted your business ventures," I said.

He laughed. "I couldn't remember anything. My memories had, "Poof!" vanished. They started trickling in slowly, and even now, fifty years later, they sometimes show up. I remember being forced to play the piano during my childhood by a cruel teacher with a witch's voice. She would yell at me and smack my hands with a ruler and be so goddamn mean it was awful. I don't remember a goddamn thing she taught me, but I sure remember the fear I felt every time I was around her. The witch."

This reminds me of the quote by Maya Angelou, I thought. "People will forget what you said, people will forget what you did, but people will never forget how you made them feel."

I asked Jim about former lovers and he said: "If a man sleeps with a lot of people in his youth, and I mean a lotta lotta people, you can store all of that away in your memory bank to return to when you're old." He pulled back his ball cap and tapped his head. "When you are old and alone, you can just go right back to the memory bank and "Poof!" it's like you're right back there."

I cringed at the image. I wanted to meet a woman to spend my life with, not live in memory land. I confessed that I had spent almost two years in Iraq as an infantryman.

"Oh no," he said, leaning against the deck railing and shaking his head. "They are a thorn in our side. I am sick and tired of hearing Taliban this and Al-Qaeda that… it is disgusting! What is happening to you young people who have to go over there and fight another endless war is disgusting!" He slammed his fists on his knees. "If people want to have their beliefs, that's fine, but keep your goddamn beliefs to yourself and don't try to make me care about them. God… and the awful way they treat women over there, it is so sad. So, so sad. I view women as majestic beings who should be respected and encouraged to participate in the doings of life, while over there they are degraded, silenced, and treated as property."

"Most of the women were kept inside like dogs," I said. "At least while we were around."

"I have no sympathy for the men over there," he said. "None. Kill them all, that's what I say. Anybody who publicly executes innocent women, gays, and free-thinkers should be executed from this planet because they are the ones fucking it all up."

While his opinion is extreme, I thought, *it is comforting to know that I have his support for what I did over there. I don't need to beat myself up any longer because I actually did a good thing by fighting and killing the bad guys.*

Sam kept to himself for a few days watching movies, reading, meditating, praying, and listening to the radio. I watched him shave with an electric razor and a small mirror near the fire pit when a tall, skinny old timer with a quivering voice, said, "Oh, you're shaving over there, huh… well, I'll give you some privacy, then," and he continued walking.

Other than that, I didn't see much of Sam.

I did not know why I was brought to the trailer park, but I knew that I was meant to be there. God works in ways that I do not understand. The old-timers were overflowing with wisdom, hope, and perseverance, three qualities I needed to learn to move forward with life. One week prior, I entered Mexico in a manic attempt to escape responsibilities or die trying. But now, a week later, I had three friends, three crushes, and a few locals who recognized me and talked with me any time I saw them.

I closed the drapes on the day, poured myself a three finger glass of whiskey, and sat at the computer typing until long after the lights in the trailer park stopped shining.

6

SPIRITS OF ANCIENT WARRIORS

Pressure Canner | Hearst Church | Hail Storm | Spirits of the Apache | Electrical Charge | Apples by the Heater | Covered Motorcycle | "What a Life" | Spaghetti and Garlic Bread | Fungus Attacks the Hawk | Richie Helm | Expelled | Railroad Work in Alberta | One-Eyed Indian Romanian Bullies | Wet Cigarette | No Church Service in Pinos Altos | Saint Vincent Catholic Church | Bilingual Service | Opera Purgatory | Big Red Button | Confess Your Sins | Everyone is an Alcoholic | Lost Tarantula | The Man With the Withered Hand | Bad Joke | Asking Big Questions on a Rock while High on Bud Cookies

1

I wrote in seclusion for two days. I was like a pressure cooker ready to explode, I could not take in any more information without releasing pressure. The apples were moved inside, a pot of soup simmered, and a feeling of hibernation was in the air. Thick, dark storm clouds rolled in with a howling wind that sounded like ghosts in the trees. A cold breeze made me miss Alaska. I took short walks through Pinos Altos to break up the sedentary nature of writing. Down dirt roads while admiring small rock walls and rock gardens inside stick fences, until reaching the Hearst Church where I stood in admiration of its weathered beauty.

The church had six wooden stairs and a handrail that led to a gothic archway with two wooden doors from the late 1800s. Two arched windows on either side of the door came to a point at the top and were wood framed with knotty pine. The work was crafted by a master. The bottom half of the building was tan adobe with peeling stucco in the bottom left corner that revealed old handmade bricks. An exposed log beam was set directly over the door. Above the beam was a small circular window with a star inside that was surrounded by hundreds of shingles that resembled bird feathers. The church reminded me of an A-frame cabin back home, or the glass pyramid in Memphis. I imagined the settlers building it back in 1898, and the fear felt by the persecuted natives.

Suddenly, thunder roared behind me and a bolt of lightning flashed near the mountains.

"Thor!" I yelled, raising a fist.

A deafening sound grew closer as clouds billowed overhead.

"Holy shit," I whispered, walking up the church steps to find cover.

The sound of thunder and whatever-the-hell else was coming grew so loud that the rest of the world seemed to stop. Suddenly, I could see a wall of hail coming at me. I leaned against the old wooden doors as hail struck and bounced around. Thunder roared and lightning crashed as I wondered if the spirits of Mangas Coloradas and the Apache had returned for justice.

They shouted in my imagination, *You burned, tortured, murdered, and erased our people, but you will not kill our spirits!*

As lightning flashed nearby, an electric charge raised the hair on my arms and filled my body with an energy I had never felt. The hail moved on, yet it was still heard with the howling wind and roaring thunder. I rolled a cigarette with shaky hands and smoked it in admiration of nature's power.

"Spirits are here," I whispered.

I stood in the archway for an hour as black clouds rolled around in the sky like ocean currents in the ocean. Finally, I walked down the stairs and turned to stare at the star in the circular window.

I grew up thinking that a star in a circle represented Satanism and witchcraft, I thought. *What does it represent here?*

I returned to the trailer park with an undeniable feeling of God's presence inside and outside of me.

Boyd was cleaning his pistol on the top stairs of his bus. He looked at me with a straight-face and I nodded, he looked back down at his pistol as if he had not seen me.

"Where ya coming from, Rob?" asked Sam from an open window in his bus.

I laughed, *Nobody can do anything in the park without somebody watching.*

"I just went for a short stroll is all," I said.

"This is a heavy front," he said, looking at the clouds while exhaling smoke. "If I were you, I'd cover that bike of yours. You don't want a beauty like that to get damaged by hail."

"Good idea," I said. "I'll do that now."

I went inside and filled three paper grocery bags with dried apples to set on the windowsill near a small electric heater. I used a bungee cord and the tent to cover the bike. I went inside to eat soup with bread and butter and to lie on the floor reading Jack London as flickering streams of sunlight kissed my face.

"Life ain't so bad after all," I said.

2

I awoke to Jim pounding on the door with an empty bowl in one hand and a nearly empty bottle of Vodka in another.

"So this is your life?" he said, standing by the door as I reheated the soup. "It sure is quiet."

I laughed, "My life is not always like this."

"Is that right?" he said, glancing around. "I find that very hard to believe. You are a very strict man, an orderly man. I am the opposite, I have no order."

"I am a strict man," I said. "And I hate to see you go, but I have to continue writing my story. Here, take this…" I filled his bowl and lathered two slices of bread with butter on a paper towel. "Stop by later for more."

"Don't forget," he said. "I have a story to tell you that will knock your socks off."

"What kind of story?"

"A love story," he said. "A love story that will change the world."

"I'm looking forward to it," I said. "But right now, I have to work on another story. So please give me some time before you tell me your love story."

I opened the door and led him outside. He stood silently on the porch for a few moments as if pondering the next move, until he slowly walked back to his camper. As day turned to night, Jim returned to ask if I could drive him to town for food and booze. I agreed. We drove to Albertsons in silence where he used a shopping cart to walk down every aisle before checking out with two pounds of discounted buffalo burger and two donuts. He gave me a donut, and we ate them in silence on our way to the liquor store where he bought a liter of Crystal Palace. He was peppier on the way home, insistent on telling me his one-of-a-kind true love story.

When we returned to the park, he insisted that I wait outside his camper. After a few minutes of him crashing around inside, he stepped out with a plastic bag full of meat, tomato sauce, spaghetti noodles, garlic, onion and garlic bread.

"Carry this," he said. "Let's cook at your house."

I wanted to deny the request, but I didn't have a legit

excuse. So we walked to my place where he sat on the plaid couch drinking green tea with warm milk, cinnamon, and honey.

"Mmm…" he said, with foam on his bushy mustache. "This is good! And there is no booze? None at all?"

"No sir," I said. "No booze."

"You have to be kidding me!"

He sat behind me on the two-cushioned couch as I prepared the meal. It made me anxious to have my back to him, but I could hear him breathe and knew that I could react if he made a sudden move.

Is it the war veteran in me, or being the victim of a creepy molester baseball coach that makes me so weary of Jim? I wondered. It has a lot to do with his strange comments and creepy stares. But seriously, what could an old drunk like him do to a young man like me? Anything, if I get complacent.

I minced the onion and added it to a few tablespoons of bubbling vegetable oil. The sound and smell enveloped the trailer. When the onions turned translucent, I added a pound of buffalo burger and cooked it until it was brown on all sides, before pouring in a can of tomato sauce and adding salt and pepper. When it was nearly done, I added diced garlic and then set the burner on low before filling a pot with water to cook the noodles. I felt Jim's eyes on my back, and I tried not to pay him any mind.

"You know what you're doing in there," he said. "You are just like Sam, a master chef."

I laughed off his remark, recalling my college roommates

who would scoff at the fact that I was making spaghetti with canned sauce and non-organic noodles.

"My mother used to have my brother and I cook when we were young," I said. "One day each week we got to pick what we were making. We went to the store with a list of ingredients, shopped for the best prices, and paid. We cooked the meal with mama's help, and then served the whole family. It was a special task that taught my brother and I a lot more than how to cook."

"Sounds like you have a good mother," he said. "I bet those skills paid off."

"Yes sir," I said. "They sure did. Did you bring a bowl because I don't have an extra?"

"I forgot."

"Do you mind eating out of a pot," I said. "Because I could put it in a pot for you." He looked at me with disgust.

"I will head back to my place for a few things," he said.

"I might have paper plates," I said, searching the cupboards. "Got 'em."

"I'll head home for a real bowl," he said. "Who wants to eat spaghetti on a paper plate, anyway?"

"True."

"In my household growing up," he said, "we had a lot of kids! Seven of us, plus Ma and Pa, and whoever else came over for supper. There were always people over for supper. We each had our own bowl to clean and keep track of. You see, we ate out of bowls. Bowls! Not out of what the food was cooked in. Heavens, no. That's how people get sick."

I laughed, "You are more orderly than you know, Jim. Since I usually cook for myself, I don't see the point in dirtying up another dish. So I typically eat out of what I cook in."

"That is ludicrous," he said. "I can't believe it. I can tell that you have cooked a lot by the way you move around a kitchen. My god!"

Quit watching me, I thought.

"Now… is the food done yet, because I'm hungry."

"Go back to your place and grab a bowl," I said. "It'll be ready when you get back."

He leaned back and flung his weight forward to stand from the low couch. He stood for a few seconds in place before slowly walking outside.

Even though I planned on being alone this evening to write and drink, I thought. *It's kind of nice having Jim's company. Even if he gives me the heebie-jeebies sometimes, I'll bet he's an innocent old man nonetheless.*

I put the garlic bread in the oven, dropped the noodles in the water, and tasted the sauce. It was perfect for the company and the occasion. Jim returned with a full drink in one hand and a wet bowl in the other. We ate silently together for the second time of the day. Wind blew against the trailer and caused the candle's flame to flicker. The park's sign creaked by the road.

When we finished, I did the dishes and put the leftovers in plastic containers as Jim talked about a woman from his past who called him out of the blue a few months back. The only woman he ever proposed to—the only woman who ever rejected him.

"She told me, way back when I was still a young man, 'You are going to have to clean up your act if you want to marry me.' And you know what, I wasn't ready to clean up my act, and I still ain't!" He laughed. "That was forty years, ago. Forty years! Wow! Can you believe it? The time sure flies, young man. And then she calls me out of nowhere to ask if I still want to marry her. Ha! How she found me, only the good Lord knows. But I don't need to bother having a lady around telling me what to do. 'Wear this, eat that, don't say this, watch that...' and of course, 'Quit drinking so much!' I would rather watch television all day than be bossed around by a self-righteous bitch. I'm happy as a clam!"

Are you really as happy as you think you are, Ol' Jimmy Boy? I wondered. *Am I? Are any of us?*

He finished his drink and then popped most of the bones in his body while standing.

"Thank you for dinner," he said. "I look forward to telling you my love story tomorrow."

"Thank you for the ingredients," I said, handing him a bowl of leftovers. "You paid for it all."

He walked outside without another word. Ten minutes later, when I stepped on the porch to smoke, he was on the other side of Sam's bus staring at the black clouds in the black sky before he turned to stare in my direction. We looked at each other for a few moments of eerie stillness until he drunkenly waved and I waved back and then I went inside and locked the door. I took the Buck knife out of the bedroom and placed it on the refrigerator next to the door just in case he came back and tried to knock down my door.

3

I awoke to an inch of snow on the ground and still falling.

Thank God I brought the apples inside, I thought. *They would have been ruined.*

Sam invited me over to smoke a joint, where he told me about a fungus that had infected his body and left him hiding from view. He was reclined in his chair with a stack of books on a TV tray just beside him. He was an arm's reach from a two burner stove, a sink, a microwave, a blender, and a satellite television. A few paces from a toilet, a hot water shower, and a laptop with wireless internet. It seemed like a good place to be. A rash covered his face and eyelids that was so irritating that he blinked slowly and rubbed his eyes often.

"What have you been up to in here?" I asked.

"I've been watching YouTube videos on alternative methods of treatment for this fungal issue," he said. "Anything from fasting to colon cleanses to Native American medicine. And I can't pass up a good storm chaser video. I love watching videos on tornadoes and hurricanes. The power behind the weather is fascinating. People who say that God doesn't get angry have never been stuck in a bad storm."

"Sounds like a pretty good time, despite the rash."

"It could be worse," he said. "Like when I was kicked out of high school at seventeen because of a bomb threat that I didn't do." He used Vortex binoculars to scan the eastern sky for the ISON comet. "Richie Helm was in a band and everything—a real hot shot around town. He was out of school but still dating a girl who was in school—and he really wanted to spend time with her but he didn't know how to get her out of school. So Richie and I went back to my parents' place to get a bite and he comes up with a brilliant idea and he says to me: 'Hey Hawk, dial up the school will ya,' so I called the school without asking more about it. I had the number memorized from all the times I excused myself from school. So the phone begins to ring and I hand it over to Ol' Richie Helm, and all he says is: 'Der iz a bomb in ze school dat will detonate in fifteen minutes,' with a thick German accent, and then he hangs up the phone and we start laughing."

"Uh oh," I said.

"Everyone was evacuated from the school, including Richie Helm's girlfriend. Well, not long after, the police came to my house and arrested me on the spot. I had been kicked out of school two days prior from an altercation with a teacher, and so somehow or another they linked the call back to my house."

"Damn," I said. "Did you get in trouble?"

"I confessed to everything, and I was given community service and expelled from school. When I was done with community service, I went to Alberta to build and repair railroad tracks."

He described the arduous days of labor required to build a railroad track, and a one-eyed Indian friend whose brother had shot his eye out with an arrow when they were kids."

"The one-eyed Indian could fight like three men, and he was smaller than me by at least an eighth. He won a fight with two Romanians who stormed our bunkhouse one time, I had nothing to do with it. I wrestled one guy while he knocked out the other, and then he did the same to that one. When they came to, they tucked tail and ran out of there without saying a word. That one-eyed Indian could move his hands so fast you could hardly see them. Like this…"

He threw combinations like he was back in the bunkhouse fighting Romanians.

The old man hasn't always been an old bird who stays in the nest, I thought. *He was a wrangler, a railroad worker, a stone house builder, a brawler, a defender of the weak, an ice-road trucker, an explorer, a motorcycle enthusiast, and a lover of women and woods.*

He continued, "The one-eyed Indian and I were all excited after the fight, giving each other high fives and praising one another's abilities. We were both only seventeen years old and we had just taken on two big thirty-five year olds—so we felt good about ourselves until one of the female cooks, a fine woman she was, came running inside bunkhouse yelling: 'The Romanians just busted up the bar. They grabbed some knives and are headed this way! Get ready!' And she ran out as fast as she ran in. So I turned to the one-eyed Indian and I said, 'Well, brother—the second time's a charm,' and those big Romanian bastards kicked in the bunkhouse door with a knife in each hand. But we were waiting on the other side, and the one-eyed Indian punched the first one square in the nose and knocked him out before he could say 'Bucharest', and he did the same thing to the second guy. We could've been hurt pretty bad in that one."

"Sounds like it," I said. "You've lived quite a life, Sam."

"Isn't that why we were on put on this planet?" he asked. "To take risks, make mistakes, and live life to the fullest. Okay, Rob, I am going to take a nap. I'll catch you later."

4

I woke up Sunday morning to the storm's passing and the return of clear skies.

Thank God, I said. *I am ready to get the heck out of here, but I don't know how confident I would be to ride the bike in snow. Even if it's only an inch or two. I can't get trapped here.*

I put the apples on the roof while wondering how long it took the Nepalese families I saw who did the same thing on stone roofs with apples in straw baskets. Although I felt connected to them from thousands of miles away, I was tired of moving the apples and ready to be done. I made a cup of coffee and walked to Pinos Altos to see if the Hearst Church had a Sunday service. Negative. I decided to ride to Silver City to find a church service to attend.

Sam heard the engine and called me over to the bus where he was smoking out of an open window with his shirt off and eyes swollen. I told him that I was headed to church and he looked surprised. He denied the invite, he needed a few more days of healing before going in public. I could not understand why such an intelligent, capable, tough, and tender man lived alone in a trailer park, and why my mother was only attracted to lazy indoorsmen instead of active outdoorsmen like Sam.

Couldn't my mom have given me a cool step-dad, I wondered. *Somebody to teach me about hunting, fishing, and living off the land. Instead, she married an insurance salesmen Mason whose only time spent outdoors was playing golf, and a Muslim extremist doing life in prison.*

"I ran out of tobacco," he said. "I found two soggy butts by the fire, but the storm really doused them." He laughed while drawing hard from a wet butt.

"Take some to roll yourself a couple." I handed him the pouch.

"Thank you," he said. "Now that's what I'm talking about." He set two pinches of tobacco on a book with three papers. "Maybe you could grab me a pouch on your way out?"

"No problem."

Today is the day to count the money, I told myself. *Quit putting it off!*

I was ashamed that neither Sam nor Richard smoked when I had arrived, yet both were now smoking regularly.

It all starts by bumming a smoke, I thought, *and now they are buying their own. It really does only take a puff or two to start back where you left off.*

Although my mother was a baptized Catholic, she drifted away from the church at a young age and raised her sons with a combination of Native American philosophy, New-Age spirituality, and Christian morality. Candles, incense, and sage burned beside crystal balls and tarot cards. We attended pow-wows, prayed to God, participated in psychic fairs, thanked Mother Earth, and had crucifix necklaces. I went to church twice with another family as a young boy in Nome, Alaska, twice with my mother in Seward, and every Sunday during basic training to escape from cleaning the barracks with a toothbrush. While stationed in Italy, I prayed in world-class cathedrals covered in stained glass and felt a presence I could not name. I observed strict Muslim rituals in Iraq that made me admire their discipline and faith. I attended Spanish speaking churches in Guatemala and Mexico where I felt an overwhelming feeling of peace and love, and I participated in Buddhist and Hindu ceremonies and retreats in Nepal, India, and Thailand that taught me that spirituality does not need to be done behind closed doors but can be practiced in rivers, streams, and mountainsides. I have always been on a quest for faith, understanding, and a regular practice—yet I am unable to fully believe any religious tradition to this day. Even though I cannot give my all to one religion, I love to sing, chant, pray and meditate, and anytime I do those things my life is less chaotic and more peaceful.

A hundred or so people were attending the ten o'clock mass at Saint Vincent de Paul, and since the majority of parishioners were Hispanic, the sermon was bilingual—so everything the priest said in English was repeated in Spanish. It must have lasted at least two-thousand years.

The band was the worst church band ever. A silver haired lady with thin hair in a thin perm played piano. She must have been a hundred and twenty years old. She was unable to turn the page while playing and every time she stopped it threw off the young Hispanic guitarist, three back-up vocalists, and the lead singer. I could barely hear the back-up singers because an elderly lady with short brown hair and a glare sang so loud and out of key that I felt like I was in an opera purgatory. She stared at the crowd with piercing brown eyes to curse anybody who covered their ears or showed signs of displeasure.

I laughed-out-loud on two occasions because of the discomfort and embarrassment I felt for the band. The congregation tried to sing from their little books while following the numbers on the wall but all I heard was the opera singer and mistaken piano notes.

Is this what God wants? I wondered. *For his people to sing a bunch of shitty songs?*

The red-faced priest with a five finger forehead had

blondish grey hair and blue eyes. As I watched him enter the room and greet the congregation, I did not like him. As soon as he started talking, I understood why.

"Who here can tell me a sign of the end of times?" he asked, in English and then Spanish. Nobody raised their hands. "Anybody?"

Thirty seconds of tense silence passed as he scanned the room in disgust.

"Let me inform all of you of a sign that will be shown when the end of the world is imminent." He annunciated the letter "s" like the snake, Kaa, from *The Jungle Book*. "Because it is quite obvious that none of you have been doing any of the studying that I have assigned."

Heads dropped, shame sunk in.

"When Israel is completely and utterly surrounded by military forces from different nations, there will be one Israeli man who will push the big red button. One! All it takes is the one Israelite, my people, just one, and that big red button is going to be the explosion of all explosions that will end everything. Just before the explosion kills everything and everyone on this God forgiven planet, Jesus will appear in the sky. He will come down from the gates of Heaven for those who have lived righteous lives and accepted Christ into their hearts. All others will go straight to Hell to live in forever damnation. To Hell! That is why I urge you, my fellow followers, come to confession and confess your sins. Accept Jesus into your hearts! Because if you do not confess and be forgiven by God, you will spend eternity at the gates of Hell. Do not only bring your butts to the booth," he said, smiling at a group of teenagers in the front row, "but bring your sins, too."

What a creepy thing to say, I thought. *While looking at teenagers. Sorry buddy, but you're not making the Catholic Church look any better after all of the rape allegations.*

Since I do not believe his fear-based propaganda, I focused on the stained glass to numb out the negativity. One disturbing work of stained glass showed a man with a sinister grin, jet black hair, and a huge forehead wearing a white robe and holding a tiny baby boy in his left arm. He had his right hand on top of a young blonde girl's head who had two pigtails and stood at the exact height of his privates. I could not get past the sinister gaze of the man in the stained glass, and the way the priest stared at the teenagers in front. I left the church feeling ashamed and angry that Mangas Coloradas and millions of others had been tortured and murdered in the name of Christianity. I stopped at the liquor store for a bottle of whiskey and two pouches of tobacco to quiet the thoughts and to focus on writing.

S

I arrived at the trailer park around 12:30 and was called over to join Sam, Richard, and Jim around the fire under the sun.

"How are you guys so hot all the time," said Jim, pulling a shawl over his neck. "You're in shorts and tee-shirts while I am freezing in my sweatshirt."

"It's because you don't have any heat in your camper," said Sam. "And because you're just skin and bones, Jim."

I backed away from the circle and their heads turned in unison.

"Where you going?"

"To go climb around on some rocks," I said, pointing toward the distant hills.

"Why?" asked Jim. "There's no booze, no food, no women. So why would you go? I never could understand how people can have fun without booze. It's just not normal."

Little do they know I just bought a bottle of whiskey, I thought.

"No shit," said Richard, "I picked up a box of Sauvignon a few nights ago and I can't stop sipping on it."

"You see," said Jim, with both eyes open. "Everyone is an alcoholic! Everyone!"

For the first time in my life, the powerful four-word-question popped into my head.

Am I an alcoholic?

———

I grabbed a marijuana cookie and packed some snacks and water in my pack before leaving. I stopped at the museum to check for hours and noticed a young backpacker on Main Street wearing two thick rope necklaces carrying large crystals. He carried a huge backpack and was talking to an older man in a white Volkswagen van searching for a runaway tarantula.

"It's mating season," said the man with a grey beard and glasses. "Peter Parker always escapes during mating season. I'm just trying not to run him over." He sped away.

The backpacker reached his right arm across his body to unzip a small pouch on his left hip. "I found this on the road earlier while I was walking," he said. He held up a small, black metal eagle with a missing wing.

"Good find," I said.

"It was a sign from God," he said. "Thank you, God." He put his hands together in prayer. "And look at this." He pulled down the sweatshirt sleeve that covered his right hand and held up a disfigured hand with a thumb and a pointer finger only inches from my face.

"Pretty cool, huh?"

I shrugged.

Not really, I thought. *That probably sucks.*

"I am going to heat this eagle on a fire and brand it into my gimp hand," he said. "Right here." He pressed the eagle to the top of his hand just below the two fingers.

"Sounds painful."

"I don't think I'll regret it," he said. "Maybe I will."

"Do it if you want," I said. "And then don't regret it. What's your name?"

"Coleman. And yours?"

"Nice to meet you, Coleman," I shook his good hand. "Robert. Robert Stark."

"What do you a call a guy without arms and legs floating in a body of water?" He asked.

"I don't know."

"Bob," he said, laughing to himself. The man with the withered hand walked toward the highway to hitchhike elsewhere. I could hear him say "Bob" while laughing and walking away.

Is he always walking away just like I am? I wondered. *Escapism, that's what they call it.*

I found a dirt road that led to the Continental Divide Trail where I climbed around on some rock formations. I climbed to the highest point in a series of hoodoos, ate the marijuana cookie, and laid naked on a warm rock questioning whether or not I was truly an alcoholic, and wondering why the hell I took myself so seriously.

7

CONFESSION OF A NEBRASKAN FARM BOY

Real Laborer | Four-Wheeler Ride | Sweat Lodge | Six Willow Poles | Cache Full of Tools | Tired and Hungry | A Love Story | Jim Hesitates | Construction Site | Business Man | Have a Snip | Can't Sleep | Confession | Nash Rambler | Leave out the Details | Hunting Partners | Jesuit Priest | Buck Knife on the Refrigerator | Your Feet | "I'm Not Wanted" | Desperation Sets In | One Hundred Dollars | Snow Storm | Fiftieth Anniversary of JFK's Death | Sam's Advice | Fresh Snow | Departure | Lodi, California

1

The second week of my stay at the trailer park, I rode on the back of Sam's four-wheeler to a "secret meditation area."

"Don't go telling anybody where it is," he said, "but you can show one or two."

Like I will really remember, I thought.

We took back roads into the woods and then draped a camouflage cover over the four-wheeler for concealment. Sam searched at the base of trees until uncovering three waterproof sacks full of tools buried in small hollows and wrapped in leather and twine. Rats had eaten much of the twine and shoulder straps. In the bags, Sam had a half-mile roll of 17-gauge wire, a tool used for installing barb wire, an ice pick, wire cutters, two pairs of pliers, channel locks, a mallet, a kukuri, a spade, a drawknife, and extra handsaw blades.

"The government says we can't be back here doing this type of thing," he whispered and walked as I followed. "We are supposed to follow their rules and trust that they are managing the land the way God intended." He laughed. "Look what they did to the buffalo, the bear, and the wolves. It is the same thing they're doing to the salmon. And we can't even enjoy the beauty of our own country without trespassing on government property. It's hypocrisy."

I smiled at the sound of dry leaves and breaking twigs underfoot. Quiet rocks inside a pine forest. The smell of juniper was accompanied by the sound of songbirds. We carried the bags a half mile to a creek past a series of pools until reaching a waterfall beside two rock faces. We unloaded the gear on a flat rock next to the pool and took a breath of misty air.

"Pretty nice, ay?"

"Fucking incredible."

"The entrance to our sweat lodge will be two or three steps from this pool," he said.

He knelt by the pool and used both hands to wash his face before taking a deep breath and unpacking the tools. We followed the creek downstream searching for six willows he had cut and peeled a month prior that were washed away in a storm. On the way, we stopped at another cache with two handsaws tucked under the roots of a Crocodile Juniper tree.

"This way you don't have to pack things in and out all the time," he said. "People really start to wonder then. The government would be all over us, putting us in handcuffs and locking us away."

We found the willow poles two hundred yards downstream coated in a clear mucus-like substance and slippery algae, they were slippery and difficult to drag upstream. Back at the site, we leaned the poles against a rock face as water crashed three feet away and mist surrounded us. It felt good to be alive. Sam used a heavy wooden mallet to pound rebar stakes into the hard ground. He let me do the last one, and it took me five times as long as it took him because the hammer was so heavy I could hardly lift it with one arm.

"Never swung a hammer before?" said Sam.

"Not Thor's hammer."

"If you think this one is heavy—you oughta try my hammer down in Big Bend."

"There are hammers bigger than this one?" I said. "I didn't think that was possible."

He laughed, and kept working. He used the mallet to pound six large bolts with wire attached at head height into the lateral face of the rock opposite the stakes. He tied the wire from each bolt to a single willow pole that became a ledger. He tightened the wire on the new ledger until the willow pole was solid against the rock face. He then used the kukuri to notch out both sides of a different willow pole and wired it to the ledger and then bent and wired it to the rebar stake. His precision and force with every strike of the tools was impressive. It was obvious that he had done a lifetime of labor. After bending and attaching the first pole to the stake and ledger, we started on the second pole which cracked and nearly snapped. He used the kukuri to cut out the center two or three feet of the pole to provide more flex. He needed to rest after the second pole was done so he offered me the kukuri to mirror what he had done. Every time I swung the curved, Gurkha machete it deflected from the wood instead of cutting it. My angle was all off.

"Set the kukuri up to the wood," he took it with his left hand and set the blade at an angle on the wood. "And then use the hammer." He struck the backside of the tool with the heavy hammer and it sliced through the wood with ease. He notched out the third pole in a few minutes with that method. I tried to do the same, but I was unable to swing the hammer accurately with one hand while holding the blade at the right angle with the other. I felt inferior to a man twice my age who used his hands in ways that I could only dream of. I started feeling bad for myself and wanted to walk away from him so he wouldn't see how weak I was. I started getting mad at my mother for marrying dipshits who didn't teach me how to work. I started getting mad at my father who couldn't handle the pressure of parenthood and took the long distance route.

Here is a man with arthritis in his joints, a fungus spread across his body, and a bad back from a motorcycle injury—and he is outworking a healthy, young man who should be able to outwork him. I am pathetic.

Then I remembered that Sam Hawk had been romping around the woods doing this type of work since childhood, while I was skateboarding and playing baseball in a subdivision, or chain-smoking and reading.

We are different men with different skills, I reminded myself. *Does he have the patience and communication skills to sit for hours and write stories to entertain people? What am I saying? Nobody is reading my stories.*

I tried to stay positive while doing my best until his break was over and he gently took the tools from my hands and finished notching the last poles. I was relieved that he was not yelling at me and calling me names, but I felt like I deserved it and that maybe he should. I held the willow poles firmly while he used channel locks to tighten the wire. We stood the six poles as they bent from the ledger on the rock wall to the rebar stake in the ground with a healthy flex.

"We have a rib cage," he said, smiling in satisfaction. "Now—to build a body."

"We are students of Dr. Frankenstein."

He laughed, "Exactly."

Maybe if I stick around, I will become more capable with my hands by helping Sam with this sweat lodge, I thought. *I could use the skills back home.*

"Why don't you go find six more willows along the creek about the same diameter," he said. "Use the handsaw to fell them. Drag them back and we will peel them with a drawknife and leave them to dry for a couple weeks before we wire them to the rafters as purlins."

I followed the creek downstream into a grove of willows in a low area. I found six trees with matching diameter. I cut their limbs and then cut them down while wondering which animals ate willow in New Mexico.

It's a primary food source for moose back home, I thought, *especially in winter.*

I dragged them to the worksite and used a drawknife for the first time to peel the bark. It was my first time using a kukuri and a drawknife, and I felt good about learning how to use different tools. When I finished peeling the first one, Sam laid it across the rafters a couple of feet from the ground and then wired it down.

"There's no reason not to wire them in now, they'll dry in place."

It was getting dark by the time the six purlins were peeled and wired in place. We rolled a cigarette and smoked by the falls, admiring our day's work. We packed the tools in the bags and silently walked the same game trail by the creek to stow the tools under the trees. We uncovered the four-wheeler and slowly rode back to the trailer park.

That was the first time I walked in the woods since being in the military where I performed SLLS, I thought. It felt good to use those same stalking skills that I had been trained in. To get an adrenaline rush while being quiet and mindful. Hell, maybe it's time to start hunting.

"We just broke the law in probably a half dozen ways," Sam said over his shoulder. "Trespassing, harvesting trees on government property, utilizing a motorized vehicle on government property, among other heinous crimes. The one-world government would rather that we cut down the Amazon rainforest using oil from the Saudis and exploited workers from South America, and then ship the timber using barrels of diesel than to use our own forest to build our homes. The last thing the American government wants is self-sustaining people who know how to live off the land. That would not feed the war-machine, the economy."

"It's a lot easier to buy lumber from the store than to cut your own," I said.

"Yes it is," he said. "If you don't count the destruction of the Earth's ecosystems and cultures in the name of convenience. Not to mention the countless hours spent at work to earn enough money to buy the lumber. But hey, what do I know? I am just an outlaw breaking the government's rules to enjoy God's creations."

At the trailer park, we ate grilled pork chops with beans and vegetables by the fire while Boyd cleaned his pistol on the bus steps. I was tired and hungry from the labor, and it felt good to be tired and hungry from labor. It was the first time I had done manual labor since being on the land the previous summer, and my hands already had blisters. We ate in silence while listening to quiet voices and the sounds of a fire. I looked up at the stars and down at the embers, watching orange sparks rise and meet the dark sky every time Sam poked the coals. I wondered when I would return to Alaska to work the land, and I became excited at the thought of continuing to pursue my dream of farming.

Jim arrived drunk and hungry. He collapsed in a chair mumbling things I could not understand before Sam cooked him a pork chop and covered it with beans and handed it to Jim. Jim thanked him and stumbled home to eat alone.

2

On Wednesday evening after dark, Jim pounded on my door demanding to tell his story. I did not see the point in arguing, so he came in and sat on the couch while I sat at the table with the computer open ready to type.

"I don't know where to start," he said, watching my hands move on the keyboard. "Are you really writing what I am saying?"

"Yes sir," I said. "I've been typing all of my life. Let's hear the story."

"You really are something special," he said, standing to look over my shoulder at the screen. "Holy christ!" He sat and stared at the ceiling as his swollen fingers clutched a plastic cup of clear liquid. "I wouldn't know where to start... because it's really a kind of love story. A love story between a friend of mine, and me."

He set the cup on the counter and crossed his arms over a paint-stained sweatshirt.

"We actually fell in love, ya know, and that's what the story would be about. And it's quite a provocative story, for a lot of reasons. The main one is that we actually did love each other, and that is a rare thing to find in most relationships."

"Ain't that true," I said.

"Why does anybody fall in love?" he asked. "But we did, and we quickly started a romantic relationship. And this is in Nebraska, where people don't keep secrets. They just hide things under old rugs and act like nobody knows, but everybody does." He took a deep breath and closed his eyes while leaning back on the couch. He sat in silence for a few minutes as I rested my fingers on the keyboard in anticipation.

"I am going to have to rest," he said, standing to look over my shoulder at the screen. "It is beautiful," he said. "Absolutely beautiful. I have never seen or done anything like this in my life."

He was stalling, and I was not going to push it.

How long had he been carrying this love story in his heart? I wondered. *Why was it so provocative?*

"What do we have to eat?" he looked at the stove and patted his belly.

I served him a bowl of soup and two slices of buttered bread. We ate in silence. I didn't know what to say. I recalled the many times I had seen him staring at my trailer and at me, and I felt uncomfortable.

But no matter what I told myself about how I should act, the thought of him staring at me all of those times made me edgy.

"Now, to continue the story," he said, and I opened the laptop to start typing. "I was raised a Catholic, and I have not done confession since I was a boy. And to be honest with you, I have never confessed this story to anybody."

"I am honored," I said. "But you know Jim, it's late and I've had a long day. So why..."

"It was an incredible deal," he said, with his eyes closed and hands behind his head. "The most profound thing of my life was that relationship, and it still goes on. It's amazing how love never dies, it keeps growing and growing until you die, and then it grows exponentially after we pass on."

"How does it still go on?"

"I would really like to get into this thing with you, in-depth, but it might be a little graphic. There is nothing more relevant than getting into the details, though, because that is what love is all about. Love is about an accumulation of physical, intellectual, emotional, and spiritual encounters that two lives share."

"That's deep, Jimmy."

He took a deep breath and rocked three times before standing and leaving without another word.

3

Despite being dog-tired, I could not sleep.

Almost two weeks prior, I was thrilled to grow closer with Sam, Richard, and Jim, but I was beginning to feel paranoid and ready to return to my off-grid life in Alaska where nobody fucks with me.

What was I thinking trying to open up with people again? I wondered. They always let you down. Just get back on the bike and keep riding. The apples are dry and packed away, and I don't have much going on here anyway. Maybe those guys are right, I should be out there living life to the fullest rather than hiding away in a rented trailer letting life pass me by.

I rolled over in bed and looked at the envelope on the carpet.

I have to pay rent in two days if I want to stay another week, I thought. That is seventy-five dollars. I wonder how much money I have left? I looked at the envelope. Hell, I will open it tomorrow. Tomorrow. What the hell are you so afraid of, Robert? Reality? Quit running from it like a coward and take some responsibility. Plus, you have created a bad habit of drinking alone in this trailer and chain-smoking, and you know that you shouldn't be drinking so much. Hell, I might be an alcoholic after all. If I keep on this way, I am going to end up like my grandfather who died of cirrhosis after Vietnam, or like Jim—living and drinking alone in a broke down truck camper. Alone and drunk for the rest of my life isn't my idea of a good life. If I don't make up my mind about staying or going, my mind will be made up for me. How much money is in the envelope will determine everything. I stared at the envelope trying to summon the courage to face reality, but I just couldn't do it. *Tomorrow,* I repeated. *I will count the money tomorrow.* The conscious choice to avoid responsibility made me feel like a coward.

I spent the next day reading on the couch behind closed drapes. I put the Buck knife on the table next to the computer so it was easy always within arm's reach. I smoked inside with a window open. I did not want Jim to return, I did not want to hear any more of his love story, and I did not want to be at the park any longer. I thought about going to the restaurant to talk to the waitress and grab the guitar but I did not want to talk to anybody. That night, Jim returned to tell his story with a cup of vodka and a joint.

"Okay," he said, puffing on the joint and passing it. "I am ready."

I opened the laptop and typed with the joint between my lips.

"Joseph Saint-Veltri was my lawyer when I was suing Weld County, Colorado for a massive settlement," he said. "Hell, they had me thrown in jail for... What the hell was it? Larceny! Larceny of mortgaged property. You see, I had bought a car from Weld County Buick Distributorship, which was owned by MacArthur. You know General MacArthur?"

"I've heard of him," I said. "But I don't know the first thing about him."

"His brother owned a car lot where I bought a Buick, and it was really a nice car. It was an old leather, two-door hardtop with push button windows. A beautiful car, a beautiful car, and I went off to do business."

"Bidness," I said, trying to catch up as he laughed.

"That car really had a lot to it," he said. "It was a functional piece of equipment and it was beautiful. I'd take it up to the ranges and look at the cattle, and I always had a bottle of Jack Daniels so those Jack Mormon boys could have a snip. You know, just a snip. And they'd get drunker than the good Lord." He laughed and poured the cup of vodka into the coffee. "Because they would never drink, but they'd take a bottle of Jack Daniels and we'd give it to them and they'd go off and get wild drunk. It was funny, it was real funny, but I never did make any deals with them, never did buy any cattle. Only with one guy up in Longmont, I don't remember the details, but it was up by a ski area somewhere, and I got the sale and they brought all of their cattle down and I sold them. I got one of the highest prices in the country on that sale, it was something like thirty-two dollars a hundred pound. Anyway, it was the last sale I ever did. They didn't want me around there no more. I had too much money. So I built a bar in

Colorado Springs near the Kelker Junction Concert Hall. I put together a business down there..."

"Bidness," I said. He laughed, took a swill, and a few deep breaths

"I put together a business down there, I had about three or four businesses going on at the same time. I had a building under contact with Breckenridge, Colorado, a ski area.. That was years ago when they just started. I had that bar in Colorado Springs, and I tell you that place was funny. It was real funny. I've got to show you pictures sometime, you'd get a kick out of it."

"That would be cool, Jim," I said. "I would love to see the pictures."

"They're not really good pictures though because I lost most of them over the years. But anyway, I built a bar. It was a big old warehouse and I had acoustics sprayed all over the ceiling, and we opened and our prime objective was Fort Carson because we could get all of the college kids from there. And we all just had a good time. A damn good time." Suddenly, his face turned red and he locked his jaw while staring at a wall of memories. I touched the cold metal handle of the Buck knife and unbuttoned the sheath. "Then the city cops started messing with me," he said. "Before that, I had my own police force, my own security force. But then the city cops started messing with me and I got into all kinds of trouble for nothing. They threw me in jail, and fucked around with me, and then I started losing it. I started losing the businesses."

He took a deep breath and exhaled a raspy sound before sitting quietly for a few minutes. I wondered why the police had harassed him, and if it had anything to do with his drinking?

"Cops can mess up your entire life," he said. "They did mine. You know, I've never talked to anybody about this stuff."

"I am honored," I said, looking over the screen at his bewildered blue eyes.

He walked outside and I started heating a kettle of water before stepping outside onto the dark porch to smoke. He returned with a full cup of vodka which he poured into a half cup of coffee.

"Maybe we should have more of that smoke," he said.

For a man without much money, he sure consumes a lot, I thought. *Or is that you?*

"Smoke it if you got it," I said.

He lit another joint and we smoked it until it was gone, and then he stared at the ceiling in silence.

"Whatever came of the businesses?" I asked.

"We used to go hunting, pass hunting, shooting, for geese and birds, ducks, and such. We'd go up on a hill and they'd come down and fly past you. They'd come off the water and we would just stand there and shoot them and take them home and roast them. Good birds. We'd go to Yankton, South Dakota from Norfolk, Nebraska and we'd go up in the hills. We were just teenagers when we met on my Dad's worksite and I had a Nash Rambler, and we were sleeping back there and we started touching each other and before I knew it it was all over. I was in heaven. Absolute heaven! We got up the next morning and we did some more hunting. It was true love, I tell you. And I have never been able to love again after having a taste of true love."

He grabbed his empty cup and walked out without a word. It was 11:30 p.m and I was tired, so I tidied the living room and then lay in bed trying to sleep while wondering about Jim's story and life.

I was awakened by a pounding on the door at 3 a.m.

"Wake up!" Jim shouted. "I need to confess the rest of my sins."

I tiptoed into the living room and grabbed the knife from the table, removing it from its sheath and standing by the door. The doorknob rattled and shook as he tried to open the door. He slammed on the door with his shoulder or arm or something else.

"I'm sleeping, Jim," I said. "Leave me alone."

"Open up," he said. "You are my Jesuit Priest, and I need to make a confession."

"I am not a priest, Jim, and I'm sleeping," I said, taking slow, deep breaths to steady my nerves. "Let's finish the story tomorrow."

I heard him pacing on the porch and then walk down the stairs. I peeked out the curtains to see his silhouette facing the trailer. He returned twice to knock on the door and wait on the deck for a response. As I heard his footsteps move around the trailer and stop outside the bedroom window, I held the knife tightly while lying in bed waiting. I slept light for the rest of the night, echoing the words of my former first sergeant in Iraq.

"Sleep light, freeze tonight... Stay alert, stay alive, men!"

The next morning, he was hammered drunk when he knocked on the door demanding to finish the story. I opened the door with the knife within arm's reach.

"What was up with you trying to break down my fucking door last night?" I asked.

"What are you talking about?" he said. "Please, I need God to forgive my sins before I die. You are my Jesuit priest."

"I am not a fucking Jesuit priest, Jim, so please quit saying that."

"Please let me finish the story," he said. "I need atonement for my sins."

His eyes were full of desperation, craziness, and booze. Letting him inside was not an option.

"I want to enjoy the morning silence," I said. "Maybe you can finish the story later if you sober up."

He stormed off and returned multiple times to pound on the door and beg.

"Go home and sleep," I said. "Come back tomorrow."

"I need forgiveness so I can get into Heaven."

"People are trained to be priests," I said. "I am not one of them! So leave me the fuck alone!"

I packed my bag in preparation to leave in the morning. I tidied the trailer and organized the food on the shelf for a future tenant. I turned a loaf of bread into enough peanut butter and jelly sandwiches to feed me for two days, and I filled three empty jars from a pot of black beans. I kept the drapes closed and door locked to prevent any altercations between Jim and I. While I wanted to learn more about him, I did not want to be around him when he was drunk. I was sad at the thought of saying goodbye to Sam and Richard in the morning. I enjoyed their company immensely, and I knew that I would not see them again in this life. But it is what it is, we all have to carve our own way down the mountain.

The moment I had been avoiding had finally arrived, I could not put off counting the money any longer. I picked up the envelope from the carpet by the bed and held my breath as I really felt it for the first time in weeks.

It feels thin, I thought, *like there is hardly anything in here. I should have done this weeks ago.*

I reached my hand inside and almost gasped.

"One-hundred dollars," I said. "One-hundred dollars! That's it! Somebody must have snuck in and robbed me."

What the hell am I going to do? I thought. *I don't have a debit card or a credit card. This is all of the money that I have to my name. What do I know?* I took a deep breath and whispered, "Be calm. It will work out." *It is the 21st of November, I have $100, and I have to pay $75 for rent tomorrow if I want to* *stay another week. I have enough food to last me a week and some basic camping equipment that would keep me from dying outdoors. In one week, I will receive a disability check that covers my mortgage in Alaska, and leaves me with $450 dollars until December 1st.*

Pounding came from the front door as Jim yanked on the doorknob and pleaded to be heard.

I have to leave, now. I can't deal with Jim any longer or I might either kick the shit out of him or kill him.

Jim walked around the trailer while scraping something against the wall. Was it a knife? Was it a gun? I didn't know, and I didn't want to find out.

I could put the bike in storage and ask my mother to buy me a ticket home? How will I call her? I will use Sam's phone. Okay, that's an option. I could sell the bike in Silver City and use the money to either fly to Mexico or fly to Alaska and return to the property? How long would it take to sell the bike? No telling. Where would I stay in the meantime? The woods. I could go back to Arizona to stay with my buddy, Whitelow. I am sure that he'd take me in. But he has four sons and a cousin staying with him already, I'd be a real burden to him. I could go back to Santa Fe to stay with my cousin, but those Buddhist monks are probably happy that I'm gone. Hell, maybe I could hook up with the elf girl and see if I could stay with her for a couple of weeks. No, no, no, that's not the right thing to do. I could take my tent and find a place to camp while exploring the area like I want to? But it's cold at night, and I really don't have the proper equipment or the money to buy it. These are all options.

Jim pounded on the door again and I bolted up from the bedroom and ran to the front door and swung it open and stepped up to his face and yelled, "Get the fuck out of here you sick fucker or I'm going to kick the holy shit out of you." And I shoved him backwards down the stairs and he lost his footing and rolled onto his side.

"I just wanted to finish telling you my love story," he said innocently.

"Go back home and don't come over here again or I'm going to tell the owners and they're going to boot your ass out of this fucking park."

I went inside with my heart beating and my pulse racing.

Calm down, Robert. Calm down. Think, think, think. Aunt Kathy lives in Lodi, California with Grandma. I don't know if $100 will buy enough gas to get there, but I can sleep on the side of the road and eat PB&Js along the way. I have to try, I don't have a better option. It is around 1,200 miles, and I would have to fill the gas tank at least four times. A gallon of gas is around $3.50, so I can travel roughly 250 miles on $17.50. So I will spend around $70 on gas, if my math is correct. I sure as hell hope it is. I can make it in two nights, and I can camp to save money. Hell, I've never been to Lodi before, and I don't know exactly where my aunt lives or if she'll even let me stay there, but she is my mother's sister—so she has to take me in.

4

It was the fiftieth anniversary of the assassination of President Kennedy when I woke up to make coffee and leave. Sam stopped over and mentioned the bad energy of the day. I was apprehensive to step outside in fear of seeing Jim, so I invited him in.

"The Alabama guy and his girl split last night," he said. "She threw a glass of wine in his face before leaving, glass and all. His face is pretty cut up."

"Good for her," I said. "Nobody should be talked to like that."

We paused as he looked around the place.

"Looks like you're hitting the road," he said.

"It's my last day of paid rent, so I either have to pay for another week or leave tomorrow. So I'm just going to leave today in case another storm comes in."

I left out the part about only having a hundred dollars to my name.

Sam clinched his jaw and nodded, "I understand," he said. "I will miss having you around, but you are young with a good head on your shoulders and a bright future. There is a big world out there, full of highs and lows, good guys and bad guys, love and broken hearts—and you don't want to miss it by hiding inside a trailer surrounded by castaways."

I nodded and I almost cried.

"I've learned a lot from you guys since being here," I said. "Thank you for the great food, funny stories, and hospitality."

"Anytime. There's a storm coming this way from the north. It's supposed to snow tomorrow, so you are you making the right decision to leave today. And like I said, there's bad energy around here today. You take care of yourself, ya hear?"

I nodded and he left.

I scrubbed the stove and sink, took a final shower, and sat inside the warm trailer with closed drapes to finish reading *Starrover* to leave behind. When I was done with the book, I set it on the counter next to the food and I dropped to my knees like Sam and prayed for protection and guidance on my journey west.

I strapped my pack on the back of the bike and fired it up. As it warmed up, I went inside to put on riding gear and to do a final walk-through to make sure I wasn't forgetting anything. I got on my knees again in the small living room and thanked the trailer for providing me a dry home for two weeks.

Richard, Sam, and Jim moseyed over when they heard the engine, nobody said a word. They patted my back and nodded their heads and clinched their jaws. Sam held out his hand.

"You needed a pocketknife," he said, "and it matches your jacket."

"Thank you guys for opening up about your lives," I said. "And for welcoming me into them. You never really know how you will impact another person, but I will say this—you guys have changed my life completely. I will never forget you. I left a gallon bag of dried apples on the porch for each of you."

Jim was the first to step forward and give me a hug, he was followed by both Richard and Sam.

"You're a good kid," said Richard. "I'll sure miss you."

Jim and Sam nodded, as if they, too, believed that I was a good kid who would be missed.

I left the Continental Divide RV Park and turned left on the Trail of Lost Spirits Highway to ride south to Silver City and west toward the Golden State of California.

S

I rode hundreds of miles only stopping for gas, sandwiches, and bathroom breaks. I rode through LA around midnight and pulled into a business district somewhere on the north side of the city where I found a dark office building to pull the bike around back and take a few hour nap in the grass. I kept riding until almost Bakersfield where I pulled over at a rest area to set up my tent and sleep for eight hours. I arrived to my Aunt Kathy's house in Lodi sometime in the evening with five dollars to my name.

I stayed in her barn in my tent for three weeks trying to process the trip and to determine the next move. She fed me some of the best home cooking I'd had in years, and got to know me for the first time. In turn, we started to love each other like an Aunt and nephew should. She also provided me with enough beer and pot to keep the edge off—and she didn't give me shit about not having any money. Not once. She loved and accepted me just as I was— a lost war veteran who couldn't get my act together no matter how bad I wanted to.

My grandmother and her Chihuahua lived with my aunt, and I got to know them better, too. And I got to know her better, too. After a week of listening to her yell, "Shut the fuck up!" at my Aunt's adopted son, I realized that she was only yelling for fun. She got a kick out of it. And everybody else already knew that. So I would sit in her room drinking Natural Ice Light with her and she would sneak some of my cigarettes and tell me not to tell her daughter. She let her chihuahua lie on her bed and she'd whisper sweet things to it and talk at the TV like they could hear her. She retold the same stories, hardly ate, and laughed so loud I could hear her from the barn. Her husband came home from Vietnam a different man. He drank himself to death in a shed in the backyard leaving her to raise six kids alone.

I flew home to Alaska a week before Christmas because my mother was crying to my aunt about her new boyfriend who would beat the shit out of her. Aunt Kathy begged me to go home and take care of her, and I agreed. When I finally reached my mother's apartment in Seward, a large black man walked out with a smirk and a backpack as I walked in. I didn't see him for two weeks while I stayed in her apartment over Christmas.

Because she was the apartment manager, she put me in an empty apartment below her where I continued to drink every day despite not having any money. I always found a way. I stayed there all winter without a job. I wrote now and then, only when I was clear-headed enough to make any sense. I drank and smoked all day every day. I hid from life and responsibility. I ran from people. I prayed for sobriety at night, but then smoked and drank the next day. It was a tortuous existence that I do not wish on anybody.

I planned to return to the farm in the spring of 2014, but I broke three bones in my ankle on the day I was leaving. I spent the entire summer fully dependent on friends, family, and God. That was the beginning of the end for me, when I finally realized that I needed people, and that people loved me, and that I wanted to live a good life rather than just survive.

After blacking out on money loaned from an acquaintance, and waking up with my crutches by my bed and not knowing how the hell I got there, I was done. Done with hiding. Done with feeling like shit. Done with spending all of my time and energy on booze. Done with being fucking depressed all of the time. Done with making a fool of my family name. It was time to buck the fuck up and face life rather than hide from it.

I thought about the guys at the trailer park, and that gave me courage to make positive changes and not give up no matter what. I did not want to end up alone, but I knew that if I did not stop drinking I would. I recalled what my mother told me when I returned home from Iraq.

"If you keep drinking like you are, you're going to end up just like my Daddy. Dead before you're forty-five from alcohol poisoning."

I knew that she was right, and I wanted to live. I wanted to have kids, a wife, a farm, and an author career. I wanted to make my mother and father proud. I wanted more out of life and I was ready to make the necessary changes.

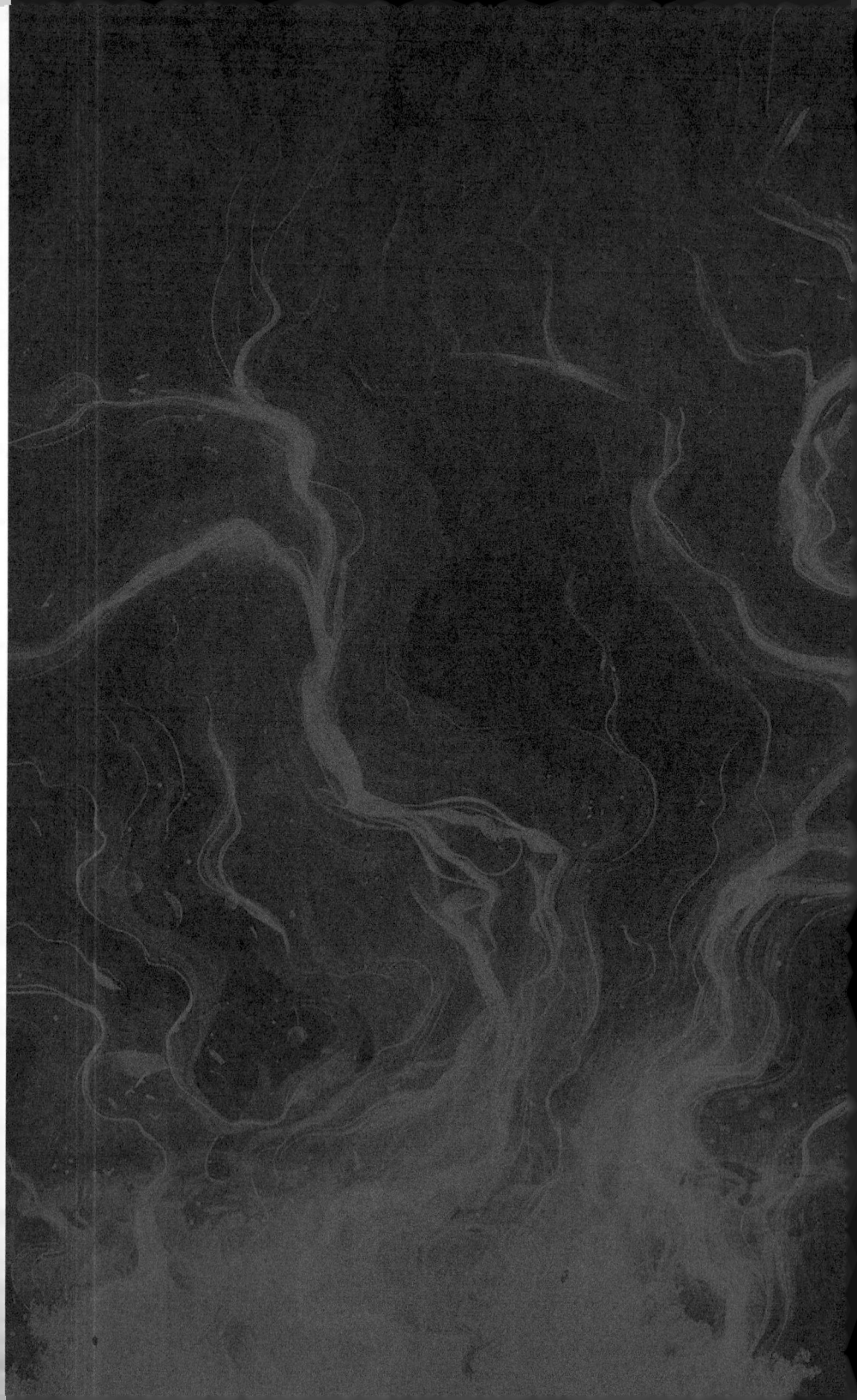

PART III

HERO OF
THE VALLEY

THREE YEARS LATER

"Blessed are the meek, for they
shall inherit the earth."

MATTHEW 5:5

1

Skagway, Alaska

MAY, 2018

Father's Death | Subconscious Searching | What is Love? | Rebuild Our Brotherhood | Moving to Olympia | Chasing a New Girl | Brother Moves to Phoenix with $10 | Abandoned Again | New Friends, New Apartment | David Bowie | Changes | A Return to My Birth Town | A Soft and Gentle Cousin | Reunion With James | Invisible at a Golf Course | Using Tools I Learned in Recovery | Fighting Family at a Gathering | Cigarette Burns and Piss Stains | Not Keeping My Word | Hugs From New Friends in Recovery | Flight From Seattle to Juneau

My father died last week, I guess I will never have the chance to know him after all. Do we ever really know anybody? For thirty-three years, I have subconsciously tried to win his interest—to no avail. I have searched the eyes of every bearded homeless man intent on finding my father, but he refused to be found. Twice we met in person. Twice. We spent a total of three hours together before he died. Three hours. Who is counting anyway? Twice he said he loved me. Twice. I never felt it. I guess you could say that my father and I were not close.

I love my brother, James. At least, I think I do. I try to forgive him and look past his mistakes. To help him in a responsible, non-enabling manner. I try. I listen when he needs ears and talk when he needs distraction.

I returned to my birth town of Caldwell, Idaho to reunite with my brother after our father died. James was living in a car in Phoenix, Arizona after following a girl he met online a week after we rented a two-bedroom mother-in-law place in Tumwater, Washington where we could rebuild our relationship. I would finish my college degree while he worked in a nearby store driving forklift. We agreed to split the costs. That was after six months of paying for his every meal and cigarette when he came to live on the farm after his divorce. I was sober, and so I refused to buy alcohol and pot, which meant that he was sober, too. I was excited to live together, to grow closer, and to support each other after our mother's death. Meanwhile, he was searching online for the next girl to latch onto, and he found her.

She was a curator in a Phoenix museum, which meant that she had money and a successful career. This boosted his ego like he wanted. She was in Tacoma on business and found a man online, so he left me in the mother-in-law house with an empty room while he ate out, partied, played pinball, and attended live music events in the Seattle and Tacoma—all on her dime. When the time came for him to fly to Phoenix with his new girlfriend, he had a ten-dollar bill that I gave him and a new girl on his arm.

"When I die, nobody is going to say that I wasn't romantic," he said laughing.

I didn't think it was romantic at all. He had two sons in Alaska who needed his love and two different mothers who needed his support, but he was too busy running away from responsibilities and feeling sorry for himself to be there for anybody. I couldn't blame him, he learned it from our father—I just hoped that he would break the cycle. When they left, I was alone again reminded of the feeling of abandonment. I tried to escape the avalanche of self-pity by studying, writing, making new sober friends in recovery rooms, riding my bike, paddle boarding, and quitting smoking cigarettes.

His new girlfriend called a week after he moved into her Phoenix apartment begging for help to get him out. I could hear him yelling in the background to hang up the phone. I told her to call the cops. What more could we do? Maybe our mother was right, he was beyond help—give him what he really wants, to go back to prison to live off government handouts. The phone was hung up while she screamed. My brother and I did not talk for months after he moved away.

He later told our cousin that he left because he was being judged too harshly by me, and that I was not accepting of who he was. That is true. I was sober and working to better myself as a person, and he wanted to drink, to be depressed, and to be abusive. I was not, and am not, supportive of those actions.

After two months I moved out of the $850 a month mother-in-law house into a friend's one bedroom apartment. I rented a space in the living room large enough to roll out a sleeping bag and to have a mantel for prayer, with full access to the kitchen and bathroom. It was $300 a month. I grew in faith, community, acceptance, and sobriety alongside somebody doing the same. It was a transformational year in Olympia, and I was thankful that James went on his own way.

My brother called six months later while I was in a seminar on Celtic Folklore. When I called after class, he bawled and told me that our father had died from a heart attack.

"Our uncle said that his heart was 95% clogged," said James.

"If you're going to do something, do it right," I said.

I could not understand his emotions, because it seemed like nothing more than a stranger's death to me. It was like shoveling a long driveway full of heavy snow with a tiny shovel while wearing tennis shoes without socks. Cold and uncomfortable. The feeling was opposite of when Mother died. But I loved her, I know I did, and she loved me.

I left Olympia in the car that my mother passed down headed south on I-5 through Portland then east on 84 along the Columbia River. Through Hood River and The Dalles, Hermiston, La Grande, Pendleton, Baker City and Ontario. I traveled through forests, valleys, high desert, and wide open farm land until reaching familiar road signs in western Idaho. I did not cry once, but I listened to a lot of David Bowie. I have a tradition of listening to "Changes" on repeat anytime big changes take place, which seems to happen every three to six months these past few years. I stopped at a Dairy Queen for the first time in my life because of my roommate's suggestion. He was right—it was a lot of food for the price.

I found my cousin's apartment near the Nazarene Bible College in Caldwell. Some folks from the Nazarene Church in Anchor Point went to school there. I don't fit in with them, but it was neat to walk around the campus and see the young people pursuing a life dedicated to God rather than the millions of other options. Hell, when I was that age I was kicking down doors in Iraq pointing my rifle at people's faces. My cousin's rental apartment was a three-minute walk from McDonald's and Dutch Bros, a five minute walk from Starbuck's. My brother's Ford Explorer was parked out front with piles of trash, clothes, and blankets inside. I didn't know how he bought it and drove it, but somehow he made it happen without a license, insurance, or a bank account. I assumed he was living in it. I was nervous about walking inside to see him drunk, and I tried to set my resentments aside to be a supportive brother in a time of loss. I tried.

Is recklessness a genealogical trait? I wondered. *Because I have always been reckless.*

My cousin opened the door and we hugged. He is doing well for himself. He drives a parts delivery truck for Napa and is with the same girl he has been with for five years. He smoked pot all day, steers clear of tobacco, and rarely drinks. Although, he admits to going out of his way during deliveries to find new Pokemon Gems, it could be a lot worse. He is a soft man with a soft voice, soft hands, and a soft body. His ears are gauged and he has artistic tattoos on his arms. I respect and admire his laid-back lifestyle and gentleness.

His girlfriend hugged me and led us outside where they smoked pot in lawn chairs and scrolled on their phones. My last remaining family member was smoking a cigarette with stoned red eyes.

"My brother." He stood to hug and rub our heads together. He smelled like stale booze, cigarette butts, resin, and piss. "How was the drive?"

"Beautiful," I said. "I love Oregon. I could live there again. Yours?"

"Fast. When I heard the news, I left work and booked it. I'm sure they can maintain the fairways for the millionaires without me for a couple of days."

"So that's what you're doing now, working at a golf course?"

"Yeah. It's a decent gig. Hot as fuck, but I get to run machinery and I really like that."

"Cool."

"I get to see a lot of basketball players and actors who come out to play. It's that kind of place."

"You get any autographs or make any connections for your Hollywood career?"

He laughed, "No, brother. They don't even look at the workers. We are told by the boss to be invisible when the big shots come around, which is kind of fucked if you ask me."

It was our first time hanging out since I quit smoking,

and I was nervous about caving in. So I cut the conversation short to use the bathroom, and I stayed inside instead of going back out. We spent the next three days in Caldwell and Nampa meeting family we did not know, going to a cremation office, shopping for books at thrift stores, eating street tacos from food trucks, watching movies, eating from the dollar menu at Jack in the Box, and hanging out. It was great to be around him again, I had sure missed him. But I was quickly reminded of his active struggles with addiction when I was asked to remove him from a family gathering in honor of our father because he was trying to fight every man, woman, and child. I brought him to our cousin's apartment where he stumbled to his car while mumbling something about chicken heads. When I went to check on him a few minutes later, he was asleep in the driver's seat with a cigarette burning his jeans, the car running, and the door open. I led him inside where he passed out on the couch. He pissed himself during the night and nobody mentioned it the next morning. I did not cry or write or smoke or drink while I was there, even though I wanted to do all of the above. Instead, I went to the nearby Nazarene campus to pray by a pond, I drank too many double mocha lattes at Dutch Bros, and I ate too many Big Mac meals at McDonald's. They were better options than getting drunk and stoned and throwing away the sobriety time I had worked so hard for.

An uncle I had just met asked if I could say some words and a prayer as family gathered to spread our father's ashes at our grandmother's grave site. I agreed, but I laid awake all night long trying to conjure the words to describe a man I did not know and I could not come up with anything. Also, I did not want to be around James after he tried to fight everybody and then pissed on the couch. So I bailed before anybody was awake the next morning to return to Olympia. I am my father's son.

I drove the same route west while listening to Nick Drake and Iron & Wine. I was disgusted and disappointed in my brother, but there was nothing that I could do for him. No matter how sad the situation was, I did not cry—because crying would not help.

Perhaps I am cold and detached like the professionals say about people with PTSD, I thought. *Perhaps my time at war made me unlovable and distant. Or maybe it's the simple fact that my Dad ditched me when I was a baby and he didn't want anything to do with me.*

I made it to Olympia by dinner time where I received dozens of hugs from friends in recovery rooms who had heard about my father's death. I laid on the floor in my army sleeping bag excited for the flight to Juneau the next morning. I would stay one night in Juneau before boarding a ferry for Skagway to attend a writer's conference for the second year in a row. I checked out fancy clothes from the costume shop on campus just so I could fit in with the other writers.

Eventually, this dream of being a paid author will pan out, I thought. *And now that my mother and father are both dead, and my brother is too far gone, I don't have to worry about hurting anybody's feelings.*

I was exhausted when I boarded the plane the next morning so I planned to sleep during the flight. But as the jet reached cruising altitude and I closed my eyes, an unfamiliar assault of emotion came over me. So I pinched my leg, grabbed my pen and journal, and wrote.

2

What if you went through your father's belongings after he died, after believing your entire life that he did not care about you, and you found a tote with every newspaper article you ever wrote alongside letters you sent from war? What if your father lived in a '93 Ford Explorer with eight solar panels, two batteries, and a small bed of dirty blankets on a sleeping pad. What if the only clothes he had were four shirts, two pairs of pants, two mechanic suits, and two pairs of underwear and socks. What if your dad had a full garbage bag of empty Coors Light cans, Muscle Milk, Starbucks Ice Coffee, Capri Suns,

Raisin bread, Mandarin oranges and oysters? What if you knew he recycled by the card in his wallet, which also revealed that he worked as a cab driver, lived without a bank account, and had seventy-five dollars in cash. What if the only books he had was an action series from an unknown author a collection of poems written by a man with a note inside that read, "To Bertis, the Hero of the Valley." Would you wonder why he was called the 'Hero of the Valley', and which valley he was the hero of? What if your dad was a stranger, an entity whom you did not believe existed but secretly hoped was the most amazing human on the planet. Would you try to piece together his life and learn some facts, or live in imagination land?

All I know about my father can be summarized in a few pages.

Bertis Levi Stark was sixty-two years old when he died. Born on May 15, 1956, in Gold Beach, Oregon, he was the youngest of nine siblings. He married my mother, Sheri Lynn Moore, when he was twenty-three years old— the same year my brother was born—1981. My brother was born in Caldwell, Idaho, where my father and mother's families both lived. The family of three left Idaho to live in a Jayco trailer in California where our dad worked on oil platforms while our mom tended the baby.

Our dad climbed the highest ladders without fear.

"He wasn't afraid of nothing," said his older brother, an uncle without teeth. "He worked there for three years while I couldn't stay three weeks. He was a hard worker, your daddy. When he worked."

I want him to say, "Your daddy," a hundred thousand times like I have heard people say about their own fathers who stuck around.

I wondered, *Why was he was so afraid of being a family man? Why did he live in a car in the woods with few belongings, even as somebody with a hard-work ethic? Is hard work all that it is cut out to be?*

Three years later, in 1984, my parents returned to Caldwell to have a second son in the same hospital. That was me. They returned to California to live and work until Mom left Dad when I was less than six months old to live in Nome, Alaska, with her older brother. The events leading up to the divorce and the move are one-sided, since I never heard Bert's story. I did not meet my father until I was a twenty-five year old college student living in Bend, Oregon. He arrived in the same Ford Explorer that he died in, and the first thing that he did was remove his shirt, raise his fists, and ask if I could fight.

"Yeah, I can fight," I said. "But I don't want to fight you."

He laughed and assured me that I would have a lean fighter's body my entire life, and that the best thing our mother did was to take the kids away from him. We walked along the Deschutes River in Drake Park where he told me a story about meeting his father for the first time.

"We were on a walk just like this one," he said, puffing a cigarette. "When we noticed a bum passed out in the grass." A man was lying on the grass with his head on a tree root. "My dad said, 'What would you do if I kicked that man in the face?' I shrugged and said, 'I don't know.' So he walked up to the guy sleeping in the grass and he booted him in the face with steel toed boots until blood poured out of his ears. I was twenty-five."

"Please don't do that," I said.

"I wouldn't."

I learned then that my father was compassionate.

His eldest sister had not seen her baby brother in thirty years. We met for the first time after the memorial service.

"You look, talk, and act just like your daddy," she said. "He would stand back quietly with his hands by his side observing everybody until he exploded with passion. He was so handsome, especially with a mustache. Your mother was so pretty. I am so sorry to hear about her passing."

I shrug, because that is what I have learned to do, it is easier than talking. My aunt's husband has a trimmed gray goatee, kind eyes, and a callused hand. They were married at eighteen, over fifty years before we met. He fell in love with her when she was fifteen and he was sixteen. The first time he dropped her off after a date, he realized that he had to get her out of the house.

"I wasn't raised in the best house," he said. "And I have seen a few things, but I have never seen a household as violent as that one. I had to save the love of my life, so I did."

They ran away together, and they stayed away together. I almost cried at his story, learning about my father may have affected me more than his death.

What if you were thirty-three years old and both of your

parents died within three years, how would you grieve? Jesus was reborn at thirty-three, crucified, and resurrected, or so the story goes. You know that you are not Jesus, but you believe that you, and everybody else, are created by God and are a part of God's body. Does that help you to grieve and to move on?

My father's brother confesses to using drugs for thirty years before getting sober. Now he reads the Bible every morning and drinks light beer in the afternoons.

"Everybody's sobriety is different," he said.

I don't believe what anybody says, especially not myself. I shrug my shoulders more than I talk, because I know that when I say something that doesn't really matter it matters a great deal, and that I love books and writing and music and all things that do not require vocal cords. Although, I would give up books for the rest of my life to have my parents alive and happy.

"Your dad didn't visit me until I quit using," said my new uncle. "Then he came over here to see for himself, and decided to stay fifteen days. Every day he said he was leaving, but he never did, until one day, Poof, he was gone. Like a witch, or a warlock, or a ghost. Your daddy was a ghost."

"Where did he go?"

He shrugged, "Nobody knows where your daddy lived. He liked it that way. He didn't want anybody to find him. He said he hated kids, dogs and people, not in that order— but let me tell you, every damn kid, dog and person who met your daddy loved him and wouldn't leave his side. Just when your dad was getting comfortable somewhere or with somebody, he would up and leave. Poof. He loved it here at my place, said he didn't have to sleep with a knife in his hand or a gun under the pillow."

What if you found a few knives and a gun in his belongings but the knives were dull and cheap and the gun was an air-soft gun— would you assume that he didn't want to hurt anybody?

"Your daddy always said what was on his mind," said my so-called-uncle. "A guy came over while he was here, and I told your daddy that I didn't like him or want him around cause he stole from me, so Bert walked right up to him and got within a few inches of his face and yelled, 'What the fuck do you want?' And the guy mumbled some shit and tucked tail without looking back." He laughed. "Your daddy was a tough man. Someone you did not want on your bad side."

My other uncle, the one I had never heard of with a handful of teeth, swollen red eyes, and an unquenchable thirst, told me about the time my daddy robbed and burglarized a church when he was seventeen and did prison time.

"That always haunted him," he said. "Don't think he ever quite got over it."

When I asked him for another story, he said, "Bert was brave and tough— not a guy anybody wanted to fuck with."

My uncle's train of thought was interrupted when a teenage cousin in eighth grade walked by in short shorts and a tank top.

"Who is that?" His eyes grew wide and he licked his lips. "Who is that?"

"It's your granddaughter," said his daughter, a first cousin you had never met. "You don't remember your own granddaughter, you sick fuck?"

"She good looking," he said. "A fine looking girl."

Everybody shook their heads and walked away from him.

I don't believe what he said and I don't want to talk with anybody else, but I want to hear more people say, "Your daddy."

Supposedly, my dad owned two percent of a cab company, whatever the hell that means. He had pictures in his tote of people I did not know. Three pictures of a handicapped girl with down syndrome, one of which showed her on his lap. A few pictures of the woman he spent time with after my mother. Pictures of me and my brother and my nephews. He had two bags of tools, a battery charger, a first aid kit, and empty joint containers. He had a pocket pad with notes about car parts and a single poem written on a napkin.

He had driven from his Oregon Valley home to Nampa, Idaho to hangout with his brother where they drank whiskey and stayed up late burning half a cord of firewood. He slept in his car like he always did, and he told his brother the next morning that he wanted to be cremated and to have some of his ashes spread in the same burial plot as their mother's. His brother went to the store for eggs and bacon and when he returned, Bertis, was dead in his car with the engine running and the heat on high.

"It's like he was trying to warm up after all of those years of living in the woods," he said.

Supposedly, when friends, coworkers, hotel owners, restaurant workers, and dozens of others found out that my father died, they cried. I did not.

3

Juneau, Alaska

MAY, 2018

Kissed the Ground in Alaska | No Buses on Holidays | Remembering Past Visits | Meat on a Stick | Walk Uphill Through Downtown Juneau | People on Bar Stools | Wood Smoke and Salty Air | Raven Eats a Plastic Bag | Green Enchiladas | Talking to a Friend in Recovery | Early to Bed Early to Rise | Chuck Norris Kicks Ass | Pod of Humpbacks | Epic Boat Ride | Flat Rock for a Tent Site | Acceptance is the Key

I t was raining when I landed in Juneau, which is no surprise. I kissed the ground anyway. The buses were not running because of a holiday so I could not camp near the ferry terminal in Auke Bay unless I hitchhiked. I paid a hundred dollars for a room across the street with continental breakfast, a shuttle downtown, and a shuttle to the ferry dock in the morning.

It seemed reasonable. As I walked to a small store for snacks across from the Nugget Mall, the memories surged in.

Mother and I went to Juneau in 2001 to visit her husband and my brother who were both incarcerated at Lemon Creek Correctional Center. We stayed at a hotel near the airport, rented a car, and drove every mile of road. We loved road trips. I visited Mother in 2003 after basic training and airborne school. She had moved from Seward to Juneau to be closer to her husband so the long distance phone calls would not bankrupt her. Unfortunately, they did. I visited Juneau another time in 2004 when James was on-the-run staying with a sixteen-year-old native girl (he was twenty-three) whose parents owned a house but did not live in it. I visited another time after I was out of the military in 2007. Mother had moved to Arizona after her husband was transferred, and James was living with a different girlfriend while working at the Alaska Brewing Company. His girlfriend managed a Subway near the Nugget Mall and she brought us free sandwiches every day. She was really sweet. We drank and smoked pot and cigarettes and sat around telling stories of our adventures or going for long walks in silence. I later visited two gay friends living in Juneau in 2010. One worked as a pilot and got me a free flight over snowy mountains and a glacier that spanned hundreds of miles into Canada. All I could see in every direction was the glacier. It was the most beautiful flight of my life.

I rode the shuttle downtown and walked around for a few hours. I ate meat on a stick near a cruise ship and watched people from a bench. A raven was eating a plastic bag as tourists took pictures and laughed. I grabbed the bag and said, "Take the fucking bag away," and they mumbled something in another language and walked away. I rode the tram up the mountain and gazed across the water at Douglas Island. I was surprised at how developed everything had become since I first visited in 2001. I guess that's what seventeen years will do to a tourist destination and a state capital. I walked past a bar with people on stools staring outside at people walking by, I was grateful to be clean and sober and tobacco free for the first time since grade school. I walked uphill on a narrow one-way street until reaching a dirt road that leads back to a valley. Wood smoke from a chimney mixed with salty, Alaskan air. I smiled, I was so happy to be back in the slow and quiet Alaskan capital after living in Washington's busy capital for the past year. I was ready to finish college and return home to write my first book and work on the farm.

I walked downhill to the water to order a bowl of clam chowder at a restaurant my mother and I used to eat at. I sat at a table outside for ten minutes without service until leaving to sit on a bench and admire the size difference between a tiny float plane and a gigantic cruise ship. *It's all about perspective,* I thought. *Mother's death was the cruise ship, father's death was the float plane. Hell, maybe it's was more like the meat on a stick.* Maybe it was much bigger than that, like the hidden glacier that carved valleys for hundreds of miles without being known or heard. Quiet and catastrophic.

The shuttle took me back to the hotel and I walked across the parking lot to a Mexican Restaurant where I used to eat with my mother. I had green chile enchiladas and talked on the phone with a friend in recovery about the struggles we faced. I would miss her when I left Washington, but it is what it is. I am like my father and brother, I love women, but I am unfit to be a good partner. Probably because I don't feel like I deserve love. Having a distant parent who never called created serious abandonment issues. The enchiladas were delicious. People drank margaritas with salted rims like Mother and I did in the same restaurant twelve years prior.

It had been nearly four years since my last drink and I was unwilling to throw away my sobriety for anything or anyone, especially after seeing the destruction that alcohol instilled on my family back in Idaho. I would defend my sobriety with my life. So after dinner, I returned to the hotel to eat snacks in bed and watch Chuck Norris movies until falling asleep.

The next morning, I stuffed fruit in every pocket, ate scrambled eggs with bacon, toast, and cereal, and drank five glasses of orange juice before catching the shuttle at 7 am for the ferry dock. No rain and few clouds, it was a perfect day to be on deck admiring forested mountains, islands, and waters. While on the ferry and waiting to embark, a pod of humpbacks breached nearby and spouted water. It was a welcome party from God, a warm embrace from a parent, a smile from the Cosmos that said, "You are right where you need to be."

With mountains and forest on both sides of the boat, I stood on deck observing the sparse habitations, a glacier, a lighthouse, five dolphins, three eagles, another pod of humpbacks, and a vast body of water that reflected the sky. The boat ride was fucking epic. Nearly five hours later I arrived to Skagway for the second year in a row. The year before I had driven 1,000 miles from Happy Valley into Canada and back into Alaska to attend the conference. That, too, was epic. I walked past the airport and over a narrow foot bridge that spanned a creek to a trail that leads to Smuggler's Cove, where I found a large rock by the water to pitch a tent. I put down a sleeping bag and a sweatshirt for a pillow and then opened the tent door to lie in bed listening to waves and watching boats return from a day on the water. My mind entered unexplored territories.

I was an orphan. Both parents were dead. My dad's dad was still alive, but we had only spoken once on the phone and never met in person. All of my other grandparents were dead. No aunts and uncles who reach out. Nobody to impress. Nobody to win over. I was alone—I was sober—I was exactly where I was supposed to be. No matter how hard I tried, I could not escape my bloodline. I had to quit trying. I was a middle-aged thirty-three-year-old who took himself too seriously, and tried to make up for insecurities by judging everybody. Whether I like it or not, I am the combination of my mother and father. The sooner I accept that fact, the better my life will be.

4

Skagway, Alaska
MAY, 2018

Hero of the Valley | Reality or Imagination? |
The Bible | Honor thy Father and thy Mother
| August 21, 2017 | Seattle's Best and Pike
Street Coffee | Imagination or Reality?

Why did the poet call my father 'The Hero of the Valley?'
I called my cousin, Athena, who I was raised with
in Nome and saw as a sister, to ask the question.

"You could find the poet and ask him," she said. "It could
solve everything,"

She was always so logical.

"My imagination will create the answers that I need," I said.

My father died with a full set of teeth, a head full of
thick sandy hair with streaks of gray, and a salt and pepper
beard that covered his collar bones. He had piercing blue eyes

that darted around behind orange tinted sunglasses. I often wondered what he did with his days and nights, but I will never know. Before our mother died—James met with our dad at the Seattle Airport where they sat in the parking lot smoking bud, cigarettes, and drinking beer. They visited for an hour, until our father gave him a King James Version Bible with the margins of most pages covered in legible penmanship explaining our father's thoughts and interpretations.

On one of the first pages it says, "Get on your fucking knees and pray."

"It should be in a museum," James said, when he drunkenly removed it from a glass case to show visitors.

When James's wife filed for divorce, she kept the house, the boat, the cars, the money, and the child. James took the Bible and gave it to me for safe keeping. On November 1, 2016, I started Genesis. On July 4th, 2017, I finished Revelations. I read only the Bible the entire time, which is difficult to do for a person who reads 2-3 books at a time. And while I was inspired and changed from the words, stories, and characters—my father's notes made the biggest difference of all. He was no longer just a drug addict who abandoned his kids. He was a brilliant, motivated, self-disciplined, religious man. For the first time in my life I began to honor my father, shortly after learning how to honor my mother. In turn, I looked at myself in a more positive way than ever before.

I didn't have the chance to tell our father how much his words meant. Even when my brother and I watched the solar eclipse with him on August 21, 2017 from a hotel in Reedsport, Oregon. Our father paced around our room for five minutes before leaving to "check out the town." He returned thirty minutes later with a bag of Seattle's Best 6th and Pike Street coffee, and then he left. It was the first and only time that we were all together since I was a baby. I have a picture to prove it.

He died shortly after on May 21, 2018.

I had watched many moons go from black to full while wondering if he was also watching. I had wondered many times if he was at peace with God while staring at the night sky? Perhaps he was called the 'Hero of the Valley' by everybody who knew him? Perhaps he gave away his money to charity and wrote poems on barroom napkins without intent of being labeled as a poet, but just for the sake of poetry. Perhaps he stood up to logging companies who wanted to clear cut old growth forests, and he made a conscious decision to minimize his use of fossil fuels by using solar energy and only driving when he needed a resupply. Perhaps he saw the positive and negative effects of capitalism, and he chose to work only when he needed money instead of live to work. Perhaps he supported artists by attending their readings and performances, buying their books, CDs, and paintings, and giving them away as gifts to spread the word. Perhaps he worked on farms under-the-table where he was valued for his hard-work ethic and abilities as a mechanic. Perhaps his friends trusted him to babysit when they went out for dinner and drinks, and he refused to sit the kids in front of the TV but read to them and played with them instead. Perhaps he was a lover of music, philosophy, religion, and literature, but not too pompous to read novels that would be scoffed at by the *New Yorker* and never mentioned in *Poets & Writers*. Perhaps he volunteered at a food pantry, rang a bell for Salvation Army, pushed shopping carts for old people, and recycled everything. Perhaps he refused to buy new clothes and reused everything. Perhaps he built a bird feeder to hang from a side mirror so he could sit and watch birds eat while reading *Walden*. Perhaps he fished regularly and mainly subsisted on fresh and foraged foods. Perhaps he never bargained with farmers and artists because he knew the hard work it takes to produce a quality product. My father, Bertis Levi Stark, is the Hero of the Valley.

Skagway, Alaska
JUNE, 2018

Some folks at the writer's conference showed sympathy about the fact that my father had died a week prior, others showed pity. When they discovered that I did not know him, though, most people gave me a cold shoulder and moved onto lighter conversations about horses, avalanches, fishing, and poetry.

"I am sorry to turn the conversation into something dark," a woman said. "But I am so sorry to hear about your father's death."

"It is not dark to talk about death," I said. "I will happily talk about it anytime."

She turned away to talk about the politics of hair and to criticize Alice Munro and Flannery O'Connor for always writing about the same things. I left during every break to watch clouds and listen to birds. I went to the river to be alone while trying to be present, resisting the flood of thoughts trying to sweep me downstream into the ocean of darkness.

The keynote guest of the conference was the sweetest, gentlest man I have ever met. Pico Iyer arrived with his lovely wife, Hiroko. Although Pico is a successful and famous author, he asked about my writing with genuine interest and then listened to me talk for fifteen minutes about my work after he signed a copy of *The Lady and the Monk* and *Video Night in Kathmandu*. I told him about my first step-father and my second step-father, about my brother's prison time, my tours in Iraq and my difficult transition out of the military. I ended on the death of my parents. When I looked at him after I was finished speaking, tears ran down his cheeks. I almost cried.

"Please email me a copy of your novel," he said, with a British accent. "I would be most delighted to read it."

Hiroko sat beside me in the Arctic Brotherhood Hall the next morning as writers laughed and talked like intellectuals drinking coffee and eating snacks. She folded a paper crane with me and spoke about the difference between kindness and pity.

"Kindness is when you truly feel the pain that somebody else is feeling, and you take it upon yourself to help ease their suffering," she said, quietly in broken English. "Pity is when you see that somebody is suffering but it does not create an emotional response."

I cried as she disclosed the effects of the bombings on Hiroshima and Nagasaki and how the wars impacted her family then, and still today. The paper cranes represent hope, they bring honor and memory to her dead relatives and childhood friends. She mentioned the importance of prayer and compassion for healing the inner wounds, and then she touched my shoulder with a gentle hand and smiled as she held up three tiny paper cranes in the palm of her soft hand.

"I pray for you," she said. "I will pray for you."

She told me that my parents were in Heaven, which surprised me because she was a Buddhist. I left the Arctic Brotherhood Hall and skipped the first class to cry by the river.

The next week, I emailed Pico Iyer a draft of my manuscript, not expecting such a famous and gentle writer to take the time with my vulgar war story. A week later, he wrote back praising the power of my story and convincing me to change it from a work of fiction to a memoir. He challenged me to remove the distant and dissociative narrator and to tell the true story of my life and family. And by doing so, he believed, it would help heal my wounds and the wounds of others.

Happy Valley, Alaska

September 6, 2018

I spoke with an uncle named Jimmy Lee on the phone for the first time today and he told me a few things about my father that I did not know.

My great, great grandfather, Robert Milton, my father's grandpa, ran from the law out east after robbing a train and possibly killing a man on board. He got away with a pile of gold that he buried at the base of an oak tree on family land in North Carolina. He moved to Silver City, Idaho to work in a mine and anytime he saved enough money to go east in search of the hidden gold, he did. And he always came back empty handed. It is said that the gold is still buried under the same oak tree. Robert Milton was not a large man, but tough and quick to fight. Once he went with his daughter, Lily, who was known as a white witch, to a bar where he had her wait outside while he had a drink. An hour later, he was thrown outside by two large men. He dusted himself off, told Lily to wait for a few minutes, and then stormed inside to clear the bar. Over seven men were bloodied when he was finished. Afterwards, he walked his daughter Lily down the street and bought her an ice cream.

My great Aunt Lily, the white witch, was known as an intuitive with extra sensory powers. She could foretell events and explain dreams. Supposedly, every family member on the my father's side is intuitive yet only the women share their abilities with others. Instead, the men fight.

My father was on top of the world when he married my mother and had us boys. He was working hard in California to save enough money to move us into the nicest apartments in Caldwell, Idaho. He planned to move the family back to Idaho soon. Our mother was a gorgeous, classy woman who spent all of her free time with her children.

My paternal grandmother, Cathy Milton, hated her son Jimmy Lee, and the four eldest kids. She beat them regularly. They reminded her of her first husband, my grandfather Red, the man who left her. After he left, she married a man with the last name Springer who treated the kids like his own until he died young. She later married an abusive Navy Seal who beat the four oldest kids regularly with a belt. One time he ordered them to line up against a wall with their backs to him, and they did. They were too big to be beaten with a belt anymore, so he was going to use his fist. He ordered them not to move or it would be twice as bad. He stood behind my daddy first, and then he ordered him to turn around and face him like a man. My father did. The Navy Seal went to punch him in the face and my dad moved and the Navy Seal broke his wrist on a wall stud. My father left the next day and did not return for five years. He was fifteen-years-old.

My father stayed with my Uncle Jimmy Lee at his home in Arizona a couple of times and never seemed to get comfortable. "He was ahead of his time," Jimmy Lee said. "Too smart for his own good. A very deep and contemplative man. He would disappear for a couple of days and I would find him in the front seat of his car writing in his journal. He was the most comfortable alone. Your mother leaving him with you two boys broke his heart. He never recovered. Your dad moved from place to place, job to job, his entire life after that. It's like he couldn't quite figure himself out, so he kept running."

Uncle Jimmy Lee could never understand why his mother beat him so often and why she let the men treat her kids so badly.

"That woman is on the long road of purgatory," he said. "I hate to say it. But there is no way she is in Heaven. I forgave her a long time ago, but I don't know if God did. I'll tell you one thing though, Robert. If there is any man who God wants next to him in Heaven, it's your daddy. Bertis was one of a kind."

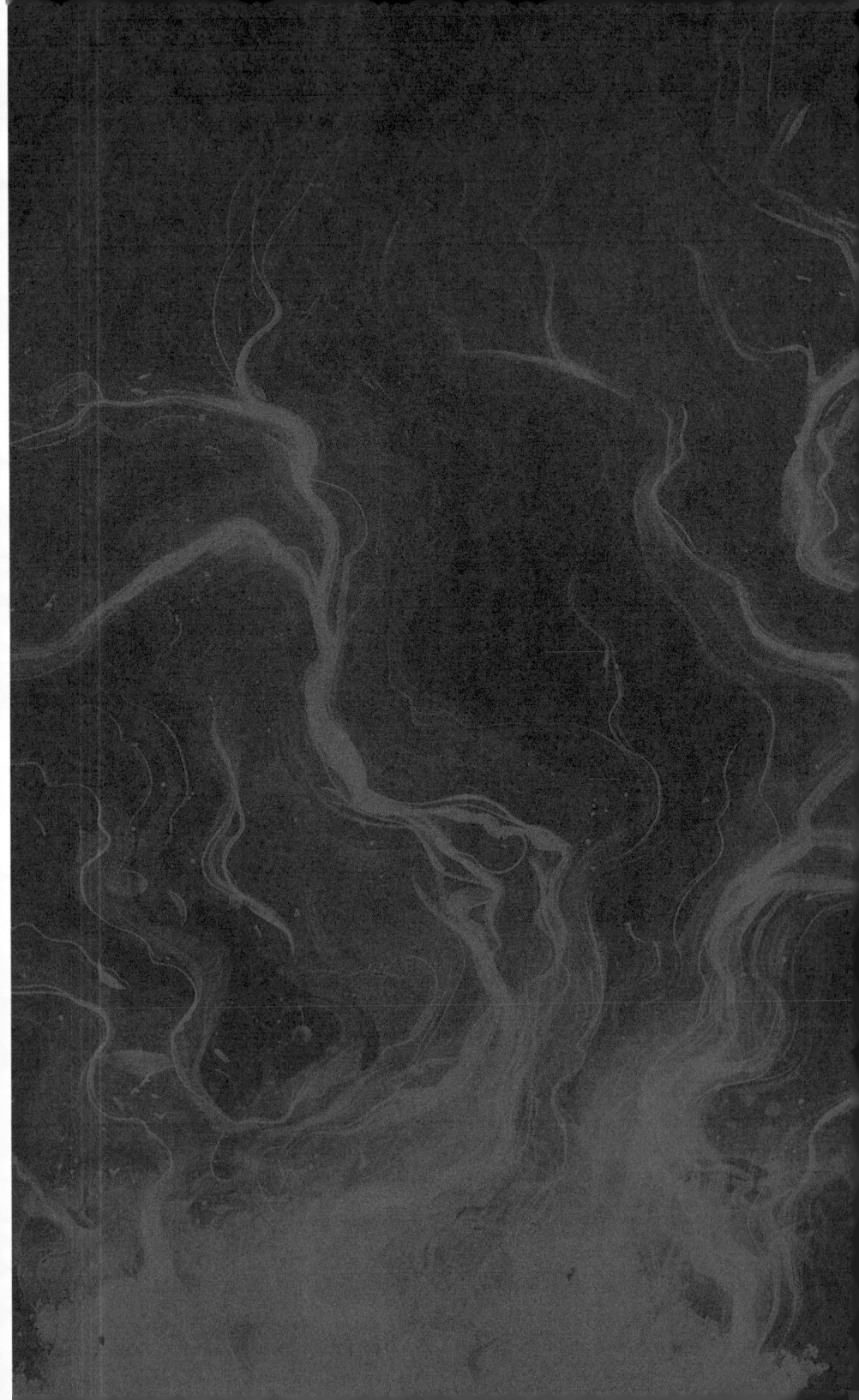

PART IV
COUNTRY BUBBLE

FIVE YEARS LATER

"To know oneself is a radical
revolutionary act."

SAVANNA STARK

1

Happy Valley, Alaska

AUGUST 30, 2023

A Sober Father of Two Daughters & A Husband |
Istanbul the Cat | Chubby Dad Makes Changes | Less
Processed Foods, More Fruits & Vegetables | An Oath
to My Health | Primrose and Marlena | Wednesday at
the White's | Covid Baby | Breaking Covid Lockdown
Rules | Harvesting Chickens | Chicken Heaven |
Quiet & Peaceful Country Sounds | Gratitude

lassical music plays from the loft upstairs as our oldest
daughter, Primrose Flora Lynn, sleeps alone in a warm
bed that she and I share. She is three years old and still unable
to sleep alone for more than a few hours. She loves to snuggle
all night and run wild all day. Her mother is sneaking a bite
of brownie in the kitchen under the watchful eye of a resident
mouse that has made our home its home. Somehow it has

eluded our cat, who must have a reputation among wildlife in the neighborhood. Istanbul is a killer calico with grey, spotty fur and a small frame. She kills mice on the regular, an occasional rabbit, too many songbirds, and a bat. How she killed the bat, we will never know. She leaves guts on display near the front and back doors or inside on the floor.

Savanna Joy Stark is my wife of four years and our daughters' mother. She is sneaking bites of brownie because her husband, yours truly, is on the first day of intermittent fasting. I have become the stereotypical chubby dad who lacks self-control with late night snacks, and has no time or energy to exercise. So I am making subtle changes with the hopes of being stronger and healthier when I turn forty in July. My new rule of not-eating-from-eight-to-eight will be broken on occasions and I don't plan on shooting myself in the head because I have a bowl of cereal at 9 pm.

On top of the eight-to-eight rule, we, as a family, are eating only local meat, increasing our fruit and vegetable consumption and reducing sugar, flour, and processed foods. Because I have become both soft in body and heart, and while I support the softening of my once-hardened-heart, I do not support the softening of a once-hardened-body. We will see how long this lasts, because I married a baker and I love her treats.

So I, Robert Joseph Stark, do solemnly swear that I will support and defend the constitution of my one and only body and mind against all enemies, foreign and domestic; that I will bear true faith and allegiance to health; and that I will obey the orders of God Almighty and the orders of Wendell Berry, Chico Herbison, and Vandana Shiva, according to regulations and the Uniform Code of Food Justice. So help me God.

Marlena Joy, our one-year-old daughter, is currently snuggled up with her mother in the downstairs bedroom on a wool Stokke mattress. Mama and Mars have slept together every night for the past year while Prim and I have done the same. While I miss sleeping in bed with my wife, I am grateful to sleep together in a safe home every night. I know that millions of people do not even have a place to call home, and millions of others live in constant fear. Our time will come, and we will miss these moments of snuggling our children and forming healthy attachments.

During the Covid lockdowns of 2020, we started a weekly tradition of eating dinner at their place and we have continued the tradition ever since. Wednesdays at the White's. Nana has planned, purchased, and prepared hundreds of meals and desserts to share with us. Our weekly dinner is a highlight of the week and a staple in our life. Barry and Donna White have become grandparents to our daughters, friends and family to us. Marlena was standing on their heated concrete floor with a smirk on her face like she was keeping a secret as she wobbled on unstable legs. She squatted down then stood up, squatted down then stood up—before taking the first tiny step. We cheered as she smiled so big that it will not be forgotten.

Marlena has one blue eye with a yellow ring in the center and one green eye with a yellow ring in the center. She barely has hair that is naturally formed in a mohawk. She crawls around our three-hundred and eighty-four square feet of downstairs, and through endless piles of chicken poop outside in hot pursuit of the chickens and ducks. She crawls after our dogs who try to escape having their hair pulled, after her big sister who sprints around the house laughing and shouting, "I am running from the monster," and after the cat before crawling to the dinner table or to her mother to eat breast milk with hummus, smoked salmon, oatmeal, and cheese on the side. Sometimes she eats all of them in the same meal.

Primrose was born during the Covid quarantine of 2020. (Lest not forget the Covid quarantine!) Her mama and I stayed in our country bubble out here in Happy Valley for almost the entire year. It was the first best year of my life, every year since has been the next best year. She is a lucky kid to have both parents in her life every day, and to grow up in the woods chasing squirrels, eating fresh peas, doing chicken chores, helping in the garden, and watching out for her little sister. She is happy, confident, helpful, and compassionate. She wants to do everything her parents are doing, and we do a lot. So naturally, she is learning more than most kids her age.

I was harvesting chickens the other day with my brother, who is staying in the yurt for who-knows-how-long after returning from work, when Primrose insisted on coming outside to help. I had a yellow crate with five chickens by my feet, a sharpened hatchet in my hand, a spruce round with two nails to hold their necks on the ground, and a crying daughter begging me not to kill *her* chickens.

"We raised these chickens for food," I said. "Now Daddy has to kill them so we can eat. We eat meat, and if we don't harvest our own meat somebody else has to do it for us. It is the way of life." I wore the same bloodstained pair of Grundéns bibs that I wore commercial fishing in 2009, and to process salmon and chickens and a moose. "When you scream at me not to kill your chickens," I continued, "it makes me feel bad for doing what needs to be done. So please, stop screaming or go inside, because we need meat for our family, and I want to do this in peace."

She paused.

"You kill chickens for us to eat?" she said. Her hand on my leg as she looked down at the chickens in the crate.

"Yes ma'am," I said. "For us to eat."

"Primrose kill chickens, too."

James and I laughed.

"No, Prim, this is Papa's work."

"I want kill chickens, too."

"Maybe when you are older, Prim, but right now I need you to stand back so I can do what needs to be done."

She stepped back.

"First, we pray," I said. She held one of my hands and one of her Uncle's hands as we lowered our heads. "Thank you, God for these chickens, this property, and this home. Thank you for this family and the many blessings you continue to bestow upon us. Forgive us for killing these chickens, Lord, and know that we do not do this in enjoyment, but to feed our family. Be with their souls, Lord, and with ours. Amen."

"And Uncle," said Primrose. "Thank you, God, for Uncle."
James laughed and shook his head with tears in his eyes.
"And thank you, God, for Uncle."

I slid open the hatch on the yellow crate with my right hand and grabbed a chicken by its feet with my left hand. I stretched its neck to squeeze between the nails as it stared at me with a blinking eye. James turned away, Primrose stared.

"Thank you, chicken," I said, raising the hatchet in the air. "For feeding our family."

Thump! The hatchet went into the water-logged wood.

The head dropped to the ground as I held the convulsing headless body to set in a wheelbarrow lined with a tarp covered with plywood. I plopped the head into a stained white bucket and reached into the crate to grab another bird.

"Go Daddy, go!" Primrose yelled. "Kill them, Papa! Kill them!"

"Primrose," I said, quietly. "This is not a time for celebration. Please stop cheering and shouting. This is a time for silence."

She quieted down as a cold north wind shook a towering young cottonwood and spruce boughs waved across the forest. Jeff Kirchner's old Ford pickup passed by on his way to the hay farm up the road. A generator powered a neighbor's house, probably the big diesel at Kevin and Tessa's place, a half mile away. I have talked to them twice in twelve years, but we wave at each other on the road. Marlena cried for milk inside. Breath left the chickens as I stretched their necks between the nails on the blood-covered round. The dull thump of the hatchet going into the wood after it cut their necks made me smile. Primrose came closer and closer until she was holding my leg.

"Please back up a little so you don't get covered in blood," I whispered.

"I want to, Daddy."

"Okay."

A chainsaw ran on high a mile away. I imagined chicken souls flying away from headless bodies to chicken heaven where corn is plentiful and bugs aplenty. They waddled on strong legs in a field of clover and corn, chasing each other and playing in the sun, taking dirt baths and swallowing small pebbles. Not once stepping in their own poop.

After a couple minutes, six birds were dead and Primrose was ready to go inside to help Mama make a quiche.

James and I plucked feathers after I scalded them. It was our second season harvesting chickens together, and we were faster than the previous year. I cleaned the birds on a bleached white table using water in a garden can to rinse them off and remove the blood from the table before doing the next one. I put the birds on a baking sheet to be carried in by Savanna, who vacuum sealed them and put them in the freezer. James had vanished into the yurt after he plucked two or three birds. An hour later, he was walking off the property to smoke pot on the road. He didn't come around until the chicken was roasted and dinner was served. Savanna had stuffed, buttered, and smothered one bird in herbs to be roasted for supper in a cast iron dutch oven. It was served with homegrown mashed potatoes and steamed peas and brought to Nana and Bampa's for a family feast. The chicken that we bought nine weeks earlier as a tiny chick and raised free-range in God's green forest fed six adults and two children with leftovers for two dinners at home. The bones and weird parts were used for broth, the cornerstone of our soups.

I thank God every day to have married such a practical, caring, and hard-working woman. Not too many years past, I almost lost hope of meeting a woman who wanted a similar lifestyle, until Savanna entered my life when I least expected.

2

Happy Valley, Alaska

AUGUST 30, 2023

How I Met My Wife | Two Sober People | Dating Someone
Else | When the Hermits Come to Town | Lost My Chance
| The Silent Approach Did Not Work | Root Beer and French
Fries | Smothered by a Local | Music Festival | A Judgmental
A-Hole | Ask Your Sponsor | Going to the Movies | Beautiful
Boy | Giving Her Space | A Dozen Eggs | Campout in the
Living Room | Two People with a History of Trauma | "Restraint
of Pen and Tongue" | Quitting Smoking | Fear of Abandonment
| Voices of Doubt | I Chose Not to Listen | Dreams Come True

I n 2015, I met a sober vegan working at a bakery in Homer,
Alaska who was the prettiest woman I had ever seen, hands
down. I wanted to marry her upon first sight, if only I could
convince her of marrying me. Call me shallow, fine. Call me
old fashioned, cool. Call me a weirdo, no problem. It's the

truth. I returned to the bakery four or five times over the next two weeks to order biscuits and gravy while waiting for a chance to talk. We spoke once, not counting when she took my orders, and that was when I discovered that she was a rare, sober vegan in a sea of alcoholic hunters and fishermen.

I was sober, too—and a vegetarian. And I had been a vegan for a year in college until returning home to my brother saying, "Damn Bobby, you are nothing but skin and bones." And when I looked in the mirror I realized that it was true.

Savanna did not give me the time of day in 2015, and I did not ask her out or even show interest other than coming to the bakery. But I could have been coming for a number of girls, or tasty treats.

Anybody who has spent time in Smalltown, Alaska knows that it's similar to being in the military. When a new girl shows up to town, even the most reclusive hermits and mountain men make regular appearances to town. And when the new girl happens to be drop dead gorgeous like Savanna, men travel hundreds of miles by plane, boat, and dogsled just to get a glimpse of her so they can retreat to their cottages in the woods and dream.

I can guarantee that I was not the only man eating cold biscuits and gravy almost every morning while Savanna was on shift.

I went out one night in my only button-up shirt with a pair of clean Carhartts hoping to get my three-minute interview. I sipped root beer and ate a plate of French fries while a band played and people danced. Two hours later, she showed up on the arm of another man. I watched them for about twenty minutes and I realized that she was with him, whether she was comfortable in smothering arms was another story, but that is what men do in small towns like these. They smother as a way to show everybody of their new prized possession.

I left the bar and drove home in a stupor. But somehow I knew that he was not the man for her—and that we would one day marry and have a family.

And then one day, she was gone.

I assumed that the relationship ended badly and he became scary so she left to clear the air and to find safety. Unfortunately, I was right.

In 2018, when I was thirty-five years old with both parents dead, a Bachelor of the Arts degree (the first in my family), four years of sobriety, and two years of celibacy—I was ready to have a family. After having tried and failed too many times, I did not want to try and fail again. I was researching Master of Fine Arts programs across the country in hopes of furthering my education while making connections in the literary world. I also hoped to meet a woman to marry and start a family with. Because there was not a single woman in my area that I was interested in.

Before sending out applications to colleges, I decided to attend a music festival in the tiny village of Ninilchik just to let loose for a night and to forget about school and other work-related activities. And just as I was packing up to leave the festival, I saw her.

My dream girl... the prettiest girl I had ever seen... the girl I wanted to marry... was sitting down drinking water by herself while looking very tired. She had a small rainbow tattoo on one side of her face and three small red, yellow, and black lines on the other side.

My first thought was judgmental.

Oh God, she's probably been off partying for the past four years with other rainbow children. I am sure that she's not sober, look at how tired she is.

But I could not stop thinking about her as I drove home, and I asked God if she was brought back in order to marry me and start a family. It may sound psychotic, or slightly stalker-like, but it is what it is. Such are the thoughts of a lonely man when he sees the most beautiful woman in the world.

Three days later, I returned to the bakery to eat cold biscuits and gravy for the first time she left three years prior. She was working in back learning to bake instead of making coffee and working the register, so there was no chance of speaking with her. I returned three days in a row, and decided to eat out on the back porch in hopes of her coming outside to talk with me. It did not happen.

Finally, I told my recovery sponsor and good friend, Barry White, about the girl and he said, "You know what I used to do when I was your age and I liked a girl?"

"What's that?"

"I would ask her out."

I laughed, "Are you saying that I should ask her out?"

"No shit, Sherlock."

The next morning, I returned to the bakery to sit on the back porch and eat and I notice that she was sitting inside eating something herself off-the-clock. I nervously walked past her on the way to the back porch and then sat down hoping and praying that she would come outside and talk with me.

Finally, after twenty minutes of reading, she came outside and walked down the steps toward a vehicle.

"Hey," I said, and she turned around. "Are you still a sober vegan?"

She walked toward me and said, "I am still sober—but I'm not a vegan anymore."

We spoke for a few minutes about veganism and vegetarianism and food. Both of us were still sober yet we had both given up our vegetarian status.

"I am going to a free movie tonight at the theater," I said. "And I was wondering if you would want to go?"

She thought for a second, "Like, go with you?"

"No, no…" I laughed nervously, totally blowing it. "Not with me. But I could maybe… meet you there."

"Sure. I would love that."

My heart skipped a beat and a bead of sweat trickled down my forehead.

"Cool, I'll be there around 6:45 to get popcorn. Do you want me to wait outside for you?" I asked.

"No, I'm fine, thanks. I am sure there will be plenty of seats. But I will see you there."

She left, and I drove home on a pink cloud.

When I arrived at the theater that evening, she was at the front of the concessions line. She waved and I waved back, and then she went inside the showing room with a huge silver bowl full of popcorn. Because the movie was free, the place was packed, and by the time I ordered my popcorn previews had begun.

I carried my bowl down the lit aisle to find an empty seat passing her along the way. I noticed her seated alone out of the corner of my eye, and I wanted to give her space and not act like a stalker. So I found an empty seat a few rows ahead, with my heart racing like a lovestruck romantic on his first date.

A few minutes later, she sat down beside me and the giddy feeling of being so close to the prettiest girl in the world took over me and I knew that we would become husband and wife. I just knew it.

That was in November of 2018, and I gave her all of the space she demanded for the next four or five months. She said she didn't want to be in a relationship and I didn't press it. She said she wanted time alone, so I didn't invite her places. But when she said she wanted a dozen eggs from me, I brought her a dozen eggs. When she said she needed an oil change, I changed the oil in her car. No strings attached. We talked on the phone occasionally for multiple hours and then did not talk for days. It took every ounce of self-restraint to remain calm and not to smother her like other men had done in the past.

On Easter Sunday in 2019, I pitched a tent in the living

room of my tiny cabin and we set up a laptop to watch movies and snuggle. It was our first sleepover, the first of many. Five months later, on Friday the 13th, I married my dream girl. Nine months later, we had our first daughter.

Our relationship was not always easy, especially during the first eighteen months. She was quitting smoking cigarettes which brought highs and lows from her cravings, defeats, and shame. A spiral of self-sabotage, she tried to push me away out of embarrassment. I did not judge her because I had been there before many times. She accused me of not really being kind, but using kindness as a manipulation tactic to get her to stay around. But the more I practiced self-restraint by staying calm and not becoming defensive at her attacks, the more she opened up with me about her difficult past, her past traumas, and her past relationships. The more I learned about why she was acting the way she was the more patience I had. I grew to love her more and more with each passing day, and the love still grows today.

I wasn't always calm and patient with her.. I yelled horrible things, called her awful names, ridiculed, judged, and pushed. I am not a saint. I self-sabotaged, spiraled into self-pity, and silenced every voice in my head that said, "She would be better off without you. She is going to abandon you someday like everybody else."

But I chose not to listen to the negative voices in my head. And by the grace of God, luck, and who knows what else—we are still married today. Dreams really do come true, if we are patient enough to wait without giving up.

3

Happy Valley, Alaska

AUGUST 30, 2023

The Depths of My Love | A Hardened Man | Watching
My Daughter Sleep | A Letter from Elroy Longhorn
| How to Use My Hardness in Healthy Ways

Primrose is stirring in bed and I don't think I have much longer to write. I came upstairs thirty minutes ago because she was tossing and turning, and now I am in the recliner watching her sleep while typing. I never realized the many facets of love until being a father and a husband. I can write in detail about certain situations, about things I have seen and done—but I cannot explain the depths of my love for my daughters and wife.

I received an email a few years back from a man I served with in the army, a man I highly respected and still do. Elroy Longhorn thanked me for sending him a Harley Davidson

T-shirt from Juneau, Alaska, and in his letter he wrote, "You are one of the hardest men I have ever met." Yet here I am, watching my three-year-old daughter sleep through tear-filled eyes.

Elroy was an Airborne Ranger with almost twenty years on active duty when we met. I was a twenty-year-old kid with an eleven-month deployment as a frontline infantryman on my sleeve. Not once did we engage the enemy together. So how did I come off as being such a hardass, and how did a romantic poet and writer like me get so hard?

Perhaps, dear reader, if you read my previous book, *Warflower*, you may know some of the reasons I became so hard. I do not need to rehash the past. But now, as I watch our daughter sleep in our bed with the sounds of dogs snoring downstairs, gentle cries from Marlena, and soft whispers from Savanna, I realize that I have softened up since Elroy knew me back in 2005-2006. Back when I had to be hard. Perhaps God gave me two daughters instead of two sons to soften up this hardened heart. And while the hardness is still there, on the surface at times, I cannot help but allow the soft feminine energy in our home to uncoil a gentle side of myself that was dormant for so long.

Do I feel bad for shooting at people in Iraq? No, it was war, and they were trying to kill me. Do I feel bad for cutting heads off chickens to provide our family with meat? No, somebody has to kill for my family to eat. Do I feel bad for killing salmon to feed my family? No, I grew up harvesting and eating salmon. Do I feel bad for killing two porcupines in the orchard after recognizing the damage they did to our raspberries? No, there is a big forest out there—stay out of our food.

My hardness is still in there, I am just learning healthier ways to use it.

4

Happy Valley, Alaska

September 2, 2023

Sleep Drive | Fall Colors From Gravel Pit | Beckoning Snacks After Dark | September Growth List | Dreams of a Broken Arm | Aggressive Tendencies | Exercise Without a Gym | Alone Time | Doing the Next Right Thing | Learning to be Consistent | Primrose is Sick | Marlena is Becoming Funny | James Returns From Togiak | Rather Camp Alone | Effects on Family | Try Not to Take it Personally | The Cycle Continues | Like Father Like Son | Live and Let Live | Slow Saturday | Sauerkraut | Gratitude for a Good Meal | The Only Family Alive in the World

Marlena and Primrose fell asleep in their car seats, so I pulled off the dirt road to park in a gravel pit with volcano views. I love fall time, the time of colors. Endless shades of greens and blacks from thousands of spruce trees.

Light greens, oranges, and yellows from willow, cottonwood, and birch leaves. Reds from fireweed stalks that refused to bloom. Shades of grey in gravel and rocks that span a hundred feet in all directions from where I parked.

It is the first time I have been in this abandoned gravel pit after living here for over ten years, and I keep looking in the rearview mirror to make sure somebody with a shotgun doesn't sneak up on me and the kids. Two active snow-covered volcanoes are fifty miles away on the other side of Cook Inlet towering over the landscape. Mount Redoubt has a plume of clouds near her crest. Mount Iliamna is engulfed by thick purple, blue, and gray clouds.

It is a perfect fall day in Southcentral Alaska.

White yarrow flowers are covered by a moving blanket of tiny orange butterflies smaller than a thumbnail. A cool southerly breeze keeps away the other bugs. It is the perfect time of year to be outside with a sweatshirt and a flannel or inside with a book.

We haven't seen my brother in a few days. He returned from work, stayed in the yurt for a couple of nights, and then left his stuff in there so we now feel awkward going inside. Who knows when we will see him again? He said that he wanted to help with the fence and spend time with us, so I am trying not to be pissed and hurt by the disappearance— but I am both hurt and pissed. Once again, my brother said that he will do something— but it has to be on his schedule.

During the winter of 2022-2023, he stayed in the yurt for the second winter in a row without money. He came into our home while we were grocery shopping in Kenai, and took a tote full of old comics to sell online. I understood that they were his childhood comics, (I was the baseball card collector), but our mother bought them and he gave them to me to keep for future generations. Instead of finding a job, and borrowing a car or asking for a ride to work, he snuck in our house to take back the comics. He thought he would make thousands of dollars in no time, but it was too difficult to learn how to sell them online, and the person who was supposed to help backed out. He was pissed. So the next time he disappeared for a few days, I took them back. They were under a mounted grizzly bear without paws that he had scored from a friend who was bringing it to the dump. He hoped to sell the bear for thousands of dollars, too. The bear was in the yurt all winter, until he begrudgingly helped me bring it to the dump before leaving for work the following spring. I wasn't going to let him ditch the bear on our land like he ditched a car.

Savanna and I have kept to our new eating routine despite a batch of chocolate chip cookies beckoning from the cookie jar late at night. It seems that every edible item in the house begs me to taste them after dark.

"Just a nibble," says a tortilla chip.

"What is so bad about berries?" say the berries in the freezer. "We are good for you."

"Don't let me go stale," says the cereal. "That would be wasting food."

"You worked hard to catch, clean, and smoke me," says the smoked salmon in the freezer. "I am the healthiest food on the planet. Just a taste."

I refuse their pleadings because I know that it is all in my head. I already had a big dinner, I don't need to eat more.

I confessed to Savanna this morning, "It's like my body is screaming all night for something that I am not providing."

"It is," she said, "it's called sugar."

I read a passage in *The Imitation of Christ* that says, "[C]ontrol the appetite, and you will more easily control all bodily desires." I believe it, and I want to gain better control of my appetite, my anger, and my inability to think positively of myself for longer than a few hours.

So I decided to add two things to my "September Growth List."

1. To stop cursing completely. (Out loud of course. Writing does not count.)

2. To resist all forms of aggression towards my wife and kids.

Although I am not beating my girls, I could be gentler, more patient, and kinder. I want to be. I want to be the dad who never yells or scares his kids. With daughters who choose not to do wrong because they don't want to disappoint their Daddy, not because they are afraid of him. Primrose woke up the past two mornings with her arm on my chest saying, "I had a bad dream, Daddy... you broke my arm."

I cannot let that happen.

I can fly off the handle from the tiniest thing and I don't know why. I talked with a military buddy, Whitelow, the other day who said the same thing.

"It's like I am right back at war," he said. "I black out when I'm pissed, and when I come out of the blackout—I realize that it's my poor kids who I am yelling at, not the Iraqis."

Violence, fear, and aggression are stored inside my body waiting to explode. It is terrifying to know that I can, and have, destroyed and taken lives. It is vital for me to work out every day, to balance quiet time with loud time, and to feel a higher purpose and guidance through God. What works for others? I don't know. But I know that these things work for me. I have been praying and asking God to remove my anger so I can better serve my family and community. To remove the feelings of abandonment I carry from my mother and father so I can be loved and provide love. To replace my violent tendencies with patience and tolerance. Prayer works, as long as I remember to do it.

I exercise on a regular basis thanks to the lifestyle I choose to live. Whether carrying water to animals, splitting and moving firewood, shoveling dirt or snow, a new building project, mucking out the chicken house, preparing garden beds, and the many other repetitive movements required to plant, water, weed, and harvest a garden—not to mention the fact that our family takes bike rides and walks. I work out every day without ever going to the gym. But I haven't figured out how to balance writing time with farm time, and work with playtime. No matter what, every day is centered around four things: my sobriety, my relationship with God, my family, and my writing.

Savanna and I try new schedules to provide alone time for both of us, but it can be so hard to carve out the time. Alone time is necessary for me to be a decent parent, husband, and person; not to mention that I am trying to make a living writing books. Savanna insists that we do not need equal alone time, and not to feel bad about taking time to write. She believes that my first book is changing people's lives for the better and that I have found a calling that requires my attention. It sure as hell doesn't feel like it most of the time and I am grateful when she says it.

This is all part of the next step in my journey toward a healthier person. I turn forty next year and I want to be healthier, stronger, and more confident than I am now. I have been sober from alcohol for nine years, from tobacco and marijuana for five years. I have had the same counselor for four years, the same recovery sponsor for five years, and the same wife for four years. I am learning how to work and talk through uncomfortable situations rather than run away. I am on the right track, with so much work to do.

Primrose is sick. She is stuffy, with a cough and mild thrush. She is snoring and Marlena is asleep with her head cocked to the side. My little one year old is becoming so funny and playful. She dances around by bopping up and down on her knees. She crawls away from her sister and then looks back in hopes of a chase. She laughs when tickled and smiles when she sees me for the first time holding out her hands to be picked up. Being their father is the greatest blessing I have received, and I am so grateful.

Savanna is at home doing schoolwork for an online herbalism course, and the kids are waking up… Time to drive…

James stopped by in a borrowed car to grab a change of

clothes from the yurt. The car smelled like sweaty feet, cigarettes, and pot. He is storing things in our yurt after working for two months as a forklift driver at a fish cannery in Togiak. He stayed with us for a week or two until he decided to camp in the cold woods alone rather than be around his family. Who knows what the hell he's doing out there? I can only assume he is drinking and using, two things he is not allowed to do on our property. He stops by for a few minutes every few days to grab something on his way to help somebody else. Savanna and I try not to take it personally, but we do—and it hurts our feelings terribly. It is especially hard on Primrose who gets used to seeing her uncle and visiting with him in the yurt, until one day he simply vanishes only to stop by for a few minutes to pack things up and to run away again. It breaks her heart every time, and she is quiet the rest of the day with a week of angry outbursts and being withdrawn.

Why would somebody choose to camp alone in the cold rain rather than stay with their family in a warm home? We assume that he is smoking pot and cigarettes and drinking all day while talking on the phone to his new girlfriend in the Philippines, without the nuisance of spending time with his nieces and feeling like a burden to us. He is one of those guys who always feels like he is an inconvenience, no matter how many times we say he is not.

I try not to take it personally or to assume the worst, it is hard to do given our past. All my life he has chosen others over me. From teenage friends to girls to gang members in prison and on to the new girl, the new shitty friends, and then another new girl. Over and over and over. I can't imagine how his sons feel; oh wait, I can—probably how we felt with a father who did not reach out because he was too busy feeling sorry for himself about things he did in the past or by chasing the next fix to relieve the pain. It fucking hurts every day. It hurts worse every time he chooses somebody, or some substance, over us—even though I should be used to it by now, I am not.

Why am I so hard and judgmental of my brother? Doesn't everybody choose a potential spouse over their kin? So why do I take it personally? I need to start loving and accepting him and to stop judging and wanting more from him.

Hell, I have so much work to do on myself.

Marlena is asleep on Savanna's back as she uses the food processor to slice homegrown cabbage and beets to pack in jars for sauerkraut. She is skipping dinner to finish the task. A second batch of chocolate chip cookies is steaming on the countertop. Yum! So much for lowering our sugar intake! Primrose is in a feverish, lack-of-sleep daze on the couch watching *Molly of Denali*. I am eating dinner alone. I bow my head to thank God for our family's blessings, asking for guidance, humility, and wisdom. Dinner is halibut coated in lemon pepper and mozzarella, a side of sautéed garlic and cauliflower, sauerkraut, and pickled radishes over brown rice. A garbanzo bean, kale, pepper, and chicken broth soup steams in a bowl on the side of the plate. Ever since I was served a bowl of soup on a plate as a teenager at the Ranting Raven in Seward, my favorite meals are served with a bowl of soup on a plate. My wife knows that, so she treats me to such things more often than I deserve.

I stick my nose in the steam and inhale. I am grateful.

"Thank you so much, Savanna."

She stops her work just long enough to look at me with blue eyes and a smile.

"You are welcome."

It is a slow Saturday on the land, I love slow and steady days because I feel at peace when I work slowly. I ran the chainsaw for half an hour to buck up logs from trees we felled last season while clearing land to expand the garden and to plant a lawn. The wood will heat our home this winter and be used to heat water and cook soups. I tried to start the truck without luck, so I removed the battery to bring to Barry's to charge and test. We organized the shipping container we use for storage and started putting things away before snowfall. We walked to the creek as a family in observance of our wild neighbors. Mushrooms bloomed, fireweed leaned, and black spruce trees looked tiny and withered in the muskeg like something out of a Dr. Seuss book.

I read a quote today in *The Imitation of Christ* that said, "Whoever loves much, does much. Whoever does a thing well, does much." I want to stop doing a hundred things in a day and to love my family and do a few things well. When I pack my day with tasks, I am stressed, rushed, and short-tempered.

I moved out to this land eleven years ago without farming, carpentry, and mechanical skills, yet I have stuck around and learned more than I could have ever imagined. Why have I lasted out here while so many others have come and gone? Is it my love of learning? My desperate need for a peaceful, quiet life? My desire to care for the Earth and to grow food as an income? My goal of leaving behind healthy land for future generations? My dream of having a family farm to raise kids with American values from generations before? My goal of being a paid author who needs away from people to write? Or is it simply the fact that I receive a check every month from the Veterans Affairs that paid for my property? Probably a combination of everything. Whatever the answer is, buying and moving to the land was the best decision I ever made.

Girls asleep, dogs in beds, cat inside with rain on fur, light on in hen house. Rain patters on the tin roof, a light breeze enters the bathroom window that is cracked for fresh air. It is very dark, too dark to see my hands. A kerosene lantern lights atop the table lights up the house. Savanna and I cuddle on the recliner in the living room beside the wood stove watching northern lights dance above spruce trees outside the north facing windows. An occasional dog barks in the distance, a rooster crows, a generator purrs, and a vehicle drives by. A distant owl can be heard. While eight billion people seem to be fighting, hustling, starving, saving, struggling, moving, and worrying—we often feel like we are the only family alive in the world.

And we like it that way.

S

Happy Valley, Alaska

September 3, 2023

I Love You, Daddy | Mistakes Happen |
Nobody is Perfect | Fighting the Urge to Sulk |
Misdirected Anger | Like Father Like Son

Primrose was lying beside me in bed last night with her three-year-old arm over my chest moments from falling asleep when she whispered, "I love you, Daddy."

I almost cried.

I am a dad; a father of two daughters. Two girls who look to me for comfort, protection, adventure, guidance, shelter, fun, food, and security. A model for future mates. I am so far from perfect that the pressure almost makes me buckle. I try to be present and to refuse the temptation to sulk. I try.

Today, in the Ninilchik Three Bears grocery store—a store roughly the size of two gas stations combined—I told

Primrose to "Go ahead and get the Pringles," after she begged for a small can for a minute. After I agreed, I looked at the list of ingredients and I wanted to take back what I said, but she was looking so cute and happy with the can of Pringles in her hand, I just didn't have it in me. When I was about to ask her to put them back she said, "Pleeease Dad," with that cute little shoulder shrug, side-faced look and pouty lip.

"Okay, okay," I said, conquered.

As we were about to check out, Savanna and I changed the answer. Mama was the firm one who carried our wailing child outside of the store as her little sister stayed in daddy's arms as I paid for coffee beans. The cashier, who was older than my mother when she died, said, "Please—let me buy the Pringles for the poor little girl. She wanted them so bad."

"She sure did," I said, "but we have chips and salsa at home. Thanks—but no thanks."

"Two girls," she said. "Looks like you have your hands full, Daddy."

"I wouldn't trade it for nothing," I said.

And I meant it.

Did we make the right decision to put the Pringles back? Probably not. Hell, I shouldn't have said yes in the first place! Besides, it's not going to kill you to eat a small can of Pringles a couple of times a year. Either way, I am not going to drink or lose sleep over it.

A few days ago, we went to the Ninilchik beach to beachcomb. I was in charge of packing the girls's outdoor gear. The wind was howling and the rain was falling sideways and when Savanna was dressing the kids in the car she said, "Oh, Primrose doesn't have her fleece."

Which I knew was a subtle way of saying, "Why'd you forget the fucking fleece, Bob!" But I didn't say anything, I just put Primrose's rain jacket on and the two of us went outside because Mom and Marlena refused to enter the storm. Fifteen seconds later she said, "Daddy, it's too cold! Too cold! Can I get in the car?" Since she was still sick, it was an obvious answer. So Mom and the girls played in the front seat while I ran the dogs two hundred yards to the tide line and back.

Sometimes being a Dad is *almost* too overwhelming to bear. Sometimes I feel like I am doing everything wrong. Sometimes I am doing everything wrong. Sometimes I get mad at the kids when I am really just mad at myself. A similar feeling comes when I let my wife down, or like I am not doing enough, or like I am stepping on her toes and in the way. It is double trouble when I feel like I let the kids and wife down. I will retreat somewhere for a while to keep from bringing the whole family down. I take the car and sleeping bag and drive somewhere in the woods or by the water to park and be alone.

The apple doesn't fall far from the tree, if ya know what I mean.

Happy Valley, Alaska

SEPTEMBER 4, 2023

Berry Harvest | Raising a Fence | Porcupine
Annihilation | Family Time | Deep Talks on the
Beach | Not Taking Things Personally

Today we harvested a half gallon of raspberries, a half gallon of Saskatoons, and a handful of beets for the neighbors. They gave us three handfuls of string beans and loaned us a wire stretcher to tighten the fence that we are installing. Primrose jumped on the trampoline for a few minutes before helping Daddy unroll and stand a hundred feet of six foot tall welded wire fence. We fed chickens, ducks, and goats; harvested seven eggs, and gave the animals fresh straw, hay, and water. I counted twenty hens, three roosters, three ducks, and seven chicks. The hawks didn't completely wipe us out this year. Our raspberry plants are trying to bounce back after being annihilated by porcupines last year. The spiky bastards. We didn't plant berry plants just for something to do. We want fresh fruit!

We drove to Homer for Savanna's counseling appointment at 11:30. I went to a new playground with the girls where Prim played, I shot hoops, and Marlena slept in the car. Mama's appointment was ended after fifteen minutes due to a medical emergency that required the counselor's help. Addiction, depression, suicidal ideations, and isolation are abundant. We are thankful that we are not there.

We went to the beach to sit on a log and watch a man with a cowboy hat ride a horse through the surf. We ate homemade quiche and Prim balanced on logs while Savanna and I talked about following our own dreams rather than other people's, and how to keep from taking other people's emotions personally until they become ours. We talked about what we want to do with our individual lives and how to unite our lives in a way that each person in our family is living a purpose-driven-life that is deeply fulfilling. It was a heartfelt, deep conversation that required vulnerability and active listening. I am a better person and a better husband because of it. In turn, we are a better couple.

It was a slow, peaceful, fun, and playful day with a little bit of work and a whole lot of family. The days that I live for.

7

Happy Valley, Alaska

SEPTEMBER 5, 2023

Fall Colors | Haircut | Marriage Life is the Best | Bath
Schedule | Savanna in a Sports Bra | Working Out
With Rocks | Like Daddy, Like Daughter | Howling
Wind | Tossing Pebbles Into the Creek | James
Helps With the Fence | Double Rainbow

To get the kids to fall asleep in their car seats I drove on our dirt road for three slow miles of mud puddles, falling leaves, open muskeg, and blowing blades of yellow grass. I love full time parenting in the fall time with so much beauty to share with my children. Even if they are asleep some of the time. Alders with catkins, ember red fireweed, a bright-green recently-cut oat field, and hay bales.

I laid in bed last night feeling dirty because of my long hair. It is time to cut it. It is between my shoulder blades, faded on both sides, and tall on top. It is a mullet, no doubt, and it looks pretty fucking rad, but it gets greasy and hot and I feel nasty sometimes. I told Savanna about it this morning and she pulled out the clippers and scissors and with both kids on my lap she cut my hair in the living room while wearing a sports bra.

Hubba Hubba! Marriage life rocks!

When she finished, I trimmed my beard and mustache, did pull-ups and abs, then used rocks for shoulders and curls while listening to The Stooges and NOFX. When the pot of water was steaming on the stove, I poured it into a metal tub in the bath to dilute with rainwater. I sat in the bathtub using a souvenir metal coffee cup I bought in Canada ten years ago to pour water over my body and a rag to scrub. I love our old-fashioned form of bathing. I take one to two baths a week, using roughly five gallons of water each time, always while listening to James Taylor or Nick Drake.

The kids watched *Winnie the Pooh* while Savanna put together an order for our online business in a sports bra.

Hubba Hubba!

After she took a bath, we ate a skillet of fresh potatoes, fresh peppers, and fresh eggs smothered in Tillamook cheddar and served in three greasy corn tortillas. Add a little hot sauce and you can't beat it!

We try to take baths every Wednesday and Sunday, the same days we water the plants, to make things easier for everybody. If we have full rainwater barrels, we will throw off the schedule.

We fed the animals and collected eggs as a family today. "Chicken chores" is what Primrose calls them. She loves them, and Marlena is learning to love them as well. Primrose makes money every week to put in her piggy bank and she can use the money to buy things she wants. A month ago, Prim and I threw scratch down for the birds and I held her hand and said, "Let's watch them for a while," and I leaned against a spruce tree watching the birds for health issues. Ever since, she says, "Let's watch them for a while," and she leans against the same spruce tree and does what her daddy did. Like daddy, like daughter.

The south wind crosses a muskeg field behind our property and whips down our driveway into the Stariski Creek Valley. Because of the wind, and Savanna's wet hair and upcoming online class, she stayed inside while the girls and I ran the dogs to the creek on the four-wheeler where we tossed pebbles from a low bridge in the narrow creek. Marlena practiced standing while holding onto the railroad tie guard rails. She looked at me every time she stood, walked, and fell. When I wasn't watching the kids, I watched the grass blow while listening to the creek accept their rocks. How blessed we are to live where we do. And lucky, too, no doubt.

I fell asleep putting Prim to bed and woke up an hour later. I am beat. James showed up in a borrowed car to grab stuff from the yurt. Primrose sprinted to him and yelled "Uncle" but he was too busy, or drunk or something, to stop and give her attention. I asked if he could help with the fence and he was obviously inconvenienced by it, and said that he could the next day. He left without saying anything to

Savanna or Marlena. He arrived on time the next day and we worked for three hours standing and stretching a quarter of the fencing. I was thankful for his help. It rained, it blew, we worked. Four hundred feet of six-foot-high welded wire with a strand of barb wire above. I hope we finish by winter, I want to keep moose out of the orchard, and dogs out of the road.

We saw a double rainbow over the creek valley after dinner.

"It's a sign!" Savanna exclaimed, echoed by James, Prim, and then myself. Marlena stared at us and smiled from below.

Savanna and Prim made personal pan pizzas for dinner and brownies for dessert. Homemade pesto with mushrooms, caramelized onions, garlic, black olives, and pepperoni. I love that Savanna takes time to cook and bake with our daughters, it teaches them a lot while making them feel loved. It makes me love Savanna even more than I do already, and I thought that was impossible.

Uncle James laid on the futon after dinner watching *Toy Story* with his nieces while they took turns on his lap. I think that he is happy here with us, but he hates to be in the way and to feel like a burden. I wish he didn't feel that way, but unfortunately, I treat everybody that way at times. After so many years of pushing people away, I still treat people like they are burdens at times. I'm sure that it doesn't feel good. I am often overwhelmed by my girls's clothes, toys, and stuff that I stomp around picking stuff up. Nowadays, I run away from my feelings and family by doing a hundred things in a day. When I am in obsessive work mode, I make everybody feel like a burden instead of a blessing. I am trying to change the way I view our belongings, our chores, and our life together by being grateful for what we have rather than burdened by them. I am still a work in progress, and I always will be. I asked James to help dig an outhouse hole the next morning, and I watched him walk out to the road to smoke and then return to the yurt to hideaway. Finally, at noon, I started digging. It was only twenty feet away from the yurt, I could hear him listening to Gregorian chants while I sweated. I was positive that he could hear me moving the outhouse and shoveling by myself. He came out to help right as I finished, then complimented me on how good I was at shoveling.

8

Happy Valley, Alaska

SEPTEMBER 6, 2023

James's New Relationship | What His Priest Advised |
What is Love to James? | Christmas Presents | Anticipation
of the Fall | Preparation | Savanna, My Bride | Bravery
in Action | Two Natural Births | Full Time Teacher |
Off-Grid Chores | Work Through Nervousness | A
Certified Yoga Teacher | My Visions of Grandeur

I can't fall back asleep after napping while putting Prim to bed. I am praying for James, Savanna. I am worried about James's decision to pursue a relationship with a woman he has not met in the Philippines. Although he is happier than I have seen him in years, I only hope the happiness turns to joy and is unconditional. He says that he loves her, and that he is "one-hundred percent serious" about having children, a cat, and a home with her in the Philippines. Where his money will go far and he will only have to work for three to five months a year at the cannery in Togiak and then return to the Philippines to live a good life. I want to remind him that he already has two sons from two mothers who he does not see, and to slow down. But I don't want him to become hyper-defensive and disappear for years again. So I kept my thoughts to myself.

His priest advised him to be prepared for a broken heart. There are many young women in the Philippines looking to exploit American men for their money, he said, and even more American men looking for young Filipinos to use for sexual deviancy, It is all "the Devil's work." He advised James to attend her home church, get to know the priest, the family, and the congregation. To start a relationship focused on God and religion, not on sex.

While it is wonderful to see James so happy—it is worrisome that he is placing so much of his well-being on a woman he has never met. I pray that this high is not followed by a low of equal proportions—and that if it doesn't work out, he is safe and level-headed about it.

I am not solely focused on worrisome thoughts regarding his new relationship, I can see the positives. He is able to love, whatever that word means to him, which means that he may be starting to love himself. He is excited about the future, which I have not seen since last Christmas when he cashed out a 401k from a former employer that he didn't know existed and then bought dozens of gifts for our family that he kept wrapped in the yurt where he was living. He was so excited that he talked about the presents for a month, and it made him a little upset that we could not open them until Christmas. The entire 401k was spent by the 1st of February. What he spent it on? Only God knows. He traded us a broke down wood chipper for rent. He is learning how to communicate with another about his dreams, goals, and faith, which is a big step for somebody who doesn't talk about shit besides politics and religion. He is learning to forgive himself for past wrongdoings. And, most importantly, my big brother wants to live. He wants to live! For somebody who has been suicidal for the past ten years, this is a victory.

I will try not to anticipate his fall by continuing to pray for him and focusing on my own life. But I am no fool, and neither is Savanna, and we have discussed what will happen if he starts backsliding into depression again while ruining his new relationship with drugs and alcohol. We have our boundaries—no drinking and using on our property or around our family, but everything else is in the gray area.

AMERICAN KURD

My brother camped in
Earthquake Park
Shooting dope in light and dark
Drinking booze and using meth
Putting Faith to the test
What an awful fucking mess.
He called in tears—it's getting cold
From his hammock,
thirty-nine years old
Two sons raised by different moms
Who haven't seen him in so long
Nothing right, all is wrong.
Five hour drive in pitch black dark
Through a city full of spark
My big brother stood alone
A bike and trailer with all he owned
No "Hi," no hug, teardrops flowed.
In our small home he stayed awhile
He met his niece, tried to smile
Distant stare—jumbled words
He ate for five and fed the birds
Just another American Kurd.
He got a place, he got a job
Stocking shelves like our Ma

Obsessed with demons,
Paul and Fate
Converting to Catholic at a rapid rate
Confirmation—"before it's too late."
Until he said, "You have to call
No stopping by—I'm tired of it all."
He locked the doors and
closed the drapes
To hide away in his new escape
Same sad story of a wilted grape.
An elder native I respect
Asked me, "Are you ready yet
To let him walk, to let him go?"
"I don't know
I don't know."
Our Ma and Pa are both dead
His heart is red, head is lead
Nothing more can be said
Brother James may soon be dead.
Flowers bloom and wilt away
Bees collect on sunny days
Tides are honest, tides are true
Flame the fire with an open flue.
Is glacier ice gray or blue?

It brings me joy to watch Savanna become the woman she wants to be. To grow from an insecure chain-smoker with a warm heart trapped inside a steel cage into a loving and tender mother who is confident and courageous. I am not trying to take credit for her growth, just making mention of what I have watched transpire since we met. She carried and birthed two babies without pain medication and has been here to raise them every step of the way. She is the co-owner and manager of a small family farm rather than just as a farm hand.

Last year, when I was asked to work as a middle-school and high school teacher, she built a fire every morning, ran the generator, fed the chickens, walked the dogs, shuttled the kids all over the Southern Kenai Peninsula in winter, cleaned our home, did laundry, bathed the family, and had dinner on the table almost every night. It was crazy! And 99.9 percent of the time she had a positive attitude. I don't know why or how she is so positive and so easy to please, but it removes the pressure to provide bigger and better. She is truly a joy to be around. I hope every man can say the same thing about their wife.

She was nervous to enroll in her first college course a few years ago on macrobiotic foods, but she did it. She was nervous to drive two and a half hours to class each week at night during winter, but she did it. She was nervous to enroll in a 200 hour online Yoga teacher training course, but she did it. She was nervous to start teaching Yoga, but she did it. She is a brave woman who keeps getting braver.

While I may currently be the financial provider, heavy laborer, and big picture visionary—she runs the day to day operations of our farm and manages the emotions of our family. I am the physical support and she is the emotional support. So now, with a one year old daughter and a three year old ruffian, we refused the opportunity for me to teach as a full time salaried teacher for another year because it does not align with my dreams for our future. I want to write, farm, and be with family—not to teach writing, teach science, and be away from family. All while getting chubbier and chubbier.

Because of our decision to work from home, Savanna enrolled in two online herbalism classes to continue her education. Where will the educational endeavors land her on a professional and financial scale? We don't know. We try to trust God, but sometimes we worry and wonder if we are making the right decisions or wasting time and money. Don't we all think these things? What is most important, is that Savanna is excited to learn about plants and to be taken more seriously as an herbalist, within our family and community. Her ego is basically non-existent, so she does not have visions of grandeur like I do. (I dreamed of having books published by Penguin and reaching the top of the New York Times Bestsellers list).

She does not want to spend any day away from family in pursuit of a career that keeps her away from family.

However, she is ready for more purpose and responsibility outside of parenting.

If there is one person who comes to mind as living a spiritual life, it is my wife. It fills my heart with joy to watch her grow, learn, and become more confident every year. She is humble, driven, selfless, dedicated, honest, joyful, healthy, patient, honest, frugal, and with more integrity than anybody I have met. I am lucky to be her husband, and I don't want to fuck it up.

I lie in bed beside my sleeping three year old and watch the half moon traverse from west to east through north facing picture windows. It was a good day. Our family ate steel-cut oats with scrambled eggs and cheese in the sun on the porch for breakfast. It's hard to believe, but savory oats are delicious! We ate healthy all day and then stopped eating at 8. Savanna is on board with the eight-to-eight thing, too, and it's nice to have her support. I went to a recovery meeting with James where the subject of discussion was making amends, forgiveness, and being accountable for our actions. James and I wrestled with trees, roots, and uneven ground to stretch and stand three-hundred more feet of fencing on the north side of the property. It is great to work with him—he is patient, tough, and determined. A positive and practical person is hard to find, and I have one in my big brother.

We discussed the struggles we face as violent men, and how we deal with our past actions as we strive to be peaceful. The positive effects of writing on mental health, and the challenges that a writer faces when telling the truth about family. The struggles of parenthood, and judgmental Christians who drive people away from church and from the Bible. The colors and textures of moss and lichen in sunlight and how Mother taught us to stop and look at the little things. The past mistakes that were necessary to be where we are today. And about ways that we stay grounded, and tricks to keep from dwelling in the darkness.

Savanna listened to school recordings while harvesting red clover in the sun to dry for medicine. She is happy to be learning about plants while she feels bad because Primrose continues to have fits of rage. I listened to her talk about her worries regarding our kids without interrupting, judging, or offering solutions—which is really hard to do. And she appreciated it, she told me so afterwards.

After the girls fell asleep, Savanna and I sat in the candlelight as I rubbed her shoulders. Touch is not something we do much of anymore, with the kids and parents asleep in different beds on different floors and being exhausted at the end of the day, it can be tough. But we try to spend an hour each night cuddling after the kids go to bed. We will do anything to keep this marriage together, because the cycles of divorce and broken families has to end. As the former president, Harry Truman, was famous for saying, "The buck stops here."

Happy Valley, Alaska

SEPTEMBER 7, 2023

Teachings From Bertis | Presence | No Place for Self-Pity | Benefits of Two Parent Kids | Abusive Parents | Pat Your Kids on the Back and Tell Them You're Proud of Them | Trauma Prevention | A Cursing Christian | Not Every Christian is a Cookie Cutter | Family Time | The Root of All Evil | Forest Fires

Here are a few things that my father taught me from a distance.

1. A father is just as important as a mother, so be a good one.

2. A parent who fills both roles is stripped of the opportunity to be one exceptionally well.

3. Self-pity and the "they're better without me" attitude which lasts for years is not good parenting.

4. Being a present father is not for everybody. Know before you blow.

5. I don't understand the struggles people face, so I need to quit judging.

6. Don't take things personally. If somebody wants to be left alone, even if it is a parent, it has nothing to do with you. Tell yourself that everyday in the mirror until you believe it.

7. Many kids become great adults with only one parent, especially those with positive adult role models. However, two great parents is twice as good as one.

8. If a parent is unable to control their bad habits and is abusive to the family, it may be better for the non-abusive parent to move away and receive help. Not to abandon the other parent entirely and to take the kids away from the other parent, unless harm is imminent.

9. Abandonment issues are like war wounds or the death of a mother, they always hurt.

10. It hurts not to have a father to pat your back and be proud of you.

11. Domestic childhood trauma can be prevented—it is simple, really—don't be violent, scary, and abusive to your kids, spouse, or anybody in front of your kids *unless* you are being attacked and have to protect your family.

12. It is okay to believe in God and to be a Christian and to write curse words in your Bible.

13. You do not have to go to church and have a bunch of friends in fancy clothes with big houses and new haircuts to be a Christian. You have to devote your heart, life, and spirit to the teachings of Christ, and strive everyday to be like Christ.

14. Love your kids and family. Spend time with them every day. The time will come when you cannot.

15. To obsess over money does not make a happy family.

16. I am no better than my father. My brother was three or four years old when our mother left him. He was a present dad for longer than I have been a present dad. Anything can happen if I am not using preventative measures and keeping up on my mental health.

17. Keep tools in your car, you never know when you'll need them.

18. Words and actions cannot be undone. Don't burn down the forest with a spark.

10

Happy Valley, Alaska

SEPTEMBER 8, 2023

Grocery Run | Deep Breaths | Car Naps |
Cooking Beans | Prim is a Cowgirl | Freezing
Berries | A Slow Day After a Long Day

Yesterday was a long shopping day for the family. We left home at 10 am and arrived to Walmart in Soldotna at 11:15—out of the time-warp-warehouse by 1:30—ate Chinese Buffet—tried to buy oats and straw but they were out—left Soldotna by 4 and returned home by 5:15. If I could go the rest of my life without stepping foot in Walmart, I would. Many times, I felt myself on the verge of fury due to the vastness of the store and the enormous selection, until I focused on my breath and reminded myself not to cuss and not to be aggressive.

I succeeded in staying calm. Mission accomplished.

Primrose fell asleep when we turned onto our dirt road at

5:05 pm and she slept while Marlena and Mama wrestled in the living room and I wrote upstairs. She woke up at 6 pm as a total grouch. Yelling, kicking, and making demands. Savanna and I basically bit our tongues until bedtime at 8. It was a long day. Not my favorite, but it feels good to be stocked up on food.

Today, a pot of beans steams in the pressure canner as a quiche bakes in the oven and our baby sleeps in the car. Primrose colors while Mama listens to a class and I write. Prim had a horse-riding lesson at 10:30 am where she rode with her arms out and a big smile. She refused to ride for the first three lessons, so she led, brushed, and cleaned the horse's hooves. And now she is riding a horse no-handed. We are so proud of her.

We continue to freeze two baking sheets of raspberries and Saskatoon berries each day for winter. I am surprised to harvest any berries at all after the porcupine damage. I thank God for that, and my twenty-two rifle. I doubt that we will have enough berries to sustain us all winter, thankfully we live in a place where we can buy more. Last night, after Savanna put Marlena to bed downstairs, she came upstairs to cuddle with Primrose and I while watching *The Magic School Bus*. When Savanna was headed back downstairs, Prim wailed and screamed and begged for Mom to stay.

When she didn't, Primrose cried and said, "It's hard, Daddy. I want to snuggle Mommy."

"I know, baby. I miss snuggling Mommy, too. When Marlena stops breastfeeding, Mommy will be able to snuggle more with both of us."

I cuddled Primrose as she cried herself to sleep.

11

Happy Valley, Alaska

SEPTEMBER 12, 2023

4 Years of Marriage | Time for a Refrigerator | American Convenience | .79 Cent Wedding | 4 Guests and a Cemetery Full of Tombs | Honeymoon Pregnant | COVID-19 Lockdowns | The Only Family Alive in the World | Miscarriage Blues | The Fertile Crescent | Surge of Testosterone | Growing Balls | A Medical Emergency | From Calm to Holy $#%! | Marlena Joy Stark | Limp Arm | X-ray Results | Dad Can't Hang at Home | Substitute Teacher to Full Time | Tough Times Don't Get Easier with Drink | Pray to Remove My Selfishness

Tomorrow is our four-year wedding anniversary, and what a journey it has been.

When Savanna said, "There are three things I won't ever

give up on, my family, myself, and my cheese." I knew I wanted to marry her.

When I asked her to marry me she said, "On one condition."

"What's that?" I asked.

"We have to get a refrigerator."

I laughed, "We can do that."

She had been staying at the property for three months without lights, a refrigerator, a freezer, a shower, a hot water heater, and most of the typical American conveniences. We had two tractor batteries on the floor in the pantry connected to an inverter, and every time we wanted electricity we got on our hands and knees to flip a switch attached to an extension cord with a surge protector and multiple outlets. It wasn't the best setup, but it worked.

We were married in a cemetery at sunrise on a bluff overlooking the sea. We said our vows as thick clouds rolled over the Caribou Hills and bugs ate brains and bodies below. We promised to stay together through life and death, a promise not taken lightly. Four friends attended the wedding, the officiator—Lorita van Sky, two guests—Barry and Donna White, and a photographer, Mary McKinley. Savanna wore a long black dress she had bought at a thrift store in the town where she grew up, Lee's Summit, Missouri. It had lace on the bottom that matched her black boots. She held a bouquet of sunflowers from our garden, and her sandy blonde hair was in a French weave. She was, and is, the most beautiful woman I have ever seen. And she was even more beautiful on that day. I wore black Levi jeans and a black vest over a black long-sleeve shirt with a red tie. Leather work boots were on my feet. The wedding ceremony cost us a total of seventy-nine cents for gas to the cemetery.

While thousands worldwide struggle to get pregnant, Savanna was pregnant by the time we returned from our Alaskan honeymoon. I thank God every day for that. It has been four years since that morning at the cemetery. There have been difficult times and wonderful times, and I wouldn't change any of them. Our honeymoon was followed by a rocky path of learning to live together, to work together, to run a business together, and to parent together.

Before Primrose was born in June of 2020, we paid off our mortgage and bought a yurt to install on the property as an artist's studio or a rental unit. We left our full time jobs with a native tribe weeks before COVID-19 lockdown procedures when we were forced into quarantine by the federal government. We made more money on unemployment than as full-time employees earning twenty-one dollars an hour. Thanks to the lockdowns, we were together twenty-four hours a day every day for the first year of Prim's life.

We weathered the hysteria from our quiet country bubble, refusing to cave in to the pressures of a mandatory COVID-19 vaccination. We stayed away from town, stayed off of social media, and refused to read the news. It was a miracle that we had united our independent lives right before lockdowns because millions of people worldwide were isolated and lonely.

It was the best year of my life, up to that point. When James called crying from a homeless camp in Anchorage during the COVID lockdowns, I left home in the middle of the night to pick him up. He had been using heroin and meth for months and he looked like a train-wreck. With all of his belongings in a bicycle trailer in the bed of the pickup, my big brother shivered in the truck beside me with his hands on the heater. The smell was wretched, his speech was undecipherable. That was the beginning of his extended stay on the farm.

We worked the land with a newborn the next spring and weathered the miscarriage of our second child. We were pregnant again a month later, and I was hesitant to be excited in fear of another disappointment. But as the days turned to weeks, and weeks to months, I became confident that our second child would be born.

"I know one hundred percent that I am growing balls," said Savanna, who chose not to find out the sex of both children in utero. "Because I want to fight all of the time."

Despite Savanna's struggles with heartburn and the surge in testosterone, she provided all of the needs for a breastfeeding eighteen-month-old while being graceful and kind.

Our second child, Marlena Joy Stark, was born at home on August 11, 2022. While I was lighting candles, opening and closing windows, cooking a pot of potato soup, and doing chores—Savanna was pushing out a baby in the living room. Things were going smoothly until the midwife checked the baby's heartbeat and heard nothing. She dialed 9-1-1 and handed me the phone.

"You talk to the paramedics. Savanna, I need you to push—Now."

Savanna put a leg on a chair, and as naked as when she was born, she pushed to save our baby's life.

I was on the phone with the dispatcher trying to stay calm and to hold back the tears.

Were we going to have a stillbirth? Was Savanna going to die? I was afraid of both.

As the baby moved lower, the midwife hooked the baby's bicep with two fingers and pulled her out. In doing so, she broke her tiny arm while saving her life. Although, we did not know this at the time. The baby was placed on Savanna's chest as I cried tears of joy to the dispatcher.

The baby is alive!" I shouted. "Our baby is alive!"

The dispatcher echoed the information to the paramedics who arrived a few minutes later.

"Are you guys going to see if it's a boy or a girl?" asked the midwife.

"Oh yeah."

Savanna held up the baby and I shook my head in disbelief.

"Is it really a girl?" asked Savanna.

"Holy shit, we have two girls," I said. "Two daughters. Savanna, we have two daughters!" I squeezed her shoulders and pressed our heads together. "You are amazing!" I kissed the side of her head and she started laughing like I imagine women have done for thousands of years after delivering a baby without pain medication of any kind.

"Is it really a girl?" she asked.

"Yes, love. Another girl."

We laid together on the futon bed in the living room with our new baby while Primrose was at Nana and Bampa's waiting for the news.

James brought Primrose to their house around 3 a.m., where he sat in the driveway until they awoke around 8. He swore that he knocked on the door, but we all knew that their dog would have barked and woke them up. Why would he choose to keep my two-year old in a car for five hours instead of bringing her inside? God only knows.

"What are you going to name her?" asked the midwife.

I shrugged my shoulders.

"We had a name for a boy, but nothing for a girl," I said.

"Marlena," said Savanna, "Marlena Joy Stark."

Tears of gratitude fell as my thoughtful wife honored the little girl, Marlena, whose short life impacted me so greatly, yet who I never speak of besides in my first book.

The midwives performed routine checks of Marlena and discovered that when her right arm was lifted and released it flopped down without resistance. This discovery was suspicious, but since there was no swelling or hemorrhaging they made a note and moved on. When the midwife stopped by the following day and realized that Marlena's arm was still limp, she recommended that we bring her to the ER. We left Primrose with Nana and Bampa again and went to the hospital. Putting a brand new baby in a car seat and driving down a dirt road is nerve-wracking. Every bump means a broken neck.

"I can tell ya'll right now that this baby does not have a broken arm," said the heavyset doctor with a Southern accent and half of his shirt tucked in. "Or she'd be more vocal than she is. See—" He moved her limp arm without a grimace or a cry from the baby. "A normal baby would be crying if she had a broken arm and I moved it around like this. Not this baby. So I feel like we're wasting time even doing it, but I'll run an X-ray anyway for good measure."

A mobile X-ray machine was brought in. When the technician was about to push the machine out of the room, I asked if I could look at the results on the screen. "Go right ahead."

I looked closely at the imaging.

"Wait a second, look at that—right there." I pointed to an obvious break in her upper arm. "That looks to me like a broken bone."

She hesitated to say, "I can't confirm that, but it really does."

She left with the machine and a few minutes later the Southern doctor arrived with an embarrassed smile.

"I admit it, I was wrong," he said. "You have one tough baby girl right there. You better watch out Mom and Dad."

We laughed for probably the last time in a month.

The following month was hell trying to keep Marlena's arm in a sling despite a rash and increased mobility. She was pissed! Thankfully Savanna did everything for Marlena while I took care of Primrose. But still, I could not stand being around a crying baby and an over-defiant toddler all day every day without losing my shit.

We decided that the best thing for the family was for Dad to work as a substitute teacher to earn money and to keep from detonating on the family like a buried IED on the roadside. After a month of working at the same school every day, I was asked to come on as a full-time teacher and we accepted the job. It was a blessing for Dad to be at work and for Savanna to be at home without my short fuse. Not once did she criticize me for not being able to deal with the needs of a crying baby and an angry toddler, and I did not criticize her for not wanting to put Primrose in daycare. Although she did laugh when I wore earplugs under earmuffs to muffle the sounds.

I don't want to mislead anybody into believing that we are barely surviving out here or that we are somehow a perfect couple without any problems. Some days are rough and overwhelming, other days are easy and smooth-sailing. I lose my temper, and Savanna does the same. But nothing will be made easier by walking away or by having a drink. I have come to believe that so many marriages end in divorce because people are selfish when they marry and selfish when they divorce. I, too, am a selfish person. So I pray every morning for God to remove my selfishness and to help me put the needs of others before my own. So far, four years later, it has worked.

12

Happy Valley, Alaska

September 12, 2023

The Fence is Done | Not Such a Bad Idea | Two
Brothers Working Together | Living in the Shadows
| A Time for Everything | Building Confidence |
Crane Migration | Wife and Kids Come to Check
Out the Fence | Eating a Meal Together

James and I finished the fencing! Hooray! He helped stretch and stand every foot of the fourteen hundred feet around nine H-braces I made out of pine trees from the land without knowing what an H-brace was before I started. As we tightened the welded wire around the southeast H-brace, sunlight reflected off the high tunnel and radiated off the rough-cut spruce siding on the treehouse chicken coop. Yellow-orange birch leaves drifted onto a bed of red and white clovers.

Buying the property to start a family farm was not such a crazy idea after all, I thought.

"You know, bro," I said. "We didn't stick to the original plan when we bought the land ten years ago—but we have grown closer over time while working this land together."

"It not only saved our relationship as brothers," James said, bending the final wire clips around the metal T-post. "It saved our family—future generations included." He pulled down the green bandana he wore on his head to wipe sweat from his eyes.

"I remember when you and I stretched the plastic over the top of the high tunnel after our helpers didn't show up. We left the next day for our trip to Olympia, Washington. I look at the cleared area over by the yurt and I remember when it was a thick forest that kept the sun from touching our home. We hid in the shadows for years until that one year when we decided to stop hiding from people and we thinned out every other tree with handsaws. Remember?"

He nodded, smiled, and kept working.

"I look around here and I see so much that we have done together."

"Yeah, bro," he said. "We have done a lot out here. You have done a lot out here."

He finished hooking the final stretch of wire to the H-brace and raised his fist.

"We are done, brother," he said. "Great job!" He gave me a high five.

"I can't believe it," I said. "This has been a big project.

One I should've done ten years ago, but I didn't have the skill, patience, or confidence back then."

"'There is a time for everything, and a season for every activity under the heavens,'" he said, quoting my favorite book of the Bible, Ecclesiastes.

"From deciding to put up a fence to pricing the material. From working and saving money to buying materials and paying a neighbor to clear the land. From cutting down over a hundred trees to limbing and stacking them. Remember when we stacked the logs last year?"

"Yeah, bro. It was fun."

"From peeling trees to burning bases, measuring and marking holes to drilling them, standing posts to building H-braces and corners. From stringing barbed wire to pounding stakes, and then finally stretching and standing the fencing. This fence has taken a lot of steps, and I feel a sense of pride because of it."

"You should, brother." He patted my shoulder. "Not just with the fence, but with all of the work you put into this property. And most importantly, the work you put into your family and your writing. You are a great father, brother, and a great writer. Your stories make a difference."

"Thanks. I hope so. I am learning how to be a father every day. We didn't have a good example."

Hundreds of sandhill cranes flew south overhead as Savanna carried our daughters on her hip to check on us.

"Wow," she said, a smile on her face. "Look at that fence."

"It's incredible," said Primrose. "Good job, guys."

Marlena shouted something unintelligible to join the celebration.

"We're done," I said. "It's almost all done. All we have left are the gates."

"Oh my God," said Savanna. "I can't believe it. No more moose in the orchard or the garden! No more dogs on the road! No more worrying about our kids getting lost in the woods—Okay, okay, I'll still worry." We laughed. "Great job you guys. Thank you so much." She kissed me and patted James's shoulder.

James and I nodded with the satisfaction of a job well done. He wrapped his arm around my shoulders and pressed his head against mine.

"I love you brother," he said. "I am proud of you."

"I love you, too."

Primrose insisted on having Uncle carry her inside where Savanna had prepared a feast of roasted beets, potatoes, and carrots with sauerkraut, fried cabbage, and baked salmon. We held hands as a family and thanked God for our many blessings before eating as a family around a table that we built as the sun set on the Stariski Creek Valley and splashes of red painted the tips of spruce trees. James was gone the next morning. We gave him a ride to the airport two days later to catch a flight to the Philippines to meet his new girlfriend who he hoped to have a family with.

13

Happy Valley, Alaska

SEPTEMBER 13, 2023

Fourth Anniversary | Not All Cookies n' Cream |
Wednesday Night at the White's | Toyo Stove Upstairs
| Enough Battery Power to Run a Stove | Past Winters
Upstairs | A Date at the Mexican Restaurant in Kenai |
Cuddling on the Couch | A Peaceful Life is Enjoyable

Today is our fourth wedding anniversary! It is a miracle to be celebrated!

Our first couple of years were full of explosive fights and arguments, hyper-defensiveness matched with hyper-aggression, physical and emotional threats, and fear of being abandoned by both parties. We got through the hard shit without any long lasting repercussions, and we began to trust each other by understanding each other. We had been acting out of fear for the first two years, and we were finally able to leave the fear behind and begin to truly love each other.

We left the Toyotomi stove on 69 degrees when we went to the White's for our weekly Wednesday night dinner. It sure is nice not to only have a wood stove anymore. It is almost 80 degrees upstairs, at least twenty degrees warmer than downstairs. Savanna and I spent our first three winters upstairs when we only had the wood stove, it was so much colder downstairs. But now that we have kids, and the Toyo stove, we spend our days downstairs.

We went to Kenai for Primrose's gymnastics class and then ate at the Mexican Restaurant where we had our first official date. We shared a plate of *carne asada* as a family. Our time at home between the Kenai trip and dinner at the Whites was my favorite part of the day. Primrose and I cuddled on the couch watching *Casper the Friendly Ghost* while Marlena crawl-walked around the house as Mama thumbed through herbalism books. We harvested berries in the rain to freeze on baking sheets, adding another gallon to the freezer. I had no clue that life could be so peaceful, and that a peaceful life could be so enjoyable.

14

Happy Valley, Alaska

SEPTEMBER 14, 2023

Alone Time | Selling the Farm Truck | Payment
Plan | Mechanical Issues | A Beginner Mechanic
| Primrose Cries for Her Truck | No Clutter |
Goodbye, Unused Items | Non-Attachment is the
Key to Joy | Directing Love in the Right Places

I t is the early afternoon, and I drove to the beach to be alone
for an hour or two while Savanna watches a friend's kid.
Our teenage farmhand skipped school today to come over
with his parents to buy our pickup truck. It was bittersweet.
I am happy to see the truck go to someone we know and love,
and we are helping him out by setting up a payment plan for
the family. But I hate to see our honeymoon truck go. It was
the truck that Savanna and I borrowed from my cousin and
drove around Kodiak Island on our honeymoon. We later

bought it. Despite the nostalgia, it had mechanical problems when we bought it, and every time we fixed an issue another one popped up. As a father, husband, and amateur mechanic living in a rugged state with extreme cold temperatures, we need a dependable rig that will start every time. The Ford was not that rig. And while Primrose had great memories of taking the truck on camping trips and driving on Daddy's lap on our dirt road, her memories are few because we barely used it. Besides, it's just a truck, we can always make new memories with a different rig.

Primrose cried when the youngster and his father drove away.

"My truck, Daddy, my truck." She reached out with her arm while I held her. "Not my truck!"

"We will get another truck when the time is right, honey. One that works. Daddy doesn't have the time and energy to become a good mechanic."

Her tears fell onto the gravel driveway. We stood in silence for a few seconds as the truck drove away.

"Okay, Daddy—let's jump on trampoline."

"Let's do it." I smiled. *If only we all moved on the way children do.*

I don't like clutter, and I don't like having things around that are not being used. And the truck was always in the back of my mind as something that needed to be fixed, that took up space in the driveway, and that needed to be in the right hands.

So on day one of our fourth year of marriage, we sold the

honeymoon truck. Don't the Buddhists say that the key to a good life and rebirth is non-attachment?

It is a sunny moment on a rainy day as I sit by the ocean and stare at mountains and volcanoes with snow covered peaks. Thick gray clouds billow across the sky as sunlight streams through and turns dark blue water to the color of jade. I love my wife, my kids, my brother, my in-laws, my friends, and my extended family. None of them can be replaced.

I did not love the truck.

15

Happy Valley, Alaska

SEPTEMBER 15, 2023

Observance of Nature | Two Parents at Two
Beaches | A Quiet and Peaceful Life

Kids asleep in car seats, Mama parked on another beach in another car doing homework. Rain and wind on roof and windows play a lullaby for our little girls to sleep. The tide is low. Long, gray stretches of sand span miles with rocks, kelp, and sticks as reminders of past tides. Seagulls soar on wind currents with imaginary smiles. Golden beach grass whips around. I listen and observe and participate in the changing of the seasons. Who ever knew a quiet and peaceful life could be so good?

PURPOSE INVENTORY

- 1- 680 square foot house with septic, well, tub, wood stove, Toyotomi stove, propane cook stove, French door refrigerator/freezer, off-grid 11.3 cu/ft chest freezer, two wool beds, one futon, a television with DVD player and Super NES, a double sink, a library full of books, a dresser, two dog beds (one currently has Marlena's pee on it and is outside), a washing machine, a dining room table, 8 deep-cell batteries, 5- 100 watt solar panels with a charge controller and inverter, power in sockets, recessed lights, lamps, a fan, plenty of house plants, and a whole lot of love.
- 1- 18 foot yurt on a 24' x 24' deck with a wood stove, a futon, a rocking chair, a camp oven, and cooking utensils.
- 1- 30' x 48' greenhouse where we grow tomatoes and other hot crops.
- 57 apple trees
- 1 pear tree
- 2 cherry trees
- Hundreds of raspberry plants
- 8 Saskatoon berry plants
- Dozens of rhubarb and strawberry plants
- 50' x 50' outdoor garden space
- A tree house chicken coop
- A lean-to used for meat birds in summer and ducks in winter

- 2 bee hives with an extractor and hot knife
- Hundreds of glass jars
- A 20' shipping container with dry storage full of tools, totes, coolers, and buckets of dry food
- 20 acres of paid-off land
- 2 working vehicles
- 2.75 acres of fenced land
- 40+ golden raspberries
- 40' x 100' new outdoor garden for next year (currently in potato production)
- Hundreds of curing garlic bulbs
- 200+ pounds of salmon in a freezer
- 26 chickens in the freezer
- 2 solid friends we can count on no matter what (Barry and Donna White)
- 1 best friend and wife
- 2 amazing kids
- A vision for this land that is slowly coming true
- A little peace each day, sometimes very little
- A growing community of neighbors doing similar things
- A published book that is read by people worldwide
- A sober and present life
- A moral compass and gratitude for the good, the bad, and the ugly

16

Happy Valley, Alaska

SEPTEMBER 16, 2023

Asleep Holding Daddy's Hand | Charley Pride | Hank Williams Sr. | Out of the Darkness | Electrician Installation | Only Rained Twice | Potato Harvest | Salmon, Potatoes, and Garlic | Dimmer Switches | Who is the Rich Kid Now?

Primrose sleeps in bed while holding my left hand. She whispers things that I cannot understand. Istanbul is at the foot of the bed with a belly full of cheese from Prim's leftover pizza. Charley Pride sings a full album of Hank Williams Sr. cover songs. We listen to Charley Pride every night as Primrose falls asleep. She loves Charley Pride, just like her Daddy. Marlena took more steps today than in her entire life combined. Primrose had fun with friends who came over. A mama with two little ones hung out in the yurt with Savanna and the girls while I helped a hired electrician wire three outlets and hang five recessed lights. Today was a big day on the home front. We left the darkness for light. Before today, we used a single shop light in the kitchen and the shadows made us dizzy and tired. We used head lamps and candles to add more light. Our bathroom and bedroom did not have a light or an outlet, and they were always dark besides headlamps, candles, and night lights. Eleven years without a light switch. I don't know many other women who would accept a life like we have, let alone thrive in it.

It poured rain while we worked inside.

We dug up the potatoes the other day and James said, "It only rained twice all summer. One time for fifty-six days, another time for fifty-three days." And it was the truest statement I had heard in a long time.

We dug potatoes earlier than normal to make sure they didn't rot, and we are bringing the garlic inside after curing in the coop for two weeks to prevent mold. Our potato harvest wasn't like we had hoped, but after the cold and rainy summer—we didn't expect much. It is best to have realistic expectations rather than to be let down by unrealistic fantasies. Our freezer is full of salmon. We have five buckets full of potatoes and hundreds of bulbs of garlic. Our shipping container has buckets full of rice, beans, oats, sugar, and flour. We are so damn rich it's incredible, especially now that we have lights in the kitchen and three light switches in the house. Heck, two are dimmer switches. I grew up thinking that only rich kids had dimmer switches. With a paid off house and fertile property, a healthy family, and enough food to last all winter, I am the rich kid now.

THE FINAL CHAPTER

When Primrose was a few months old, Savanna made
the executive decision for our family to celebrate Day
of the Dead. We found pictures of deceased family members
to set on an *ofrenda* covered in dried marigolds, candles,
incense, and offerings. Every day I visited my mother, my
father, my grandparents, and my uncle. I prayed to them for
strength and guidance, hoping to honor them and the rest
of my ancestors in this lifetime. I thanked them for their
sacrifices to keep our family alive, for denying the freedoms
of solitude for parenthood responsibilities, and for keeping
our DNA going forward.

During the last week of October, Savanna baked *pan de*

dulce and we ate tons of tacos, enchiladas, and beans. When November 1st arrived, we prayed as a family over a roasted chicken, pinto beans, rice, and all the fixings for tacos diced into tiny bowls on the table. We thanked God for our families and invited our ancestors to dine with us before opening a cast iron pan full of steamy corn tortillas. James shared in the celebration of honoring our ancestors instead of trying to forget them.

As we began to eat, a bald eagle landed on the top of birch tree only twenty feet from the house. It stared across the creek valley before turning its large white head in our direction to watch our family.

"It's your mother," said Savanna, without hesitation. "She has come to remind you guys that she is still with us."

James and I nodded as Primrose cooed on the floor.

"Hi, Ma," I said, waving at the eagle. "You always said you'd return as an eagle."

"She sure did," said James. His tattooed hand covered his heart as his eyes filled with tears. "She wants to meet her granddaughter. Say 'Hi' to your grandma, Primrose."

Primrose cooed.

An electric energy filled the house that reminded me of the thunder and lightning storm at the Hearst Church in Pinos Altos. The hair on my arms stood and I was unable to speak. We ate in silence as candlelight cast shadows on the cathedral ceiling and snow drifted down from the sky. After dinner, as James prepared to return to the yurt, he shined his headlamp out the window at the eagle that was still in the tree.

"Goodnight, Mama," he said. I stood beside him looking

at the eagle. "I love you." He wrapped his arm over my shoulders and pulled me tight to press his head against mine. "I love you, brother."

"I love you, too. Our mother would be proud of us."

"Our mother is proud of us."

He hugged Savanna and thanked her for the holiday before lifting his niece off the floor and kissing her baby lips.

"Your Grandma and Grandpa love you very much, Primrose."

She stared at him with innocent blue eyes and smiled before he walked away.

I snuggled with my dear wife and daughter in our upstairs bed shortly after. I was sad that my girls were unable to meet my mother and father and that they never would. I was sad that my mother was not able to meet my girls. Savanna and I did not speak, we cuddled until falling asleep together.

I dreamed that my mother and father were walking barefoot on a beach in the sun holding hands. They were young and smiling and tan. Their hair blew in the wind and their bodies were lean and strong. They looked at me, smiled, and nodded.

I awoke the next morning with a feeling of satisfaction for all that I had done with my life and for the man I had become. In the end, after all of the shit I had been through, my ups and downs, I had become just like a soldier hoped to be. Full of loyalty, duty, responsibility, selfless service, honor, integrity, and personal courage. I was grateful to be sober, and to have bought the property in Happy Valley. To have been talked out of suicide by my dog. To have left Alaska on a spontaneous motorcycle adventure that may have saved my life, or at least encouraged me to live a good one. To have returned to the property to pursue my dream of being an author and a farmer. To have been by my mother's side as she died. To have gone through my father's belongings after he died to learn that he loved me deeply in his own mysterious way. And then finally, in the end, to have forgiven my parents, myself, and my brother. In doing so, I finally began to like myself, even love myself. After doing so, Savanna entered my life and I became a dependable, loving father and husband.

It was dark when I tip-toed out of bed and went downstairs to shine my light out the window in hope of seeing the eagle. As I moved my gaze from the snow on the ground to the top of the birch tree, the eagle turned its white head and eyes to look at me from the same branch where it was the night before.

"Holy shit," I whispered.

We stared at each other as the sun rose and cast a pink light over the forest and creek valley. Savanna tip-toed downstairs with Primrose in her arms and she passed our daughter to me and I held her in the nook of arm while I wrapped my other arm around my wife. I squeezed them both and kissed them.

"Good morning."

"Good morning."

We stared at the eagle in silence until it flapped its wings three times before swooping down into the creek valley and soaring high above the trees. It flew three circles over our house before riding the wind west toward the beach.

Please email or send a letter to Robert Stark if you want him to participate in your book club or in any other speaking engagement. If he is unable to make it in person, he will tune in virtually.

ROBERT STARK

P.O Box 986
Anchor Point, AK. 99556
SecretGardenAlaska@gmail.com

- Facebook: SecretGardenAlaska
- Instagram: Secret_Garden_Alaska
- X: SecretGardenAK
- Tik Tok: SecretGardenAlaska
- Secret Garden Alaska

ACKNOWLEDGMENTS

First and foremost. Thank you, Savanna Stark, for putting up with my ups and downs as a writer, for giving me the feedback I beg for, and for reading my drafts and telling me that I am a great writer. I wrote millions of words before meeting you, but I was not courageous enough to publish a book until after you have encouraged me for years. So I say again, I could not have done this without your faith in me.

Thank you, to the fertile land that has sustained and healed me. For providing me with a purpose and a place to live a good, clean life.

Thank you, daughters, Primrose and Marlena, for providing me with the motivation to write stories to read when you are older to learn about your father and our family history. Being your father is my life's work, and I cherish every day with you both.

Thank you, brother, James Stark, for understanding my need to write stories that may not shine a bright light on our family.

Thank you, Mother, Sheri Moore, and Father, Bertis Stark, for loving me the best way they knew how, and for providing endless teachings and guidance from the earthly life and the afterlife.

Thank you, Torvald and Laura Hansen, for being role models in spiritual living. Your shining lights radiate much farther than you know.

Thank you, Chico Herbison, my former professor at The Evergreen State College, a mentor, and a dear friend. He proofread *Warflower* and *Just Like a Soldier*, it is because of his wisdom, confidence, and guidance that I went from a closet writer to an author.

Thank you, Barry and Donna White, your friendship is priceless. Thank you for the weekly dinners, where we eat good food while talking about life. And for the way you love our kids like they are your own grandchildren.

Thank you, Najdan Mancic, of Iskon Design for designing two incredible book covers, and formatting the interior of *Warflower* and *Just Like a Soldier* to look better than if they were published by Penguin or Random House.

Thank you, Pico Iyer, for reading *Warflower* before it was published and convincing me to change it from fiction to memoir. Your gentle persuasion gave me the courage to own my story, and that has made all of the difference.

Thanks to my readers! Without you, I would not publish my stories.

For the letters, donations, book purchases, book reviews, publicity, and endless support! Thank you for reading *Warflower*, for sharing it with your family and friends, and for encouraging me to publish *Just Like a Soldier*.

And lastly, thank you, God.

Thank you to the Kickstarter backers who funded the publication of *Just Like a Soldier* prior to its release. Your support allowed me to start making a profit the day it was released.

Troy Wise
Michele Meulendyk
David Magrane
Torvald Hansen
Brie Wallace
Cynthia Edwards
Amber
Sarah Styf
Karen Van Keuren
David Paperman
Buddy Boren North
Tara
Tessa
Mary McKinley
Inkwells Bookshop
ACWP
SH
Theresa Evans
Tyler Christie
Patty Barnes
Jennifer Hubert
Shawn Weeks
Julie Atkinson Elde

Logan Paul Thompson
Travis Stubblefield
Karma Hibbetts
Cynthia Stinnett
Angela Perry-Carter
Gerald Beans
Simon K
Don Moore
Justine Larsen
Blake Mullins
Matt Worabel
Kurt P Leffler II
Matt Kruger
Logan Richmond
Keegan Fritts
Rosy Audette
Mark Teckenbrock
lizperrotti3
Mila Cosgrove
Mike Baker
Patricia Linville
Stephen Carmichael
Sarah Doran

Zach Gardner
Stefan Kasprzak
Kylee Fetterly
Johanna Kinney
Tony Stark
Kathy Vitaris
Kyler Texeira
Barry White
Eugene Chow
Daniel Clarke
Shannon Pretzel
Michelle Pajka
Hasendonckx
Kari Boulden
Rebecca Paul
Donald Miller
Judy Rough
Thomas Cook
Joseph Davis
Krista Brott
Suzanne Johnson
Leslie Jacoby
Kathy Mitchell
David Griffiths
Jess R Hall
Nichole Cox

Haley
Thomas Klingensmith
Matthew Smith
Doug Capra
Seward Community Library
& Museum
Tim Roach
Diana Davis
Ranger Fox
Joseph Martinez
Perrin E. Randlette
Kari Anderson
John Kemp
Michael Westphal
Eric Jensen
Dana Fuentes
Rich & Theresa Brinker
Timothy Glimsdale
Justus A. Miller
Amy Walker
Frank Ramsden
Sean Ulman
FelissiaW
Stephanie Roach
ZoPetra

Thank you for joining me on this journey. Stay tuned for Robert's first work of fiction to be released in the fall of 2025. Please take time to rate and review *Just Like a Soldier* on every platform you can find.

Ratings and reviews matter—especially for independent authors like me. When you are done leaving a review, follow me on social media and share my books with your family and friends.

Photo by: Savanna Stark